PATTERNS OF CONFLICT,
PATHS TO PEACE

PATTERNS OF CONFLICT, PATHS TO PEACE

WITHDRAWN

EDITED BY

LARRY J. FISK,
& JOHN L. SCHELLENBERG

broadview press

Canadian Cataloguing in Publication Data
Fisk, Larry J. (Larry John), 1934–
  Patterns of conflict, paths to peace
Includes bibliographical references and index.
ISBN 1-55111-154-3

1. Peace. I. Schellenberg, John L., 1959– . II. Title.
JZ5538.F57 1999   327.1'72   C99-931935-3

Broadview Press Ltd., is an independent, international publishing house, incorporated in 1985.

North America:
P.O. Box 1243, Peterborough, Ontario, Canada K9J 7H5
3576 California Road, Orchard Park, NY 14127
TEL: (705) 743-8990; FAX: (705) 743-8353;
E-MAIL: customerservice@broadviewpress.com

United Kingdom:
Turpin Distribution Services Ltd.,
Blackhorse Rd., Letchworth, Hertfordshire SG6 1HN
TEL: (1462) 672555; FAX (1462) 480947; E-MAIL: turpin@rsc.org

Australia:
St. Clair Press, P.O. Box 287, Rozelle, NSW 2039
TEL: (02) 818-1942; FAX: (02) 418-1923

www.broadviewpress.com

Broadview Press gratefully acknowledges the financial support of the Ministry of Canadian Heritage through the Book Publishing Industry Development Program.

Text design and composition by George Kirkpatrick

PRINTED IN CANADA

...for our families and their futures...

ACKNOWLEDGEMENTS

We (Larry and John) would like to acknowledge the financial assistance provided by two internal research grants from Mount Saint Vincent University (MSVU) without which we might have been seriously out of pocket for incidental expenses. We would also like to thank the Academic Vice-President of MSVU, Judith Woodsworth, and her office, for the generous financing of travel. This funding made possible the gathering of contributors and the shaping of the book's epilogue.

Thank you to the staff at DUET (the distance education people at MSVU) and also to Michael Harrison, Barbara Conolly, and Betsy Struthers of Broadview Press for their generous assistance in this project.

CONTENTS

PREFACE

Welcome to Peace Studies! An adventure awaits you. As our title suggests, this adventure will take you into two broad (and interconnected) dimensions of understanding. The first concerns the nature of conflict. Here matters of disagreement, contention, strife, or struggle – especially ones involving pain or violence of some sort – are explored. Analyzing this part of the terrain, at various levels, from the interpersonal to the international, involves paying close attention to what we mean when using the language of conflict and developing sensitivity to the many forms it can take.

The second dimension involves the discovery and careful investigation of various pathways that promise to take the traveller over or around or through conflict to a less violent, less troubling, future. It is the learner/traveller's task to determine, in each case, whether the promise is (or can be) fulfilled.

For their part, the authors of the various chapters in this book (who, as you will soon learn, consider themselves your co-travellers) provide definitions, examples, and arguments they have gathered along the way. These are offered in the hope that they will help you do the analysis needed for the first form of understanding and will contribute to the new synthesis essential for the second.

Informing all of this work, and a necessary part of any successful endeavour in this field of study, is what we may call *critical thinking*. Space is devoted here, not only to such things as the definition of key concepts and the development of positions, but also to criticisms of notions with which peace researchers work each day – including complaints laid against the very idea of a project such as Peace Studies. If we wish to work at solving problems, we must be open to a full appreciation of what those problems are and to worries about our solutions. We must take seriously, and consider charitably, the different (perhaps conflicting!) views of other learners. Many new and potentially illuminating perspectives are opened up as we are challenged by divergent points of view and alternative values and commitments.

This orientation or approach has had important consequences in the creation of this book. We began by inviting the most critical reviewer of our original proposal to write his critique as an introduction to the book itself (which he did – it appears as Chapter 1). We ended our work by reading one another's contributions and coming together in the same place (Mount Saint Vincent University), both to record our own take on the problem areas treated by others and to register our differences or alternative positions and arguments. Some of the results of this exchange are contained in our epilogue.

Another consequence is that we recognized a need to pay heed to all sources of information, analysis, and inspiration which belong to the subject. Thus the design here not only incorporates alternative perspectives within previously defined areas – like United Nations peacekeeping, nonviolent action, peace education, and peace movements – but also confronts an apparent split between traditional peace studies and contemporary conflict resolution studies. This is accomplished by addressing both. A deep understanding of peace and conflict challenges us to take seriously the work, both of those expertly trained in conflict management (such as the authors of Chapter 2) and those immersed in the normative, value-laden concerns of "conventional" peace studies. Here, also, practitioners of security meet with theoreticians of peace, and theoreticians of politics meet with practitioners of nonviolence. Open disagreement, unresolved questions, still unfolding perspectives and the praxis of reflection-in-action – all are integral to these essays and represent for readers an invitation to become part of a growing, evolving, and exceedingly important area of human inquiry.

Those responsible for this book (editors and authors alike) hope to facilitate active problem-solving and understanding, which, as we have already seen, require humility and openness to diverse sources of information. We see this approach as having another consequence for us as well: that we concede our limitations, disclose our partialities, and consign many real-life social and political problems, as well as our proposed solutions, to the future refinement and evaluation of the reader. Readers are invited to learn, where they can, from our example. We especially hope that you will further develop the attitude and skill of critical thinking for yourselves and take it with you into the twenty-first century.

L.J.F.
J.L.S.

ONE

SHAPING A VISION: THE NATURE OF PEACE STUDIES

CONRAD G. BRUNK

A. Why Study Peace?

The twentieth century has been described by many historians as the bloodiest century in recorded human history. Judging simply by the numbers of people who have suffered violent death or the many other terrors of warfare and social strife, they are surely justified in their claim. The majority of those killed in the two major world wars, like most of the victims of the many regional wars that followed, were terrified, innocent civilians. The latter half of the century was dominated by a "cold war" in which the superpower nations of the world, having developed weapons of mass destruction, threatened massive genocide upon each other's populations. Their weapons, many scientists believed, held the potential to terminate human life on the planet. Although this "cold war" came to an end in the last decade, the nuclear, chemical, and biological weapons it produced remain in existence and continue to place the peoples of the world at risk.

This is only a part of the bloody story of the twentieth century, however. The rest includes chapter upon chapter of border wars between smaller nations, and ethnic, religious, and revolutionary conflict, in which acts of terrorism, guerilla war, and even genocide have become commonplace. The human race has achieved many apparent economic, scientific, and political advances in the modern era, but when it comes to managing our conflicts our most recent record demonstrates that we have made little, if any, progress. Indeed, it appears that the human race has a decided penchant for turning its most impressive technological achievements to the task of finding ever more painful and destructive ways of dealing with its conflicts.

Surely one of the most important tasks for humanity in the new millennium is to learn how to handle individual, social, and national or international strife in more constructive and peaceful ways. The toll in human misery and the threat to our survival on this planet have become far too great. Rather than continuing to rely on entrenched procedures, we need to find less destructive, less violent ways of dealing with conflict at every level, from the family and the neighbourhood all the way up to the community of nations and states.

For this reason increasing numbers of educators and scholars have developed the conviction in recent years that the problem of conflict and violence in our world requires focused attention to the conditions that can turn human conflicts so quickly and easily to violence and war, as well as new ways of thinking about the alleviation of these conditions. After seeing the horrible power of the atomic bombs dropped upon the Japanese people at the end of World War II, Albert Einstein observed that nuclear weapons technology had "changed everything, except our way of thinking." What he meant by this was that the awesome power this technology introduced had radically changed the world, especially humanity's ability to threaten the life of the planet. This, of course, should have altered just as dramatically the way we think about the place of violence and war in dealing with human conflicts, but it did not. Many people concluded that the only serious way to respond to the problem noted by Einstein was to set issues of peace and conflict apart as a special area of research and education in the university.

Of course, problems of conflict and its resolution have always been the subject of study and research by the traditional disciplines represented in the university. Historians study the history of conflict. In fact, many people think that historians tend to focus too much of their attention on wars and violence, as if these were the only important events in history. Psychologists study human behaviour at the individual level, to try to understand what influences us to choose violent or nonviolent means of handling our disputes. Social psychologists, anthropologists, and sociologists focus their attention on the behaviour of social groups; political scientists try to understand the behaviour of nations and political organizations. Philosophers and theologians are interested in the moral and religious significance of conflicts and the most appropriate means of dealing with them. Even some of the so-called "hard sciences" like biology, zoology, and ethology claim insights into the problems of human violence.

But each of these disciplines tends to study only a narrow aspect of human behaviour; that is, the one that most naturally fits its own methodological approaches and assumptions. And it is clear that the problems of human conflict and their peaceful resolution are much larger than any single discipline can capture. Each discipline has important insights to offer, but none can understand these problems fully in their real-life contexts. Further, there are aspects of these problems that can fall in the cracks between disciplines. This is why the proper study of human conflict and its resolution is *interdisciplinary* — understanding the problem requires the insights both contained in and overlooked by many disciplines. Only by setting the study of conflict and peace apart as a separate *problem area* is it possible to stimulate the "new ways of thinking" necessary for our radically changed world.

B. Objections to Peace Studies

1. Is it Really a Discipline?

The points just mentioned indicate the usual rationale for the development of "Peace Studies" as an independent course of study in many colleges and universities. But some traditional academics have argued that Peace Studies really isn't a "discipline" in the commonly understood sense of that term, and therefore should not really be a separate field of study. This argument is not very persuasive, because it is not at all clear what defines academic "disciplines" in the first place. They are not identified by a common methodology, since in many disciplines there are lively debates about the proper methods to use (especially in the humanities and social sciences). Nor are they characterized by common assumptions shared by their members, since these too are constantly debated. It appears that many disciplines are defined by the range of problems, or the *subject matter,* they study. History is defined by its concern with events in the past, psychology with human behaviour, anthropology with practices of different cultures, and so on.

In this respect, Peace Studies, which takes as its subject matter the problem of human conflict and its peaceful resolution, is no less a *discipline* than many of the well-recognized academic disciplines which have emerged over time, especially in the twentieth century. But it is not necessary to establish Peace Studies as a distinct academic discipline in order to establish its value as a separate course of study, because it is clear that some of the most significant and highly respected courses of study to emerge in colleges and universities in the past several decades are, like Peace Studies, attempts to explore highly important social issues which require the perspectives of many disciplines.

Take, for instance, the emergence of Environmental Studies in universities around the world in the past forty years. Environmental issues have come to be recognized as demanding immediate, well-founded responses in personal behaviour and in economic and political policy. Understanding these issues requires input from many sciences, as well as disciplines in the humanities: physics, biology, geology, zoology, ecology, psychology, sociology, geography, political science, economics, ethics, and religious studies, just to name the most relevant. But these disciplines cannot tackle environmental problems in an integrated and coherent way in their own isolated corners. They need to be brought together around real environmental problems, where the solutions require insights from each and require each to recognize the limitations and possibilities identified by the others. Environmental Studies is one of the best examples of the importance of *interdisciplinary* research and education in dealing with critical social problems. Other similar examples in the university include Development Studies, Area Studies (e.g., Canadian Studies, African Studies), and Ethnic Studies (e.g., Aboriginal Studies). Few people today would argue that these do not have a legitimate place in the university, even though many of the traditional "disciplinarians" were highly suspicious of them when they were first proposed because they infringed on their "disciplinary turf."

2. Is Peace Studies Too Political?

Even though Environmental Studies is now an accepted and highly respected course of study, when it was first introduced into college and university curricula many people opposed it on the grounds that it was not an "objective" science. It was, they said, merely an excuse for introducing environmentalist political activism into the academic curriculum, and this was a violation of the scholarly commitment to maintaining a neutral or "objective" attitude. It is not appropriate for colleges and universities to be supporting items on the "green" agenda (like "limited growth," sustainability, or "saving the spotted owl"), which are controversial and challenge many entrenched ways of thinking and acting within our society.

Peace Studies programs meet with the same arguments. They, too, are charged with being "too political" because they are often critical of mainstream ways of thinking about government behaviour and policy. Thus they are often seen as promoting pacifism, socialism, or other "left-wing" political agendas and providing a platform for engaging students in anti-war protests and other forms of activism, rather than maintaining the appropriate level of scholarly "objectivity."[1] Now it is certainly true that Peace Studies, like Environmental Studies, looks for new ways of thinking about conflict and violence that often are critical of entrenched ways of thinking about these things. But there is nothing inherently more "political" about this than other accepted forms of critical scholarly inquiry. Indeed, most people would argue that this is just what the university is all about: the promotion of new, and often very unpopular, ways of thinking. "Politicization" *is* something to worry about in universities, but the "politicization" to be feared is not that of ideas critical of mainstream politics. It is rather that which suppresses the free expression of unpopular viewpoints for political reasons. We might also ask which is the greater threat to the objectivity of the university: a research grant of millions from a government defence department to a physics professor to study the feasibility of a laser weapon, or a Peace Studies course which investigates nonviolent alternatives for national defence or international peacekeeping?

3. Is Peace Studies Value-Free?

An important related question is whether Peace Studies is defined by a commitment to a certain set of values. Some of its academic critics have claimed that it is defined *primarily* by such a value commitment, and that this is the sense in which it is really the inappropriate introduction of a moral or political agenda into scholarly research and education. Thus it is often said that Peace Studies is defined by a common commitment to pacifism or nonviolence as a moral or political ideology, or that it shares a common opposition to patriotic nationalism in favour of trans-nationalist or internationalist sentiments. Some of its harshest critics have even claimed that it is motivated by strong socialist or Marxist ideology.

There is an important sense in which it is true that Peace Studies is defined by certain values. One of these is certainly the value of peace itself; that is, the belief that peaceful relations among people and nations are better than unpeaceful ones. This implies another closely related value central to the very definition of Peace Studies – that violence is undesirable, and that where the same human goods can be achieved by them, nonviolent means are preferable to violent ones. But these two values are, as just stated, hardly controversial ones. They would be shared by most people and should not be identified with any particular "political" agenda.

With respect to these value commitments, Peace Studies is no different from many, probably most, other academic and scholarly endeavours, which are also motivated by underlying values or goals. For example, the whole point of Environmental Studies is to find ways to ameliorate destructive impacts upon the environment. This distinguishes it from Geology, which is more often taught with an eye towards facilitating the extraction of resources from the environment (this, after all, is what most geology graduates do). Administrative and Management Studies have as underlying values such things as efficiency and profitability. Aboriginal Studies is premised upon the explicit value of preservation of cultural and ethnic traditions and practices. Even Strategic Studies, often hailed by its proponents as a "value-free" or "realistic" enterprise, is based upon national interest. These are, in each case, values appropriate to the community served by the area of study and appropriate to the area of study itself. Peace Studies is committed, equally appropriately, to the values of peace.

C. The Subject Matter of Peace Studies

As already suggested, Peace Studies is defined, not so much in terms of its methods and assumptions, but in terms of its *subject matter*, the problems with which it is concerned. This problem area has been loosely identified as that of "human conflict and its peaceful resolution." The domain of human conflict is, of course, extremely broad, because we are very conflict-prone creatures who construct many levels of social interaction and generate conflict at every level of that interaction. Individuals find themselves in conflict with others in a variety of social contexts: in families, in schools, in the workplace, and in the community. We organize ourselves within racial, religious, ethnic, economic, and political groupings which regularly come into conflict with each other. And we also form nation states and alliances in the international arena which vie with each other for power, influence, resources, and territory. If we ever encounter beings from other galaxies, we will surely add intergalactic conflict to the list!

That humans come into conflict with each other at various levels of individual and group interaction is normal and expected. Conflict is itself inevitable among beings who live together in situations where common interests meet finite resources, and where different interests lead to incompatible activities. There is nothing particularly bad, or even undesirable, about the inevitability of conflict. It is, in itself, neither bad nor good, though it can have both good and bad consequences. It can lead to misunderstanding, hostility, alienation, and violence. But conflict can also be a stimulus to creative thinking and the development of new ideas, new technologies, or new forms of social interaction, all of which can make things better for everyone. Nothing would be more boring and unsatisfying than life without conflict. The only human community without conflict, it has been said, is to be found in a cemetery!

Conflict can be defined (and usually is defined in conflict theory) simply as what results from the existence, real or imagined, of incompatible interests, goals, beliefs, or activities. It is a situation in which one party's interests cannot be fully realized without their impinging upon the realization of some other party's interests – or a situation in which one of them *thinks* that the interests are incompatible. Defined this way, it should be clear that conflict among finite beings on this earth is inevitable. It would be inevitable even if humans were perfectly good beings. It is not our failure to be good that brings us into conflict with others. It is simply the fact that, being the same kinds of beings, with similar interests, we will naturally want the same things when there is not enough for everyone at the same time. But we also have different beliefs and values, and these too come into conflict with the beliefs and values of others. This is normal and natural – there is nothing bad about it at all.

The important thing about human conflicts, then, is not so much the conflicts themselves as the *means we choose to deal with them*. These means largely determine whether the conflict leads to good or ill. Not only do we generate strife at various levels of social interaction, from the individual to the international, we also have developed habits, practices, and institutions for dealing with it at all these levels. Some of these work better than others, are better at *preventing* hostility and violence, while others seem to *promote* hostility and violence or even depend upon them.

The primary concern of Peace Studies is to understand how conflicts among human beings arise, what causes them to become harmful for some or all the parties, and what means are most likely to deal with them in less harmful ways. Adam Curle, founder of one of the first Peace Studies programs in Britain, defined the function of Peace Studies as identifying and analyzing "unpeaceful relationships" in order to "devise means of changing unpeaceful into peaceful relationships."[2] A useful aspect of Curle's definition is the way it points out that human conflicts can be handled in "unpeaceful" as well as "peaceful" ways, and that the point is to find ways of turning conflicts of the former type into conflicts of the latter type. What this amounts to depends, of course, upon what is meant by "peaceful relationships," and, as we shall see in a moment, this is a matter of much interesting debate within the Peace Studies community.

Another useful aspect of Curle's definition is that it defines Peace Studies very broadly, since it includes the study of peaceful and unpeaceful relations at every one of the levels of human conflict from the individual to the international. Peace Studies is interested in the analysis of conflict between individuals and groups in communities and in finding methods of transforming violent and harmful relations arising in these conflicts into more constructive or "peaceful" relations. This is the focus of what is often called "Community Conflict Resolution Studies." (These aspects of conflict and its peaceful management are discussed by Loraleigh Keashly and Bill Warters in Chapter 2 of this book.)

But Peace Studies is interested in conflicts at the more "political" levels as well. These include the unpeaceful relations that often arise in conflicts between the diverse racial, religious, ethnic, and political groups within our communities and nations. While most states have legal and political institutions for dealing with these conflicts – police, courts, prisons, social agencies, elected councils, and legislatures, which are designed to "keep the peace" – they often do not perform in ways that resolve the underlying conflicts or transform them into more peaceful relationships between the parties. Creative nonviolent means of confrontation and conflict transformation, such as those used by Mohandas Gandhi and Martin Luther King, Jr., have therefore been a major subject for study. (These issues are addressed here by Jo Vellacott and Nigel Young, in Chapters 4 and 5, respectively.)

Conflict between nations and between ethnic or nationalist groups within nations, which typically leads to the organized violence of civil or international war, has been a major focus of Peace Studies in the past. Indeed, during the past several decades the major impetus for the establishment of such programs in European and North American universities and colleges has often been concern about the growing destructiveness of regional wars around the world, the high risks of nuclear war during the cold war period, and the emergence of ever more horrifying military technologies, such as chemical and biological weapons. The search for more peaceful ways of managing regional and national conflicts rightfully remains a high priority. There is a desperate need for investigating new methods of intervention in highly volatile situations: peacebuilding or peacekeeping roles which do not simply multiply the violence and suffering of the people in conflict, as traditional military methods of intervention so often do. (Chapter 3, by Alex Morrison, reflects this interest.)

Peace Studies researchers and educators have also been interested in undertaking critical examination of the prevailing doctrines and ideologies that shape the mainstream ways of thinking about human conflict. This is especially true at the level of international conflict, where international relations theory has been strongly dominated by debates between "realism" and "idealism," Marxism and capitalism, liberalism and fascism, and similar dichotomies. Many people think that these debates are based upon assumptions about individual, group, and national behaviour that are outmoded and prevent the emergence of new, creative solutions to conflict at this level. Perhaps these assumptions — the identification of political power with force and violence, the idea that human individual or group behaviour is essentially egoistically motivated, that social order is dependent upon the monopoly of violence, and so on — need to be challenged. Here Peace Studies provides a useful service by examining the evidence from the many sciences which may call these assumptions into question. For example, the "political realist" assumption that social order and cooperation can only be maintained by the existence of a scheme of centralized enforcement has been called into serious question by recent research on the emergence of cooperation and altruism among insects and animals in their natural evolutionary adaptation to their environment.[3] There is reason to believe that the same might be true of the human animal in social contexts.

So we see that Peace Studies is defined by concerns with human conflicts and their peaceful resolution across a broad spectrum of human interaction. The chapters in this book speak to this wide variety of conflict issues and introduce critical challenges to entrenched ways of thinking. It is thus clear in what ways Peace Studies can be distinguished from many other disciplines and research programs. For instance, Strategic Studies, a growing area of research in universities and non-academic research institutes, generally limits its focus to international conflict situations, and it views them from the point of view of the national interest of a particular national actor or government. It tends to make certain assumptions about the interests of states and their use of power and examines conflict situations with the aim of finding the most effective "strategy" for maximizing the interests of the particular state. It provides useful input for policy-makers who are interested in serving the particular interests of their own country, however these interests may be defined (and they are usually defined in terms of economic advantage and political influence). Peace Studies, on the other hand, attempts to take a broader view, which may include the critical assessment of assumptions made by Strategic Studies and their implications for peaceful relations among nations.

D. Central Concepts in Peace Studies

1. Peace

The best evidence against the claim that Peace Studies is defined by any particular ideology lies in the existence of an ongoing vigorous debate within the field about how to define "peace," the concept central to Peace Studies as a field of research and education. If we accept anything like Adam Curle's definition of the field, as the analysis of unpeaceful relationships and the means of transforming them into peaceful ones, then the first question we must address when undertaking our study is: What do we mean by "unpeaceful" and "peaceful" relationships between people?

Curle himself defines these terms in the following way. "Peaceful relationships," he says, are "those in which individuals or groups are enabled to achieve together goals which they could not have reached separately." In contrast, "unpeaceful relationships are those in which the units concerned damage each other so that, in fact, they achieve less then they could have done independently, and in one way or another harm each other's capacity for growth, maturation or fulfilment."[4] Curle clearly includes more within the concept of "peace" than is usual in newspapers and popular language. He does not mean merely the absence of war or other forms of overt violence which kill or maim persons and does not believe that a situation is "peaceful" simply when there is a cease-fire or temporary truce in hostilities between parties. There are many subtle and inconspicuous ways in which people can harm each other psychologically, socially, and economically even though they are not actually engaged in acts of violence in the usual sense of this term.

Curle's definition of peace is an example of what has come to be known as "positive peace," because it is said to define peace in terms of the *presence* of a state of affairs that is beneficial for all the parties in a relationship. "Positive peace" is contrasted with "negative peace," which defines peace negatively – as the *absence* of certain kinds of specific violent actions, like those which physically maim or kill other persons. From the point of view of "negative peace," a situation is peaceful among individuals and groups if they are not engaging in specific acts of physical or psychological violence, such as occur in assaults in which people are seriously injured or even killed. Among nations there is "negative peace" if they are not at war or are not using the threat of war to advance their diplomatic objectives. The concept of "negative peace" is the one that we typically use in our ordinary speech when we talk about peace among nations or among conflicting political groups within a society.

Curle prefers to use a "positive" as opposed to a "negative" conception of peace because he thinks that there are many ways in which relations among individuals and groups can be harmful to some or all the parties to the relationship even when they do not involve overt acts of violence. A situation should not be called "peaceful" if persons are suffering harm from the nature of the relationship. A marriage is not "peaceful" if one of the partners is being exploited, oppressed, or prevented from realizing his or her potential as a person because of power imbalances or simply habitual ways of structuring the roles, even when these are unrecognized or unintended. A society is not "peaceful" if, as in a slaveholding society, its laws or social practices demean or impoverish certain groups or exclude them from the opportunities and benefits available to others. Those who, like Curle, prefer the notion of "positive peace" would say that any relationship of extreme injustice should hardly be considered "peaceful." Furthermore, a situation that places people in such positions is a fertile breeding ground for overt forms of violence, and thus is not likely to be peaceful even in the "negative" sense for very long.

The well-known Scandinavian peace researcher, Johan Galtung, has defended an even stronger conception of positive peace than Curle's. He calls any situation unpeaceful in which "human beings are being influenced so that their actual (physical) and mental realizations are below their potential realization."[5] Galtung has been much criticized for this view because it suggests that we have peace only when we have reached a perfect utopia! Others have pointed out that on this definition there is no difference between the concept of peace and the concept of perfect justice. We will return to this criticism a bit later.

Johan Galtung also has an interesting way of explaining the distinction between positive and negative peace by pointing out that really each of them has a "negative" definition — peace is the *absence* of something, which can be called "violence." But negative and positive peace, it may be said, refer to the absence of two *different kinds* of violence. The violence with which negative peace is concerned Galtung calls "direct, personal violence." This is what we normally think of when we hear the word. Violence in this sense has four essential elements: a) an identifiable *actor* or groups of actors, b) an identifiable physical *action* or behaviour, c) a clear physical or psychological *harm* which results from the action, and d) an identifiable *victim* who suffers the harm. The usual things that come to mind when we hear the word "violence" — such as physical assaults, stabbings, shootings, bombings — have all four of these elements.

But Galtung points out that some of the most pernicious ways people are harmed do not have all these elements, and hence they tend to be ignored or not recognized as "violent," even though they should be. People can be harmed, not only by the actions of others, but also as a result of the way the relevant relationships or social practices are structured. In these cases it is not anybody's particular *actions* but the structures themselves that cause the harm. The examples cited earlier of the lack of "positive peace" — slavery, apartheid, or an oppressive marriage — are for Galtung perfect examples of what he calls "structural violence." In these cases there is a clear "victim" who is being harmed in some way in the situation, or *by* the situation, but the victim may be unable to identify any particular *action* of any particular *person* or group as the cause of the harm. It is the way things go as a result of the relevant social arrangements that puts the person in the disadvantaged situation. The poverty and dehumanization of the slave is the result of the *system of slavery*, not the result of any identifiable act of violence on the part of the slavemaster. The fact that a specific slavemaster may be very "nonviolent" (in the sense of direct, personal violence), or even unusually benevolent, in the treatment of his or her slaves does not mean that the situation of the slaves is not extremely detrimental to them. There is a sense in which slavery "does violence" to the slaves, even though no one may be "acting violently" toward them. This is what Galtung means by "structural violence."

This distinction between direct, personal violence and structural violence makes it easier to clarify the distinction between negative peace and positive peace. Negative peace can simply be understood as the absence of direct, personal violence. Positive peace is the absence of structural violence. When viewed this way, it becomes evident that the common element in both conceptions of peace and violence is the element of *harm*. How broadly we understand the notion of peace depends in large part upon what we include as the types of harm that are "violent" or "unpeaceful."

This is not just an academic question about terminology, as it might appear to be on the surface. Very important debates about the nature of peace studies, peace research, and peacemaking turn on this issue. Consider, for example, the debate that raged among peace researchers in the 1960s and 1970s, when Galtung and Curle were writing about the issue. Many of the most visible wars occurring in the world then were "wars of liberation," in which dissident groups fought revolutionary guerilla wars against very oppressive, undemocratic regimes. Even if we agree that the goal of peace research is to find ways to help these societies restore a peaceful situation (to "turn unpeaceful relationships into peaceful ones," as Curle puts its), we must still ask whether this means finding ways to end the wars (restoring negative peace) or finding ways to end the oppression of the governments, against which the wars were being fought (restoring or creating positive peace).

Not surprisingly, peace researchers did not agree about this, nor did many of the people involved directly in the violent situation. Some people (like Galtung and Curle) argued that merely to focus on the direct, personal violence of the fighting and to advocate ways of stopping it was to take sides with the oppressive status quo which the people were fighting to end, to side with the political and economic structures that were structurally violent, and to prefer a negative peace to a positive peace. If one wanted to contribute to peacemaking in this situation, it was argued, then one should focus upon ways of ending the oppression, not just on ways of ending the war. Further, the revolutionaries fighting these wars claimed that they were not the ones who should be criticized for being "unpeaceful". They were, in fact, fighting against the structural violence of the oppressive regime and for positive peace (as well as for negative peace in the long run). They needed to break the negative peace (with direct, personal violence) in order to achieve positive peace. Those who were truly on the side of "real" (positive) peace should, they said, side with the revolutionaries. Those who merely wanted to stop the fighting weren't really on the side of peace.

Other peace researchers, like the well-known American economist

Kenneth Boulding, were strongly critical of this position. They argued that this emphasis on positive peace confuses the issues. By defining "peace" and "violence" so broadly, they said, the ideas become indistinguishable from the concepts of "justice" and "injustice," thus obscuring an important and enduring moral question that arises when we face the need to choose between peace and justice. We value negative peace too, the critics argued, and sometimes it comes into conflict with justice. When it does, we simply have to make a moral decision about which value is more important: whether the injustice is so great that ending it justifies breaking the peace by using direct, personal violence. Recognizing that this is a real choice between two *values* also forces us to look seriously for the least violent (or as we should say, most "peaceful") ways of struggling against injustice. This, Boulding argued, was exactly what Peace Studies and peace research should be seeking to do – to find effective nonviolent ("negatively peaceful") ways of fighting against injustice. So, negative peace should be the central conception of peacemaking.

Those who in this way prefer the concept of negative peace as the controlling idea in Peace Studies point out an important fact about human beings and their propensity to violence in dealing with conflict. The fact is that people nearly always believe in the rightness of their own cause. So, when they fight, they are fighting "for justice." If the injustice against which they fight is perceived to be grave, then the temptation is to use whatever means are considered necessary to succeed. This is why intense conflicts have the well-known tendency to spiral into ever-increasing levels of violence and horror. And as they do, the parties on both sides become ever more firmly convinced that their horrible deeds are justified by the end of the justice they seek. The more people use the term "structural violence" to describe the injustice of their opponents, the easier it becomes for them to think of themselves as "peacemakers" and the more difficult it becomes for them to see the violence of their own actions. The language of "structural violence" and "positive peace" helps warriors to avoid making an explicit moral choice about the justification of their own violent actions, or about whether there might be morally preferable, nonviolent ways of dealing with the conflict.

The debate about justice and peace cannot be resolved here. Perhaps the best thing to say at this point is simply that the two concepts of violence and peace call our attention to importantly different aspects of conflict and its peaceful resolution. We know that situations of structural violence are often fertile breeding grounds for the outbreak of many

kinds of direct, personal violence and that, in most cases, structural violence is maintained by the regular use or threat of direct personal
violence, which often incites those who suffer to employ violent resistance. So there is a clear sense in which it is true that the only real peace
is a positive peace. It is also clear that to be concerned about negative
peace, without taking into account the underlying conditions that produce the direct, personal violence, is to take too narrow a view. Those
who seek negative peace as a goal must also be concerned about how to
achieve positive peace (or justice) peacefully.

Different "peacemaking" approaches can give high priority to both
these values. Jo Vellacott illustrates how both the historical practice and
the theory of nonviolence address situations of injustice with methods
that do not require direct, personal violence. Loraleigh Keashly and
William Warters also show how the injustices that characterize many
conflicts between individuals can be addressed, even transformed, by
effective nonviolent strategies of conflict intervention. Alex Morrison's
chapter on international conflict points out that the peacekeeping roles
of the United Nations focus directly on the maintenance of "negative
peace" between warring parties in the world, but this often helps create
conditions of greater "positive peace" as well.

This allows us to suggest an alternative definition of Peace Studies to
that provided by Adam Curle. Perhaps we can say that its aim is to ana-
lyze human conflicts in order to find the most peaceful (negatively
peaceful) ways to turn unjust relationships into more just (positively
peaceful). This definition has the advantage of capturing the full importance of the concept of positive peace without losing sight of the
distinction between peace and justice.

3. Conflict

We often think of conflict among human beings as a bad thing – something to be avoided at all costs. Partly as a result of this perception many
people avoid conflict as much as possible. We might even think that
peace is the absence of conflict, and that the aim of Peace Studies is to
find ways of avoiding or reducing conflict among human individuals,
groups, and nations. This would be a mistake, however. The reader will
notice that the definitions of "peace" we have reviewed so far have
referred to the absence of violence – both direct and personal and structural – but not the absence of conflict.

This is because conflict is not necessarily a bad thing, although it is the *occasion* for the well-known unpleasant things people may do when they are not very good at handling it. In fact, conflict can cause many good things. Loraleigh Keashly and William Warters point out in Chapter 2 the many positive functions that conflict can play in human relations, such as fostering creative solutions to problems, facilitating personal and social change, and maintaining personal and social identities. In addition, it can be exciting and fun. This is the whole point of competitive games, of course – to engage in a contrived, but controlled, conflict for the enjoyment of the participants and the spectators.

Many people think that if they find themselves in a conflict with another person or group, it must be because someone – me, another person, or both of us – is doing something wrong. Psychologists have found that people have tendencies toward one or other of these alternatives. Some people tend to assume that they, themselves, are doing something wrong when they find themselves in a conflict. They feel guilty and tend to resolve the conflict by giving in immediately to the other party. Others assume the opposite. They feel threatened by the conflict, blame the other party, and are more likely to be combative and aggressive. Still others blame themselves *and* others. These people are either very pessimistic and fatalistic about conflict and avoid or withdraw from it, or they look for ways to reach quick compromises. None of these are very constructive ways to deal with the problem. None of them motivate the person to engage in constructive problem-solving. A person who does not immediately assume that conflict is a sign of someone doing something wrong is less likely to engage in blaming (oneself or the other) and is therefore less likely to be aggressive and competitive and more likely to look for constructive ways of dealing with the situation.

So the point of Peace Studies and peacemaking is not necessarily to find ways to end conflicts, but to handle them more constructively. Because conflict is so often the occasion for people to become nasty toward one another – to become hateful, distrustful, alienated, aggressive, and violent – we need to find ways to carry on conflicts without becoming nasty ourselves.

4. Power

Another central concept in Peace Studies, power, is like conflict, commonly understood in many different ways. Throughout human history there has been a tendency to think of power (especially political power) as synonymous with force and violence or the threat of force or violence. Western political theorists from the Greek historian Thucydides to the seventeenth-century philosopher Thomas Hobbes and modern social theorists like Max Weber and Mao Zedong have all claimed that the use or threat of force or violence was the source and measure of political power. They believed that the greater the ability of a person or state to wreak violence upon others, the greater its power. Hobbes, for example, believed that all forms of social cooperation and trust, including moral relations between people (and presumably all animals), were possible only because a strong leader could punish with violence those who refused to cooperate.[6] Apparently he had never observed "social" animals and insects, who seem to cooperate regularly, without threat from such a centralized leader.

However, throughout this same history there have also been thinkers such as Socrates, Jesus, and the Buddha, and such influential modern political theorists as Gandhi, Hannah Arendt, and Gene Sharp, who have seriously questioned this equation of power and violence. They define power in broader, more general terms, as the ability to organize persons and groups into cooperative enterprises for the accomplishment of social goals. When power is defined as *cooperation*, it leaves open the question of its relationship with violence. Threat of violence or force may be one way to exercise power, but it may not be the only or even the most effective way. As Arendt puts it, violence may be an efficient means of exercising *destructive power*, but it is an extremely inefficient and often ineffective way of exercising *constructive power.*[7]

At the centre of the argument for nonviolent action, as can be seen in Chapter 4, is the view, shared by Gandhi, King, and Sharp, that there are forms of social power, made possible by the willingness of people to stand up to threats of violence against them, which can undermine the power of those who depend upon the threat of force and violence. The argument is based upon a simple but often ignored fact: a person who threatens others with violence in order to get them to cooperate and do his or her will is powerless if those others refuse to give in to the threat. All that is left for the threatener to do is to wreak his violence upon the refusers. In doing so, he or she destroys those who are needed to carry out the purpose. This is what Leo Tolstoy taught Gandhi about the British subjugation of India: the British colonizers needed cooperative Indian colonists to do their labour and buy their goods. When Gandhi gave the Indian people the courage to resist the British threats of violence, there was nothing the latter could do to get the cooperation they sought. It is the subjugated, Gandhi realized, who ultimately have the power over the subjugators.

Part of the task of Peace Studies is to understand the dynamics and

Figure 1: Types of Conflict Resolution

	Conflict Resolution		Conflict Management		Conflict Transformation	
	Non-coercive	Coercive	Non-coercive	Coercive	Non-coercive	Coercive
Definition of Peace	Ending Conflict		Controlling Destructive Conflict "Negative Peace"		Justice, Equal Power, Etc. "Positive Peace"	
Intermediate Goals	Avoidance of Conflict; Solve Problem; Exchange; Capitulation (Giving in)	Eliminate or Defeat Opponent; "Winning"	Establish System of Rules; With Sanctions; Avoid Stereotypes, Prejudice, Alienation, and Violence; Share Power; Compromise	Without Sanctions; Compromise; Maintain Power	Strengthen the Weak Party; Change the System; Confrontation of Power; Organizing	Weaken the Strong Party; Change the System; Confrontation of Power; Organizing
Means Used	Debate; Bargaining (with Offers); Mediation; Withdrawal (Mutual or Unilateral); Negotiation (Problem Solving)	Fighting; Threatening; Bargaining (with Threats); Force	Debate; Negotiation; Bargaining (with Offers); Mediation; Voting; Ritual (dice, coin-tossing); Voluntary Arbitration; Compromise	Bargaining (with Threats); Policing (Law Enforcement); Enforcement of Vote; Coercive Arbitration/Adjudication; Compromise	Education; Moral Persuasion; Demonstration; Parallel Rule; Non-cooperation; Negotiation; Bargaining (with Offers)	Strike; Boycott; Fighting; Sabotage; Threat; Fasting; Force; Negotiation; Bargaining (with Threats)

Figure 1: Types of Conflict Resolution

uses of power. It is one of the most important elements in conflict, since balances of power among conflicting parties have a significant impact upon the "outcome" of the conflict or the way it is handled. If peacemaking is concerned with both peace and justice (or "negative" and "positive" peace), then it is concerned to find ways of managing conflict which do not simply allow powerful parties to impose unfair settlements upon weaker parties. Keashly and Warters in Chapter 2, Morrison in Chapter 3, and Fisk in Chapter 6 are all concerned with this problem.

E. Approaches to Peacemaking

One of the primary objectives of Peace Studies is to identify, test, and implement many different strategies for dealing with conflict situations. Human beings have had such strategies for as long as they have experienced conflicts. However, some are more violent than others, and some are more effective at achieving positive peace, or justice. Some aim at "winning" the conflict or imposing a loss on the opponent; others try to find some way of ending the conflict altogether by finding a "win-win" solution. Some attempt to "manage" the conflict through agreed-upon procedures (like tossing a coin or voting) or systems of rules, while others aim at actually intensifying the conflict in order to motivate one or more of the parties to resolve it in a constructive way.

Some conflicts are between parties that are relatively equal in power and resources; some are not. A strategy likely to reach a fair resolution between parties (such as a mediated negotiation) is not nearly as likely to do so if they are highly unequal. The outcome of a negotiation between two unequal parties is predictable: it will favour the interests of the party who has the greater power. So an unrestrained negotiation between unequals will not necessarily produce a more just, or positively peaceful, outcome than will an unrestrained fight between two parties of unequal strength. Negotiation is a more negatively peaceful means than fighting or war between parties, but it does not necessarily guarantee that the resulting relationship will be good (or even better). This is why methods of conflict resolution that may be good in one type of conflict may not be as good in others.

Figure 1 provides a helpful way to understand important ways in which strategies of peacemaking define their objectives differently and employ different procedures with different implications for "peacefulness," in both of the senses we have discussed. It distinguishes three very different approaches, each defined by a different underlying conception of the "peace" to be attained. Within each of these three general approaches both coercive (and violent) and non-coercive (and nonviolent) methods can be used. The bottom row provides some examples of actual conflict resolution techniques that can be used to achieve the goals of each approach. You will notice that some techniques, such as bargaining and debating, can be used to accomplish quite different goals.

The most important things to notice in Figure 1 are the three very different aims that a peacemaking approach might have. In the first, which I have called "Conflict Resolution," the goal of the approach is to end the conflict between the parties altogether. There are many ways to do this, of course, some more constructive than others. Conflict resolution is most appropriate and constructive in those situations where the parties may *perceive* their interests to be incompatible, but where there is a "win-win" solution available which would allow them both fully to achieve their goals. Careful problem-solving through negotiation, often with the help of a mediator, can be the most constructive or "peaceful" approach. A typical way to "end the conflict" is for one of the parties simply to inflict defeat on the other and "win" by imposing terms in its own favour. Complete elimination of the opponent will end a conflict, of course, but hardly in a constructive way.

In the second peacemaking approach, "Conflict Management," the aim is not to end the conflict, but rather to get the parties to live with it or to carry it on in ways that keep it within limits that are beneficial to both parties. What else is a recreational competitive game like hockey or chess but a contrived conflict that is carried on by the opponents because they both derive certain benefits (fun, exercise, thrill of competition, etc.)? The success of the game rests upon keeping the conflict within the rules that regulate it. Many real-life conflicts are like competitive games in this respect. For example, most of the political conflicts within societies can never be terminated completely. People's political beliefs and preferences don't change that easily. What a good political system does is to find effective rules and mechanisms for deciding what laws and policies to follow, without actually ending the diversity of opinion and disagreement about these things.

Democracy, for example, is a system of conflict management. It resolves questions by a set of rule-governed mechanisms like voting (majority rule), establishing rules to protect the minority (or minorities), and so on. Courts are rule-governed institutions that decide disputes by imposing an arbitrated settlement on the parties (which does not necessarily end the conflict between them). One of the best-known mechanisms for settling conflicts between good friends is through some "ritual" such as coin-tossing, straw-drawing, or dice-throwing, which the parties consider a fair procedure.[8] Another common, and very effective, conflict management device is that of compromise. In a compromise, both parties agree not to end the conflict, but to "live with it" in a way that allows each to get some of what they want. Negotiation and problem-solving cannot always end a conflict by finding a complete win-win solution; sometimes parties have to settle for compromise.

What about the third approach to peacemaking, "Conflict Transformation"? Some people find it hard to understand how *intensifying* a conflict can be called "peacemaking" or conflict resolution. Sometimes, however, it is necessary to intensify conflict before it can be resolved in a fair and constructive way. Earlier we discussed the problem of the apparent conflict between negative peace and positive peace, or between peace and justice. There we saw that a negative peace between parties that is destructive or oppressive for one of them is hardly an acceptable peace: it is not peace in the fullest sense of the word. Conflict Transformation models attempt to deal with this issue. They recognize that often, before a conflict can be resolved (regulated or terminated) in an acceptable way, it may have to be intensified first. Maybe the power balance between the conflicting parties is extremely unequal, so that one has the power to impose terms on the other in negotiation, bargaining, debating, voting — or fighting. In such cases, one must try to restore a more equal balance of power between them. Or, maybe, one party gains much more from the conflict than the other. In such cases the party getting the benefits may find it hard to see that there is a conflict to be resolved, and even if they see it they may not be motivated to enter into any resolution. These are cases in which the first step of conflict resolution has to include ways of "getting the attention" of the other party.

That is why Conflict Transformation approaches to peacemaking are usually confrontational in nature. They are concerned with finding ways to motivate unwilling parties to make peace. Often they are aimed at either strengthening the power of the weaker party or weakening the power of the stronger party. Various forms of persuasive or even coercive pressure, such as demonstrations, strikes, boycotts, non-cooperation or civil disobedience, and other tactics associated with nonviolent resistance have power equalization and motivation as their intermediate goal. The primary goal is to achieve a "positive peace." This is what distinguishes Conflict Transformation from Conflict Resolution that aims merely at beating or eliminating one's opponents. The political actions discussed in this book by Jo Vellacott and Nigel Young are important examples of the this approach.

The various chapters of this book explore very different approaches to conflict. They recommend strategies for dealing with it that are most appropriate to the relevant level of engagement, the types of persons or groups involved, the power relationships between the parties, and their conceptions of justice. All of the authors are concerned with finding conflict regulation, or "peacemaking," strategies which meet the aim of Peace Studies as we have defined it. That is, they are looking for the most "peaceful" (nonviolent) ways to establish peaceful (just and good) relationships among persons and groups of persons. These are not necessarily the strategies that are traditionally, or habitually, employed. Many of them are met with scepticism by members of the general public, not only because they challenge deeply entrenched assumptions about what are the most "effective" or appropriate responses to conflict, but also because they may be relatively untried and untested. Responding to such issues, in Chapter 6, Larry Fisk discusses why it is important for Peace Studies to be concerned with *education* about peacemaking as well as with *research*.

Notes

1 A summary of these criticisms can be found in the *International Peace Studies Newsletter*, 15.2 (Winter 1986). One of the strongest criticisms of Peace Studies as a politicization of education is made by Caroline Cox and Roger Scruton, *Peace Studies: A Critical Survey* (London: Institute for European Defense and Strategic Studies, 1985).

2 Adam Curle, "The Scope and Dilemmas of Peace Studies," inaugural lecture at the University of Bradford, 4 February 1975 (Bradford: School of Peace Studies, University of Bradford).

3 See, for example, Robert M. Axelrod, *The Evolution of Cooperation* (New York: Basic Books, 1984). See also, M. Nowak, R. May, and K. Sigmund, "The Arithmetics of Mutual Help," *Scientific American* (June 1995): 76-81.

4 Curle.

5 Johan Galtung, "Violence, Peace, and Peace Research," *Journal of Peace Research* 6.3 (1969): 167-91.

6 Thomas Hobbes, *Leviathan: Or the Matter, Form and Power of a Commonwealth Ecclesiastical and Civil* (Paris, 1651; New York: Collier Books, 1962).

7 Hannah Arendt, *On Violence* (New York: Harcourt Brace Jovanovich, 1970).

8 Rituals like these are common ways of settling important disputes within certain so-called primitive tribes and cultures, often with great success. More

"advanced," scientific cultures are suspicious of ritualistic ways of deciding disputes, since we believe that conflict resolution should be "rational." But maybe our modern societies would be better off if we tossed coins to decide very tense political disputes between warring parties!

TWO

WORKING IT OUT: CONFLICT IN INTERPERSONAL CONTEXTS

LORALEIGH KEASHLY & WILLIAM C. WARTERS

Just as she is about to place another block on top of the stack, Jessica's older brother Mark comes by and knocks them over. Jessica shrieks with rage.

It is 1:00 a.m. Saturday morning and 16-year-old Jennifer unlocks her front door to find both of her parents waiting for her in the living room. She has missed her curfew again.

He wants to go to the mountains for their vacation, and she wants to go to the beach.

Chris has asked Pat for a divorce. They have been married 10 years, have three children, and a fair amount of property.

Sara comes back to the apartment she shares with June to find that June has not cleaned up the kitchen as she agreed to do that morning.

Mark has found out that Paul, his closest friend, has told an acquaintance about Mark's financial worries despite Mark's request that it be kept confidential.

It is 3 a.m., and the Johnson's dog is barking again.

The tenant in 3C has missed yet another monthly rental payment and has not responded to the landlord's calls or notes.

Jim goes to pick up the company car he had booked for his out-of-town meeting; he discovers that his co-worker, Sam, has taken the car to run errands and cannot be found.

Linda's boss tells her that if she would be willing to be "nice" to him, he would put in a good word for her for a promotion.

It is contract time again, and the union and its members are tired of the three-year wage freeze.

The city councillors are currently discussing what site to select for the new waste management facility.

The university board of governors is debating whether to rescind their affirmative action policy.

An environmental group has built a roadblock to prevent the logging company from moving in their equipment to begin clear-cutting.

The federal government is moving to cut spending on social welfare programming.

*   *   *   *   *   *   *

All of these situations are examples of actual or potential "interpersonal" conflict, in which the perceived needs and desires of two or more people or groups of people *within a society* appear to be incompatible and are believed to be in danger of being thwarted. Take a moment and write down what you think are the key issues in each situation. For each issue, write down who might be involved in or concerned about it. As you reflect on your answers, notice the diverse nature of the settings and relationships in which conflict can occur. Our challenge is to talk about approaches to dealing with conflict that can address these incredibly diverse situations. This is a daunting task. While they may share common features or processes, each is unique, and both the common and unique features have an influence on how we might best address these problems. Some approaches may be more relevant and effective in certain circumstances than in others or will take different forms depending upon the situation.

Our beliefs about what conflict is and why it happens influence the specific approaches we choose to use when dealing with it. It is therefore important to be aware of the wide variety of perspectives on the nature and causes of conflict. We will begin with a brief review of major theories about conflict to help orient the reader. We will then move on to identify the range of conflict intervention strategies available, including strategies that the parties themselves use and strategies that third parties use. We will discuss negotiation and mediation in some detail because of the centrality of these ideas and the enormous amount of attention they have received both from researchers and actual conflict intervenors. These two approaches are closely related to one another. Indeed, mediation (which involves a neutral third party in the process) is often referred to as "assisted negotiation." The increasingly popular concepts of dispute resolution systems design in organizations will also be discussed. We will then re-examine these approaches with a more cultural lens, looking at the assumptions about human behaviour in general and conflict in particular upon which they are based. The chapter will conclude with a discussion of an alternative way of viewing conflict management commonly known as the transformative approach.

A. Perspectives on the Nature and Causes of Conflict

The many theories about what conflict is and how it develops have implications for how it may be resolved. A full discussion is beyond the scope of this chapter; however, it is useful to look at the various "families" of theories as they reflect different perspectives on how best to understand conflict. James Schellenberg (no relation to the co-editor of this book) discusses four main types: individual characteristics, social structural, social process, and formal theories. We will present each of these perspectives briefly and refer the reader to Schellenberg's work for a more detailed discussion.[1]

1. The Individual Characteristics Perspective

Theories of this type focus on individual behavioural factors and consider their role in creating or maintaining conflict. The basic idea is that social conflict is a result of aggression by individuals. Human aggression has been attributed both to a biological instinct or drive (broadly, to human nature) and to learned behaviour.

Developing the view of aggression as human nature, Freud proposed that human behaviour is the result of interaction between two very basic instincts – life (sexual) and death (destructive) – and that these two instincts are constantly at odds with each other. He argued that humans are fundamentally violent by nature. At best, violence can be somewhat controlled by creating external laws and by emphasizing and building on the connections between us. Given the inevitability of the aggressive drive, Freud said, there is a need for release of aggressive impulses; conflict is the result. This view was popularized in what is called the "frustration-aggression hypothesis," articulated by John Dollard and his colleagues in 1939.[2] In essence, they argued that frustration leads to an increased tendency to aggress against someone or something. By aggressing against the cause of the frustration (e.g., the boss) or some suitable substitute (e.g., the family dog), we can effectively release our internal tension.

Theories linking aggression with a *personality trait* also fall within the perspective of aggression as part of human nature. The most notable work in this area is that of Theodore Adorno and his colleagues on the authoritarian personality. The authoritarian individual is characterized as someone who tends to blame others for his/her problems and experiences hostility and prejudice toward outsiders. Authoritarian individuals are thought to be more aggressive and, therefore, to cause more conflict.[3]

Another view suggests that aggressive behaviour is actually a rational response to particular situations; that is, aggressive behaviour is a learned response designed to achieve certain objectives (for example, getting the toy a child wants or getting one's partner to stop "nagging"). If being aggressive allows a person to get what they want, that behaviour gets rewarded and is likely to continue. This view is based on the principles of operant conditioning in psychology. Another way in which people learn aggressive behaviours is by observing how others act and seeing the results they achieve. This is known as observational learning. The view emphasizing observational learning has been used to argue for the negative effect of television violence on children.

Whether aggression is viewed as part of human nature or as a rational, learned response, it is individual behaviour that is thought to fuel social conflict. Taking this perspective, one might focus on options for reducing conflict that control or manage an individual's behaviours. This can be done by reducing frustrations, providing opportunities to channel aggressive impulses (e.g., through competitive games), reducing the rewards for aggressive behaviours, or by providing new models for children to observe.

2. The Social Structural Perspective

This perspective sees conflict as a product of the way society is organized. The major divisions of society, such as race, ethnicity, class, and gender, are seen as the underlying foundations of conflict. A number of views fall within this category – for example, Marxism (class conflict) and feminism (gender conflict). At the heart of this perspective is the belief that there are major groupings of people within any society that do not have the same access to economic, political, and social resources. They are valued differently, and this – and the accompanying differential access to key resources – leads to social conflict. For example, some feminists argue that women are systematically disadvantaged by a male-dominated society. Similarly, a racial structural perspective argues that in the North American context people of colour are constrained and treated inequitably relative to white people. Thus the fuel for social conflict is inherent in the way society is structured. A cue that particular kinds of disputes may be reflective of structural inequities is provided when similar disputes and issues keep occurring between particular groupings of people – for example, blacks and whites, men and women – even though the individual disputants change.

Efforts to resolve structurally-based conflicts require alterations of basic social structures. Schellenberg identifies three ways in which these "alterations" may be attempted:

1. **Gradual reform** – focusing on changing social structures over time by the cumulative effect of limited interventions; e.g., affirmative action, social welfare programming

2. **Nonviolent confrontation** – working aggressively for fundamental social change but without violence; e.g., the movements associated with Gandhi and Martin Luther King, Jr.

3. **Violent confrontation** – seeking basic social change through the use of violence; e.g., violent protests, overthrow of institutions

3. The Social Process Perspective

Theories from this perspective focus on the social interaction between individuals or groups. Social conflict is understood to be not strictly the result of individual or societal structural factors; rather, it is in the interaction of individuals and groups that conflict manifests itself and ebbs and flows. Thus, while the seeds for a specific dispute may lie in individual or structural characteristics, the development of conflict lies in the interaction of people. A basic premise of this perspective is that our behaviour generally, and conflict-specific behaviours in particular, are

Table 1: Characteristics of cooperative and competitive social processes

Nature of process	Cooperative	Competitive
Characteristic Attitudes	trusting, friendly, helpful	suspicious, hostile, exploitive
Perceptions	sensitive to similarities and minimize differences in beliefs and values	sensitive to differences and minimize similarities in beliefs and values
Communication	open, accurate, respectful	indirect, misleading, threats
Task Orientation	problem to be mutually solved	contest to be won unilateral solution

Adapted from: L. Keashly, "Conflict and Conflict Management," *Applied Social Psychology*, ed. Stanley W. Sadava and Donald. M. McCreary (Englewood Cliffs, NJ: Prentice-Hall, 1996) ch.13: 248-273.

guided by our subjective interpretations of the situation. We act toward one another based on the meanings we ascribe to each other's actions and the situation in which they occur. According to this perspective, we should be interested in the perceptions, communications, and attitudes of the persons involved and in how these relate to observed behaviour over the course of the conflict. This is a very dynamic and fluid perspective, as perceptions and meanings will influence and in turn be influenced by the behaviours in the conflict.

A good example of this perspective is the work of Morton Deutsch. As a social psychologist, Deutsch has focused his research on understanding the conditions that would give rise to productive as opposed to destructive processes of conflict management. Trying to understand why some conflicts become entrenched and difficult to resolve, he proposed his "crude law of social relations": the use of a particular action will tend to elicit the same action in return. In essence, you get back what you give; cooperation breeds cooperation, competition breeds competition. Relating this to the conflict process, we can say that cooperative relations lead to productive resolution, whereas competitive relations move quickly into destructive conflict.[4] By referring to Table 1, it is easy to see how engaging in reciprocal competitive actions can fuel escalatory processes in the conflict. Suspicious attitudes mount, communication becomes more indirect and misleading, differences are exaggerated and similarities are minimized, until a "deadly" and vicious conflict is in play.

From a social process perspective, then, it will be said that while a conflict may arise from individual or structural characteristics, its movement into constructive or destructive patterns will depend upon the perceptions, attitudes, orientations, and subsequent behaviours of the people involved. Process-oriented approaches for dealing with conflict include the facilitating of constructive disputant interactions either by the parties themselves (e.g., using structured negotiation), by other persons (e.g., using mediation, arbitration, consultation), or by the system (e.g., adjudication).

4. The Formal Perspective

Theories of this type characterize the development and resolution of conflict in logical and mathematical terms, and view disputants as "super-rational,"[5] calculating costs and benefits and then choosing the most rewarding options. Adopting this perspective involves identifying key concepts about conflict development (e.g., number of issues in dispute, number of arms available, etc.), making assumptions about how these concepts relate to each other, and translating these assumptions into a mathematical form such as an equation. The mathematical model is then tested using concrete data such as historical information on past conflicts. At the heart of this perspective is the belief that there is some inevitability in the way conflicts will develop given certain conditions, and that the researcher's job is to discover these natural conflict patterns.

A popular theory within this perspective is called game theory. It relies on using games or simulations to examine the ways in which conflicts of interests (such as those that arise with resource allocation in situations of scarce resources) may be resolved. It is argued that the structure of the different games researchers develop mimics the structure and factors in various real-life conflicts and provides information on people's decision-making behaviours in conflict situations. The classic gaming situation is what is known as a two-person, zero-sum situation. In a two-person game, there are only two disputants, which simplifies conflict interactions. "Zero-sum" means that any gains made by one party are at the expense of the other. A good example of this is the prisoner's dilemma, in which police have apprehended two people for a crime. They put them in separate rooms and ask them to confess. The sentence they will receive depends not only on their response but on that of the other person, with whom they have no communication. If one confesses and the other does not, the one who confesses gets a severe sentence while the other goes free. If both confess, they both get a reduced sentence. If neither confesses, they both go free. Their best bet is to cooperate and not confess, but since they cannot communicate with one another, they do not know what the other will do. Even in what seems such an unresolvable situation, researchers have demonstrated that there is an equilibrium solution that works for both parties.

The more challenging games present mixed-motive or variable-sum situations, where there are some opposing and some common interests. A good example of this type of game is the dilemma of the social commons, in which several people rely on a single common or pasture for grazing their sheep. If each person lets their sheep graze as much as they want, the common will be depleted, and there will be no more food for any of them. Thus, to maintain a constant source of food, they must consider the needs of the others who use this common in addition to their own needs. In these situations, there is no one optimal solution. Most real-life conflicts are of a mixed motive nature.

The value of game theory is that it can be used to evaluate the strategies of the parties and to determine how they might best work together to resolve their conflict. However, what is a good mathematical solution may not be what is psychologically or socially satisfying for the parties involved.[6] Indeed, there is a whole area of research focused on understanding why negotiators do not behave more "rationally," that is, why they do not negotiate the mathematically optimal solution.[7]

The formal theories draw our attention to the critical nature of the initiating conditions in predicting certain conflict outcomes. Thus, efforts at managing conflict from this perspective focus on altering the initiating conditions disputants encounter, an approach somewhat congruent with the social structural perspective.

In sum, then, these perspectives on the nature and causes of conflict draw our attention to the variety of factors and contexts relevant to interpersonal conflict. While each perspective may be adequate to explain a specific sort of conflict, none adequately explains conflict in general. Each offers a piece of the puzzle. Each suggests the kinds of questions we may wish to ask when observing conflict. How much of the behaviour is due to the character of those involved? How much is it a result of social, political, or economic inequities between the groups of which the disputants are members? How much is it a reflection of an escalatory process (e.g., us-them thinking)? Do these factors come together in some logical, predictable way? Is there an optimal solution? These perspectives also permit us to think in a more focused way about possible strategies for dealing with interpersonal conflicts. It is to this discussion that the remainder of the chapter is devoted.

B. Approaches to Dealing with Conflict

It can be argued that conflicts are neither inherently good nor bad, but simply facts of life. While this argument is often used in the introduction of articles and books on the subject, it is clear that many of us think that conflict is not a good thing. This assumption is revealed in the terms used by scholars and practitioners of various approaches to dealing with conflict — "prevention," "reduction," "settlement," or "termination." But other terms have been used too — for example, "conflict management," "conflict resolution," and "conflict transformation." "Conflict management" is often chosen as the appropriate term as it reflects a belief that conflict is an ongoing part of life which, while it may not be ended, can at least be managed constructively. The term "conflict resolution" more clearly suggests that conflict can be *ended* successfully. Those favouring the use of the term "conflict transformation" argue that both the conflict management and conflict resolution perspectives focus on the settlement of conflict issues but pay too little attention to the nature of the relationship in which the conflict occurs. Conflict transformation advocates argue that without changes in the parties' understanding of the dispute and its connection to the nature of their relationship and their appreciation of each other, conflictual situations and relations will continue to prevail. While there will likely be disagreement as to how we have characterized the meaning of each of these terms, it is fair to say that much of the literature on dealing with conflict has focused more on management and resolution and less on transformation. We will return to this point later in the section on a critique of the Western approach to conflict. For now, we will use the term "conflict management." As employed here, its meaning encompasses all strategies that focus on either ending, resolving, or transforming conflict.

As can already be seen from the discussion of major perspectives on conflict, the ways of managing conflicts are as varied as the theories. In their recent book on negotiation, Dean Pruitt and Peter Carnevale suggest that there are three broad ways of categorizing conflict management strategies:

1. **Joint decision-making** — methods by which the parties work together on their own, or with a third-party facilitator, to determine what the outcome will be; e.g., negotiation, mediation

2. **Third-party decision-making** — methods by which a "third" person or persons not only facilitates negotiation, but *makes* the relevant decision, thus determining the outcome of the dispute; e.g., adjudication (legal system), arbitration, and decision-making by a legitimate authority such as a manager or parent

3. **Separate action** — methods by which parties make independent decisions; e.g., retreat (yielding to the other), struggle (fighting against the other), and tacit coordination (accommodating to each other without discussion)[8]

The literature on conflict management has tended to focus on the joint decision-making methods of negotiation and mediation. This reflects beliefs that joint decision-making procedures are less costly (in terms of money, time, lives), more likely to reflect the parties' own interests, and more likely to honour and support the parties' relationship than the other two types. However, joint decision-making procedures are based on voluntary participation, open and direct communications between the parties, trust in each other, shared values, and positive feeling (or at least, manageable negative feeling) towards each other. For some conflictual situations and relationships, this combination of factors is unlikely to exist, at least in the initial stages of the conflict — for example, partners in an abusive marriage or those involved in hate crimes. Often parties move to struggle because they believe they can get more that way than through using joint or third-party procedures. Indeed, struggle can help get a party's needs and goals acknowledged. Take, for example, public protests that gradually move governments to deal with structural barriers to racial and gender equality. It appears that it is only when the struggle becomes too costly, that is, when a "hurting stalemate" is reached,[9] that joint procedures become attractive. Because of the substantial volume of work on the joint decision-making methods, the rest of this chapter will focus on them, particularly on negotiation and mediation.

1. Negotiation

Negotiation has been referred to as a "basic, generic human activity ... something that we all do, almost on a daily basis."[10] Negotiation can be described as a discussion between two or more parties with (apparently) differing preferences, interests, or goals aimed at reaching some form of mutually beneficial agreement.[11] P. H. Gulliver briefly and eloquently describes typical negotiator behaviour in the following way:

> [B]y the exchange of information, they explore the nature and extent of their differences and possibilities open to them, they seek to induce or persuade each other to modify their expectations and requirements, and they search for an outcome that is at least satisfactory enough to both parties.[12]

Looking at some of the situations described at the beginning of this chapter, we can see that people could negotiate who gets what toy, joint custody, reasonable curfews, recovery of money owed, appropriate wages, environmental issues, and equitable access to education and employment. A critical element for negotiation is that the parties be interdependent; that is, each party must require the other's assistance to get what they want.[13] Being dependent on one another demands that parties assert their own desires and also consider, and at times accommodate to, the demands and needs of the other person or group. Negotiation is this process of assertion, consideration, and accommodation.

a) Approaches to negotiation

Before discussing specific strategies and tactics in negotiation, it is important to step back and consider, at a more general level, how negotiations have been conceptualized in the literature and in practice. Two major approaches to negotiations have dominated the literature: the concession-convergence model and the mutual gains model.[14] In the concession-convergence model, negotiators are depicted as being on opposite sides of an issue and gradually coming to agreement through a series of accommodations in the form of offers and counteroffers. Implicit in this model is the notion that the gains of one party will be at the expense of the other; that is, we have a zero-sum arrangement. In order for agreement to be achieved, each party must be willing to give up some of their initial aspirations. Thus, the two parties "converge" on some point between their initial positions that is acceptable to both of them. This model characterizes traditional union-management negotiations. For example, "knowing" they will need to eventually concede, the union will start by asking for a higher wage than the lowest they are willing to accept, and management will begin by offering less than they are ultimately willing to pay. Through a series of concessions, they (hopefully) will agree on a wage level that falls within each party's acceptable range. This model is known as the distributive bargaining approach because of its focus on determining how to distribute limited resources among the parties.[15]

The mutual gains model popularized in *Getting to Yes* by Roger Fisher and William Ury assumes that there may well be integrative (also known as win-win) potential in any conflict situation.[16] That is, there is the possibility that an agreement can be reached that meets the needs of all parties. Instead of focusing on "how much" of some item each party wants (their position), the mutual gains model argues that it is more important to consider "why" each party has taken the position they have (i.e., what are their interests?). In essence, a stated position (I want the car tonight!) is a way of addressing some underlying interest or concern (I need to get to the library to do some research for class). If people's underlying concerns are made clear, it is possible to come up with ways of meeting those needs that also allow the other party's needs to be met. Thus, in this integrative approach, negotiations and the resultant agreements are based on an analysis of the parties' interests. The oft-told story of the orange conflict (which has various versions) nicely illustrates the distinction between the distributive and integrative approaches to negotiation. One version depicts two sisters arguing over how to divide up the last remaining orange in a fruit basket. Through a series of offers and counteroffers, they finally agree to a 50-50 split. Upon receiving each of their halves, one sister eats the fruit and throws away the peel while the other throws away the fruit and uses the peel in a recipe. Had the sisters discussed why each of them wanted the orange (what their interests were), both could have had everything they wanted instead of getting only some of it. Thus, getting at the interests underlying people's positions may well permit the development of creative solutions in which everyone gets what they want; that is, each gets their needs met.

It is easy to see from these brief descriptions how the mutual gains approach might be seen as far more desirable than a concession-convergence approach. However, each of these approaches will be more or less appropriate depending upon the nature of the conflictual issues and the context in which the conflict occurs.[17] The distributive approach may be expected in certain situations; for example, bartering for goods in a market or in traditional labor-management relations.[18] And it may be used in other situations too, if parties do not have the time, energy, or commitment to devote to a mutual gains approach. On the other hand, if the situation involves numerous issues, and it is critical that both parties be committed to carrying out any agreement that is developed, then open sharing of information and joint analysis of the problems as characterized by the mutual gains approach will be needed. In most concrete cases, Rubin argues, "[e]ffective negotiation requires a judicious mix of both approaches..."[19]

(b) Strategies and tactics

Parties utilize a wide variety of more specific strategies in their negotiations with each other. The negotiation literature identifies five such strategies: *concession-making, contending, problem-solving, inaction, and withdrawal.*[20] These strategies involve a range of behaviours or tactics.

Concession-making (also known as yielding or accommodating) involves reducing one's own demands or desires in order to accommodate the other party. In the divorce example at the beginning of this chapter, Pat may concede Chris's demand for primary custody of the children, even though Pat had originally desired joint custody.

Contending involves either trying to get the other party to concede or resisting such pressure from the other party. Contentious tactics include threats, harassment, and positional commitments (refusal to concede on an issue). For example, in the barking dog situation, the neighbours could insist that the Johnsons get rid of their dog and threaten to call the police if they do not.

Problem-solving involves trying to identify solutions that would satisfy both parties' concerns. Tactics associated with this approach include providing accurate information on one's priorities, actively listening to the other's concerns, and brainstorming possible solutions. For example, in the logging dispute, representatives of the company and the protestors could disclose their concerns (e.g., producing lumber and preserving the wildlife habitat) and generate possible solutions that might meet both these interests (e.g., restricting cutting to limited areas with replacement).

Inaction and *withdrawal* are considered to be qualitatively different strategies from the other three as they are not oriented toward forging some kind of agreement.[21] As the term suggests, inaction involves "doing nothing," while withdrawal involves one party refusing to continue in the negotiations. Both are deemed to be examples of an *avoidance* strategy wherein one party makes every effort not to address the issues in dispute. For example, in the waste management case, the city councillors could continue to refer the issue to "committee" or defer the discussion to the next meeting.

While these different strategies are suggestive of different attitudes or mind-sets toward negotiations, the reality is that throughout the process of negotiations, negotiators may alternate between strategies. For example, in the union-management situation, the union may stand firm on the wage issue (contention), but be willing to concede on certain aspects of the benefits package (accommodation). Issues on which the parties are firmly opposed may be "dropped" from subsequent discussions or referred to a joint committee outside of the negotiated contract (avoidance). On other issues, such as vacation and leave, both management and the union may be willing to brainstorm creative solutions (problem-solving). In essence, effective negotiation (i.e., achieving a mutually satisfying agreement) requires a "matching" of strategy to features of the current situation, such as the issues, the priorities attached to them by negotiators, and the behaviours exhibited by negotiators up to that point.[22]

The notion of matching behaviour to situation is part of a broader discussion of what influences negotiators' choice of strategy. One predominant model of strategic choice is called the Dual Concern Model, which focuses on predicting negotiators' initial strategic preference.[23] This model proposes that negotiators have two types of independent concerns: concern for their own outcome and concern for the other party's outcome. These dimensions vary from weak to strong, and the combination of the levels of these two predicts a particular strategy. High self-concern coupled with low other-concern is associated with a contending strategy. Low self-concern and high other-concern is associated with the concession-making or yielding strategy. High concern for self and for other is associated with problem-solving strategies. Inaction (and this includes withdrawal) is assumed to be produced by low levels of concern for both one's own and other's outcomes. In their review of the experimental literature regarding this model, Pruitt and Carnevale found that contentious tactics were more likely under conditions of high self-concern and low other-concern. In addition, higher levels of joint benefit or win-win outcomes were found in conditions of high self-concern and high other-concern, which they argued to be indicative of the use of some form of problem-solving during negotiations.

The research suggests, then, that being strictly concerned with one's own goals can actually hinder the progress of negotiations and the achievement of a good joint outcome. By considering the other's outcomes, negotiations appear to proceed in a more problem-solving fashion with higher joint outcomes – that is, everyone benefits. (It is important to remember that the Dual Concern model concerns the preferred strategy of a single negotiator.)

c) The Social Context of Negotiation

Social norms. A frequent criticism of the theoretical and research literature on negotiation is the failure to acknowledge that negotiation occurs within a broader *social context*;[24] negotiators do not operate in isolation from everything else around them. Just as with any human social process, negotiations are shaped by social norms which influence what are considered the qualities of a "good" negotiation process and the qualities of an "acceptable" agreement. Norms regarding the "fairness" of both the outcome (distributive justice) and the procedure by which the outcome was determined (procedural justice) are relevant to negotiations. There are a variety of ways in which outcome fairness, for example, can be defined – equality, equity, and need.[25] The norm of equality requires that everyone benefits or contributes equally. Equity requires that the benefit people receive is in direct relation to how much they contribute – for example, more work means more pay. Finally, the needs rule requires that benefit accrues to those who need it most – for example, those who are less able are taken care of. While we can debate which norm is most appropriate, what is critical in negotiations is that the negotiators share the same definition or rule of fairness.[26] Negotiations can be slow and even fail when negotiators hold fast to different interpretations of fairness. To the extent that these norms are held dear (as morally right, for example), rigidity in behaviour and positions is likely to follow. This leaves little room for either integrative or distributive negotiations (how can one compromise on principle?). Some strategies to reduce rigidity include trying to move discussions away from principles to more concrete and specific issues such as wages, or trying to find solutions that have features that satisfy all definitions of fairness.[27]

Social norms vary both within a culture and across cultures. Thus the utilization of negotiation requires sensitivity and awareness of cultural differences and of how these relate to what is considered as appropriate behaviour and satisfactory outcome.[28] We will return to this point in the section critiquing the Western perspective on conflict and its management.

Group and intergroup inXuences. In many negotiations, the negotiator at the bargaining table actually represents some larger group or constituency – for example, unions, interest groups, the government, and community or grassroots organizations. In these situations, a negotiator is not acting as an autonomous individual but as a representative of a group. Thus the negotiator's behaviour in and outside of the negotiation situation is subject to a variety of *group influences.*[29] Principles derived from strictly interpersonal negotiations – where negotiators speak only for themselves – are not fully generalizable to intergroup negotiations. For example, groups or constituencies will have their own internal differences which will require continual reconciliation and which will affect negotiations with the other group. Thus negotiations occur both within and between groups.[30] What can make intergroup negotiations even more complex is that the representative may actually be a team of negotiators. This introduces the possible need for within-team negotiations and reconciliation as well.

An interesting finding is that the nature of the interaction *within* these different groups leads to similar interaction with the other group. As with Deutsch's crude law of social relations, cooperative intragroup relations lead to cooperative intergroup relations.[31]

Another finding is that even in what appears to be a conflict between two individuals, group and intergroup processes may still be relevant to understanding the processes and outcomes. For example, if two students are hotly debating the issue of affirmative action and one is white and the other is black, it is possible that their interaction is being influenced by the broader social relations between these two racial groups. The social structural perspective on conflict encourages us to consider these influences in all negotiations regardless of whether the negotiators are representing themselves or others. Thus an understanding of negotiations requires a recognition and examination of the role of group and intergroup influences.

Problems of Power. Any discussion of negotiation context would not be complete without an explicit acknowledgment of the role of *power.* Much of the research and practice literature is premised on the assumption that negotiators are equal in power, but this probably occurs relatively infrequently. Looking at the list of situations at the beginning of this chapter, it is possible to see in each one that the disputants may be more or less powerful relative to each other, as well as in a more absolute sense. Even in a marriage/divorce situation, one partner may have more power relative to the other. And such is definitely the case in sexual harassment and racial discrimination situations. Governments may have more absolute power than specific interest groups, although there are certainly examples where a specific group manifested greater influence and hence power – for example, where the military had an impact on government decisions. *Power* in this context refers to the ability to influence another to do what one wishes and often to influence them to do something they would not choose to do on their own. According to French and Raven, the bases or types of power vary widely and include:

1. **reward power** – ability to provide what the other desires

2. **punishment power** – ability to withhold desired things, or to give undesired things; e.g., being grounded, being hit, strikes

3. **referent power** – influence based on being liked or respected by the other

4. **legitimate power** – based on having agreed-upon authority; e.g., the power of managers in relation to subordinates; parents in relation to children

5. **expert power** – based on having special experience or ability[32]

One person's power is also affected by the degree of dependency of the other person. The more dependent a person or group is on another person or group, the more powerful the latter is in the relationship. Some interesting research findings are that in terms of relative power, the more powerful negotiator often concedes less, often uses more contentious tactics, and as a result often obtains higher outcomes. However, these results depend on the size of the power difference. If the other person or group is only slightly less powerful, they can retaliate and the negotiations can deteriorate into a struggle.[33] When both parties are quite powerful, with support from external resources and groups, there is less threatening and more conciliatory behaviour, as a result of fear of escalation and the severe harm that might result should they struggle.

As we work to engage effectively in negotiations, we are challenged to understand the myriad ways in which power is manifested and parties perceive their own influence and power. As noted earlier, a disadvantaged group may choose collective, and possibly violent, action in an effort to get the more powerful other to recognize them and deal with them fairly — take, for example, riots in response to a failure to convict police on charges of brutality towards blacks. Thus a "power" perspective allows us to understand more fully the rationale for apparently "undesirable" and harmful behaviour. It encourages us to find other ways in which those less powerful can have genuine influence or voice in negotiations. It also encourages us to examine how more powerful parties generate situations in which others feel pushed into violence.

2. Mediation

When individuals or groups are having difficulty or are unable to manage the conflict between them, a frequently sought after (or offered) alternative is to involve a third party to help resolve the situation. Mediation is not the only example of such third-party intervention. Some other strategies involving third parties are:

1. **adjudication** – involving a judge or jury in a court setting

2. **arbitration** – involving an independent third party who hears both sides of the problem and decides what the solution should be

3. **conciliation** – involving an independent third party who brings disputants together so they can talk; may persuade parties to meet face-to-face or may "shuttle" information back and forth; not active in the actual discussion or agreement; primarily a communication link

4. **fact-finding** – involving an independent third party who gathers information to arrive at an independent judgement of the dispute which is often only advisory; usually has little contact with the disputants other than to gather facts

Like procedures 3 and 4 (and unlike procedures 1 and 2), mediation is a strategy of conflict management that seeks only to facilitate a final decision — a decision ultimately made by the disputants themselves. But unlike all of the other procedures, mediation involves an independent third party who works directly with the disputants to identify problems and to reach an agreement that satisfies both. More research attention has been directed toward mediation than to any other intervention approach. This is likely a reflection of its ever-expanding use across a variety of settings.[34] A brief overview of the mediation process will be presented to provide a better idea of how it works. Then the question of effectiveness will be addressed by drawing on Kressel and associates' review of mediation research.[35]

a) The process

To get a clearer idea of what mediation can be, consider the following definition, provided in the context of a review of conflict, negotiation, and third-party interventions in organizations:

> By definition, mediators employ a variety of strategies and tactics to initiate and facilitate interactions between disputants, but leave the final resolution or terms of settlement in the hands of the disputants. Thus, mediation primarily relies on facilitating negotiation (problem-solving) among disputants.[36]

A variety of models have been proposed to characterize the mediation process.[37] Since the intention here is to convey a flavour of the mediation experience, a brief anecdotal description rather than a detailed identification of the stages, issues, and tactics that may occur or be utilized will be provided.

Mediation is characterized by face-to-face interaction between the disputants (or their representatives in the case of intergroup conflicts) in the presence of the mediator, who may be a single person or a number of people. Prior to this interaction, there is often preliminary contact between the mediator and each disputant to get some sense of the issues and the disputants' willingness and commitment to proceed. Once this has been established, the interactive session begins with the mediator explaining the procedures and the role of the neutral third party in that process. At this point, ground rules for constructive dialogue are identified (e.g., no interrupting, no name-calling, confidentiality). Disputants are then given uninterrupted time to tell their stories in turn, with the mediator ensuring that the process stays constructive. Based on all information, the mediator will often summarize and clarify the main issues presented by the parties. Disputants will further clarify or add more issues if they are missed by the mediator. Then the disputants and the mediator enter into a problem-solving phase in which they review concerns and interests and develop alternatives that will address these issues to the disputants' mutual satisfaction. During this and the earlier phase on identifying issues, the mediator may "caucus" (meet with each disputant separately) if the discussion bogs down or if the mediator wants to explore any reluctance or resistance on the part of the disputants. Assuming a variety of acceptable alternatives are generated, the disputants will reach an agreement, which is often written down in concrete and specific language and signed by both parties as an indication of their support. While this discussion portrays the mediation as a linear step-by-step process, often there is cycling back to earlier phases. As a result, a mediation can take a lot of time and occur over a number of sessions.

Just as negotiators make choices among a range of possible strategies, so do mediators. Peter Carnevale has proposed the *Concern Likelihood* model (similar to the Dual Concern model of negotiator behavior) to describe mediator strategic choice. Mediator behaviour is classified into four general strategies:

1. **Problem-solving** – where efforts are directed to finding an integrative solution that satisfies both parties

2. **Compensation** – where promises of rewards or benefits are used to get parties to come to agreement

3. **Pressure** – where threat of or actual punishment is used to get parties to come to agreement

4. **Inaction** – which involves a deliberate effort to let the parties handle things on their own[38]

The likelihood of a mediator choosing one of these strategies is affected by two factors: 1) the degree of perceived common ground (i.e., estimate of likelihood of an integrative agreement); and 2) the mediator's degree of concern for the achievement of the parties' aspirations. In the now familiar two-dimensional framework, mediator strategies are located in terms of their position on these two variables. If the mediator believes that there is much common ground and cares that parties achieve their desires, then s/he is likely to pursue a problem-solving approach. If little common ground is perceived and the mediator is not concerned with the parties' aspirations, then a pressing strategy is more likely. If common ground is perceived but the mediator is not concerned with parties' aspirations, then s/he is predicted to pursue an inaction strategy. That is, the mediator would lie back and let parties do the work. When the mediator is concerned that the parties achieve their aspirations but there is little evidence of common ground, s/he is likely to engage in compensatory tactics in an effort to get some kind of agreement. Like negotiators, mediators will vary their strategies throughout the course of the mediation depending upon such factors as disputant behaviour, time pressure, changes in disputant priorities, and external pressure.

b) Mediation effectiveness

The definition of success for a mediation seems to depend on: 1) the perspective from which the question is asked (disputant, third party, interested others, the courts), and 2) what aspect of the conflict is addressed (settlement or agreement, disputants' relationship, costs). Regarding settlement and agreement, Kressel and Pruitt report median (average) settlement rates of 60 per cent across all settings examined in their review, with a range from 20 to 80 per cent. When contrasted with adjudicated agreements, these mediated agreements can be seen to include more of a joint emphasis, wherein individuals compromise from their previously held positions. (The same authors note that this compromising may in some contexts have occurred as a result of mediator pressure or bias rather than disputants' actual desire to reach a mutually satisfying agreement.)[39]

In terms of compliance with agreements once they are reached: the evidence suggests that people do maintain the commitments they have agreed to, with rates of 67 to 87 per cent compliance considered typical in neighbourhood mediation centres. Given the voluntary nature of most mediation programs, these agreement indicators may also reflect the nature of the disputants themselves, who choose to enter mediation rather than use the more legalistic methods. That is, one reason settlement may be so much higher in mediation is because the disputants going into the process are already open to a joint agreement.

The efficiency and cost effectiveness of mediation relative to other procedures, particularly adjudication, is also used as an indicator of mediation success. Cases that reach mediation tend to settle more quickly than those sent through adjudication.[40] The specific financial cost difference has been a much more difficult indicator to develop and hence requires further work. What evidence there is suggests that, at the very least, mediation is not as expensive as adjudication. Another indicator of cost effectiveness is more social-psychological in nature and involves the parties' perceptions of satisfaction and fairness. User satisfaction with and perceived fairness of the mediation process are reported to be quite high: 75 per cent even for those who fail to reach agreement. In contrast to adjudication, mediation is viewed as fairer and more satisfying.

With respect to the disputants' relationship, mediation tends to improve the interaction between disputants both within and outside of the mediation setting. In a review of ten years of research on divorce mediation programs, it was found that many divorcing couples who did not reach agreement reported that they still found the mediation process valuable as it facilitated their communication and, in a few cases, reconciliation. The argument is that the focus on constructive dialogue and problem-solving between the disputants, with the mediator modelling these behaviours, creates a more hospitable and cooperative environment, which makes it easier for the disputants to try new behaviours with each other.[41]

A number of factors can influence just how effective mediation will be. The nature of the issue under mediation is particularly critical. As noted earlier, issues of "principle" or of values are extremely difficult to resolve. These are deeply felt and not easily amenable to compromise types of solutions. The disputants' relationship also helps to determine just how effective the mediation will be. The closer the relationship between the parties (family, friends, neighbours), the more likely it is that an agreement will be reached. However, many of these agreements do not hold,[42] often because there are a number of other issues involved that were not the focus of mediation. Left unaddressed, they tend to resurface and disrupt the calm that comes with settlement of other issues.

Mediation is also less effective if the power in the relationship is unequal. For example, in divorce mediation, women who are economically disadvantaged relative to their partner report less improvement in their relationship.[43] Another example of an unequal power relationship is one in which there is or has been violence – for example, spouse abuse. A great controversy rages over whether these cases should ever be mediated.[44] Finally, the more motivated both disputants are to reach an agreement and the greater their commitment to the mediation process, the more effective the mediation will be.

By far the majority of studies of mediation focus on formal or contractual mediation, in which it is the third party's recognized task to conduct conflict intervention. It is perhaps worth noting, as we conclude our discussion of mediation, that far less attention has been paid to the more informal or emergent mediation and intervention work that we all do on a daily basis as parents with children, friends with friends, coworkers with coworkers, or managers with employees.[45] One example, though, is B.H. Sheppard's work on managers as conflict intervenors. Briefly, a common finding reported in the organizational conflict literature is that managers use procedures that are quite different from the conciliatory and mediational strategies recommended by organizational behaviour experts. Based on interviews with managers about how they intervene in disputes, three styles were identified, none of which look at all like mediation. The most frequently occurring procedure (inquisitorial style) involved managers actively controlling the discussion and what disputants could say and then making and enforcing decisions. The next most frequently described procedure (providing impetus style) involved managers calling disputants together, asking what was going on, and then telling them to settle it, or else. The third procedure (adversarial style) involved the manager passively listening to the disputants, often at their request, and then making the decision, rather like what a judge would do.[46] Studies such as Sheppard's are an example of the importance of considering the context within which we identify and examine third-party intervention.

3. Dispute Resolution Systems Design

Another interesting role for a third party that has received recent attention is that of designer of dispute resolution systems. The impetus for this approach comes from at least two different directions. First, as hopefully is clear from the presentation of major perspectives on conflict, different conflicts may require different management approaches. For example, a structurally-based conflict like that produced by racial inequality will require efforts at restructuring the current system and redressing past injuries. This would definitely require some more authoritative kinds of management from the government or an organization. The second impetus is a belief that, because many conflicts are handled inappropriately, disputants need to be aware of all the options they have. In an effort to address these issues, Ury, Brett, and Goldberg have argued for the value of formally designing systems of options for dispute resolution within organizations. In particular, they advocate that joint decision-making procedures like negotiation and mediation (which they call interest-based approaches) are preferable because of the possibility of win-win solutions and improved future relations between the disputing parties. The two other approaches of third-party decision-making (which they call rights-oriented approaches) and struggle (which they call a power-oriented approach) are generally less preferable because of the damage they may cause to relationships. They argue that, in organizations, too many disputes are handled by either rights- or power-oriented approaches when the interest-based approach is more appropriate and has more desirable consequences. They do acknowledge, as suggested by the various perspectives on conflict, that sometimes interest-based approaches are not the best choice; for example, when principles are involved or when one or both parties refuse to participate in joint processes. The authors further argue that these systems should be designed in consultation with the potential disputants; that is, with organizational members.[47] This "system design" approach to conflicts encourages people to view conflicts not only as a fact of life, but also to step back from individual disputes and view the patterning of conflicts and how they are being managed. By taking a more systemic approach, the possibilities for successfully managing conflicts and preventing unnecessary ones are increased significantly.

4. A Critique of the Western Perspective on Conflict Management

In order to broaden our understanding of conflict and its management, it is important to bring to the surface some of the cultural assumptions implicit in the models of negotiation and mediation presented here. As the section on perspectives on conflict suggests, cultural context with its attendant norms and assumptions about human behaviour is critical to our understanding of the role of conflict and how it is managed. The majority of work discussed thus far is steeped in a Western, particularly American, perspective on the value of conflict. To the extent that we assume that these models can and should be applied universally, we run the risk of fuelling conflict as opposed to making it more constructive. Such an ethnocentric view can itself be a major source of conflict! Our critique draws on feminist analyses[48] and cross-cultural perspectives[49] as well as commentary from labour-management relations.[50]

Negotiation and mediation as discussed in the North American litera-ture are premised on at least three underlying assumptions: *instrumentality, individualism/autonomy,* and *rationality.* Let's look at these in turn.

a) Instrumentality

Negotiation and mediation are viewed as *tools* or means to an *end,* with the end being an *agreement* or some other form of *settlement.*[51] Efficiency is considered an important indicator of the success of a management strategy.[52] Disputants and third parties are encouraged to concentrate on particular substantive goals to the exclusion of others, such as relationship (e.g., trust, power, liking, friendships) and identity management. While these relational features are discussed within the negotiation literature, this is typically done in service of achieving a better substantive outcome.[53] For example, trust is portrayed as important because it is associated with more cooperative behaviour, which leads to a higher joint outcome. Being friendly is important because it encourages concession-making on the part of the other person, which means a better outcome. However, what remains central is settling the dispute.

b) Individualism

The norm of individualism can be seen in the characterization of negotiators as isolated individuals who are not connected to any social structure.[54] The responsibility for negotiations resides with individuals. Even the Dual Concern model and the mutual gains (integrative) approach to negotiations are still premised on the notion that the negotiators are distinct and separate individuals. This notion fails to acknowledge the relational elements (between negotiators, between negotiators and constituents, between individuals and their social groups) which highlight the connections between one individual's identity and those of others. Gray argues that this assumption actually fuels competitive dynamics during conflict, as disputants assert their "need" to be separate and identifiable in relation to the other person.[55]

c) Rationality

The third assumption is that these processes of managing conflict are and should be rational, with rationality defined in opposition to emotionality.[56] Rationality is linked to prior planning and purposeful actions. Emotions are viewed as problems because they disrupt rational thinking and prevent parties from being detached and objective. Thus mediators are encouraged to defuse intense emotions, often by reframing the issue or letting disputants vent their feelings in a private caucus. People are encouraged to avoid conflicts until they have "cooled off." Implicit in these messages is that, while having an emotional response during conflict is "natural," it is a problem because if unchecked it fuels the conflict.

In fact, emotions are extremely informative; they help disputants and mediators recognize what is important and why, as well as providing the motivation and energy to engage in management efforts. Unfortunately, this positive role of emotion is rarely acknowledged in the literature or in practice.

What is interesting about these three assumptions is that they all are associated in Western culture with being male, with the androcentric view.[57] Autonomy, rationality, objectivity, competitiveness, and efficiency are typically masculine traits and are also features of negotiation and mediation as described in the research and practice literatures. The more feminine attributes of subjectivity, dependency, connectedness, and emotionality are either considered disruptive or irrelevant in discussions of these conflict management approaches. When types of behaviour linked to masculine attributes are privileged in representations on negotiation and mediation, then those who behave differently (e.g., in a "feminine" way, or an "Eastern" way) are likely to have their uniqueness devalued – to be seen as ineffective or inefficient negotiators.[58] Alternatively, these unique ways of behaving may be incorporated into the dominant models but in such a manner that they alter the intent and assumptions upon which such behaviour is premised. For example, connectedness in the form of quality of relationship has been incorporated into discussions of negotiation and mediation but is valued as a means to achieving an agreement, and not because the relationship is an important end in itself.[59]

Lack of awareness of the monocultural bias in our models of negotiation and mediation also has practical implications for conflict involving people from different backgrounds. To the extent that we are not aware of our own cultural assumptions regarding conflict and its management, we are unlikely to be aware that others may hold different assumptions. Thus in negotiations and mediations across cultures, we run the risk of attributing "inappropriate" acts or messages to undesirable character traits instead of attributing them to cultural differences.[60] In addition, because our current models are based on a certain set of assumptions, they may not be effective or useful for dealing with certain particular conflicts. It has been argued, for example, that current conflict management paradigms in organizations effectively ignore or suppress conflicts related to the diversity of class, gender, race, and ethnicity.[61] Often these conflicts are (mistakenly) viewed as due to personality, miscommunication and misperception, or lack of inter-unit coordination. Regarding gender, specifically, there is strong evidence that the problems and disputes experienced by working women are different from those encountered by men and that the means for resolving conflicts within organizations are less effective in disputes experienced by women.[62]

In essence, the main criticism of the feminist and cross-cultural perspectives is directed to the failure of research and practice in conflict management to question the wider social conditions that give rise to the behaviours being investigated and utilized in these approaches. Why the focus on rationality and not emotionality? Why the focus on task and not on relationship? In what other contexts or cultures are these emphases different? Should we pay attention to that?

5. A Transformative Approach to Conflict Management

An alternative conceptualization of negotiation and mediation is captured by the transformative perspective, which is grounded in relational conceptions of human nature and interaction.[63] In contrast to an individualistic perspective that emphasizes self-interest, a relational view argues that self-interest can and should be balanced with connection and responsiveness to others. In their book, *The Promise of Mediation*, Baruch Bush and Joe Folger describe this balancing process as involving empowerment (being fully aware of one's personal choices and strengths) and recognition (providing acknowledgment and appreciation of others in the conflict). They suggest that these two values are often discussed independently when the most productive approach is to enact both of them simultaneously within conflict and at times of division and difference. This conceptualization affects the practice of negotiation and mediation by broadening our perceptions of what success or effectiveness looks like. Regarding negotiations, an appreciation of the relationship view suggests the value of spending a longer time in "pre-negotiations." That is, more attention should be paid to getting to know one another and developing a relationship so that, when differences arise, the parties can discuss them within the comfort and trust of their relationship.[64]

In terms of mediation, the relational view may show up as explicit efforts by the mediator to work with the moments in the process in which one party acknowledges the other's concerns (often without indicating agreement) or assertively speaks to their own needs. These times would not be interpreted as irrelevant or as pleasant side benefits on the road to substantive agreement. Rather, they would be considered the "stuff" of success. Indeed, from a transformative perspective, negotiations and mediations that "end" in an appreciation of each other and strengthening of self are successful. The dispute now has new meaning and some of the positive functions of conflict are called into play.

C. Conclusion

The intention of this chapter was to introduce you to ways of thinking about the sorts of conflict that occur in interpersonal contexts. The main focus was on how to manage conflicts, with a bias that the conflict be managed in such a way that the best for all concerned was achieved. The "best for all concerned" criterion is clearly not an objectively determined standard; rather, it relies on understanding the dynamics and social-cultural context within which the conflict occurs. It is derived and interpreted during the ongoing interaction of individuals and groups, and particular sensitivity is paid to power relations between the parties and to privilege in the broader social context.

We hope that we have encouraged an openness on your part to the variety of ways in which conflict can be managed and a willingness to consider that there may be a "legitimate" rationale for even the most seemingly "extreme" emotions and behaviours. These are, in fact, attempts at coping with the conflict as the parties interpret it. We also hope that in reading this chapter, you have reflected on your own ways of coping with conflict, and that you will somehow be transformed through that reflection and motivated to improve in your own conflict management attempts.

Notes

1 James A. Schellenberg, *Conflict Resolution: Theory, Research, and Practice* (Albany, NY: SUNY Press, 1996).

2 J. Dollard, L.W. Doob, N. Miller, O.H. Mowrer, and R.R. Sears, *Frustration and Aggression* (New Haven, CT: Yale University Press, 1939).

3 T.W. Adorno, E. Frenkel-Brunswick, D.J. Levinson, and R.N. Sanford, *The Authoritarian Personality* (New York: Harper and Row, 1950).

4 Morton Deutsch, *The Resolution of Conflict* (New Haven, CT: Yale University Press, 1973). See also his more recent "Constructive Conflict Resolution: Principles, Training, and Research," *Journal of Social Issues* 50. 1 (1994): 13-32.

5 H. Raiffa, *The Art and Science of Negotiation* (Cambridge, MA: Belknap Press of Harvard University Press, 1982).

6 Raiffa.

7 M.A. Neale and M.H. Bazerman, *Negotiator Cognition and Rationality* (New York: Free

Press, 1991).

8 Dean G. Pruitt and Peter J. Carnevale, *Negotiation in Social Conflict* (Pacific Grove, CA: Brooks/Cole Publishing Company, 1993).

9 S. Touval, and I.W. Zartman, "Mediation in International Conflicts," *Mediation Research*, ed. K. Kressel and D.G. Pruitt (San Francisco: Jossey-Bass, 1989) 115-37.

10 R.J. Lewicki, J.A. Litterer, J.W. Minton, and D.M. Saunders, *Negotiation*, 2nd ed. (Boston: Irwin, 1994) 1.

11 See Pruitt and Carnevale; also Schellenberg.

12 P.H. Gulliver, *Disputes and Negotiations: A Cross-Cultural Perspective*. (New York, NY: Academic Press, 1979) xiii.

13 J.Z. Rubin, "Models of Conflict Management," *Journal of Social Issues* 50. 1 (1994): 33-46.

14 Rubin.

15 R.E. Walton, and R.B. McKersie, *A Behavioral Theory of Labor Negotiations* (New York: McGraw-Hill, 1965).

16 Roger Fisher, William Ury, and Bruce M. Patton, *Getting to YES: Negotiating Agreement Without Giving In*, 2nd ed. (New York: Penguin Books, 1991).

17 Rubin.

18 R.A. Friedman, "Missing Ingredients in Mutual Gains Bargaining Theory," *Negotiation Journal* 10 (1994): 265-80.

19 Rubin 40.

20 Pruitt and Carnevale.

21 Pruitt and Carnevale.

22 Pruitt and Carnevale; Lewicki et al.

23 Dean G. Pruitt and J.Z. Rubin, *Social Conflict: Escalation, Stalemate, and Settlement* (New York: McGraw-Hill, 1986).

24 S.V. Horowitz and S.K. Boardman, "Managing Conflict: Policy and Research Implications," *Journal of Social Issues* 50. 1 (1994): 197-212; B. Gray, "The Gender-Based Foundations of Negotiation Theory," *Research on Negotiations in Organizations* 4 (1994): 3-36; Friedman; Pruitt and Carnevale.

25 Morton Deutsch, "Equity, Equality, and Need: What Determines Which Value Will Be Used as the Basis of Distributive Justice?" *Journal of Social Issues* 31 (1975): 137-50.

26 Pruitt and Carnevale.

27 Pruitt and Carnevale.

28 See for example P.R. Kimmel, "Cultural Perspectives on International Negotiations," *Journal of Social Issues* 50. 1 (1994): 179-212.

29 Gulliver; Pruitt and Carnevale.

30 Pruitt and Carnevale.

31 P.A. Keenan and Peter J. Carnevale, "Positive Effects of Within-Group Coopera-

tion on Between-group Negotiation," *Journal of Applied Social Psychology* 19 (1989): 977-92.

32 J.R.P French and B.H. Raven, "The Bases of Social Power," *Studies in Social Power*, ed. D. Cartwright (Ann Arbor, MI: Institute of Social Research, 1959) 150-67.

33 Pruitt and Carnevale.

34 J.A. Wall and A. Lynn, " Mediation: A Current Review," *Journal of Conflict Resolution* 37. 1 (1993): 160-94.

35 K. Kressel, and Dean G. Pruitt, "Conclusion: A Research Perspective on the Mediation of Social Conflict," *Mediation Research*, ed. K. Kressel and Dean G. Pruitt (San Francisco, CA: Jossey-Bass, 1989) 394-436.

36 R.J. Lewicki, S.E. Weiss, and D. Lewin, "Models of Conflict, Negotiation, and Third Party Intervention: A Review and Synthesis," *Journal of Organizational Behavior* 13 (1992): 233.

37 For a review, Lewicki et al.: 209-52.

38 Peter J. Carnevale, "Strategic Choice in Mediation," *Negotiation Journal* 2 (1986): 41-56.

39 Kressel and Pruitt.

40 Kressel and Pruitt.

41 J. Pearson, and N. Thoennes, "Divorce Mediation: Reflections on a Decade of Research," Kressel, D.G. Pruitt, et al. 9-30.

42 J.A. Roehl and R.F. Cook, "Mediation in Interpersonal Disputes: Effectiveness and Limitations," Kressel, D.G. Pruitt, et al. 31-52.

43 Pearson and Thoennes.

44 Wall and Lynn.

45 Discussions of these everyday contexts appear in the following: Loraleigh Keashly, "The Influence of Third Party Role on Criteria for Intervention: Parents and Friends as Intervenors," *International Journal of Conflict Management* 5. 1 (1994): 22-33; D.M. Kolb, "Labor Mediators, Managers, and Ombudsmen: Roles Mediators Play in Different Contexts," Kressel, Pruitt, et al. 91-114; B.H. Sheppard, K. Blumenfeld-Jones and J. Roth, "Informal Thirdpartyship: Studies of Everyday Conflict Intervention," Kressel, Pruitt, et al. 166-189.

46 B.H. Sheppard, "Managers as Inquisitors: Some Lessons from the Law," Bazerman and Lewicki.

47 William L. Ury, J.M. Brett, and S.B. Goldberg, *Getting Disputes Resolved: Designing Systems to Cut the Costs of Conflict* (San Francisco: Jossey-Bass, 1988).

48 For examples of feminist analysis see: Gray, "Gender-Based Foundations"; L.L. Putnam, "Challenging the Assumptions of Traditional Approaches to Negotiation," *Negotiation Journal* 10 (1994): 337-46; and D.M. Kolb and L. Putnam. "Through the Looking Glass: Negotiation Theory Refracted Through the Lens of Gender," *Frontiers in Dispute Resolution in Human Resources and Industrial Relations*, ed. Sandra E. Gleason (East Lansing: Michigan State University Press, 1997).

49 Cross-cultural perspectives are developed in P.R. Kimmel, "Cultural Perspectives on International Negotiations," *Journal of Social Issues*, 50. 1 (1994): 179-212; and P.E. Salem, "A Critique of Western Conflict Resolution from a Non-Western Perspective," *Negotiation Journal* 10 (1994).

50 R.A. Friedman, "Missing Ingredients in Mutual Gains Bargaining Theory," *Negotiation Journal* 10 (1994): 265-80; and C. Heckscher and L. Hall, "Mutual Gains and Beyond: Two Levels of Intervention," *Negotiation Journal* 10 (1994): 235-48.

51 Gray; L.L. Putnam, "Challenging the Assumptions of Traditional Approaches to Negotiation," *Negotiation Journal* 10 (1994): 337-46.

52 B.H. Sheppard, "Managers as Inquisitors: Some Lessons from the Law," Bazerman and Lewicki.

53 See for example Pruitt and Carnevale.

54 Kolb and Putnam.

55 B. Gray, "The Gender-based Foundations of Negotiation Theory," *Research on Negotiations in Organizations* 4 (1994): 3-36.

56 Kolb and Putnam.

57 Gray; Kolb and Putnam.

58 R.A. Friedman, "Missing Ingredients in Mutual Gains Bargaining Theory," *Negotiation Journal* 10 (1994): 265-80; and Kolb and Putnam.

59 R.J. Lewicki, S.E. Weiss, and D. Lewin, "Models of Conflict, Negotiation, and Third Party Intervention: A Review and Synthesis," *Journal of Organizational Behavior* 13 (1992): 209-252; and Pruitt and Carnevale.

60 P.R. Kimmel, "Cultural Perspectives on International Negotiations," *Journal of Social Issues* 50. 1 (1994): 179-212.

61 A. Donnellon and D.M. Kolb, "Constructive for Whom? The Fate of Diversity Disputes in Organizations," *Journal of Social Issues* 50. 1 (1994): 139-55.

62 P.A. Gwartney-Gibbs and D.H. Lach, "Gender and Workplace Dispute Resolution: A Conceptual and Theoretical Model," *Law and Society Review* 28. 2 (1994): 265-96.

63 Robert A. Baruch Bush and Joseph P. Folger, *The Promise of Mediation: Responding to Conflict Through Empowerment and Recognition* (San Francisco: Jossey-Bass, 1994).

64 Roger J. Fisher, "Generic Principles for Resolving Intergroup Conflict," *Journal of Social Issues* 50. 1 (1994): 47-66; and S.V. Horowitz and S.K. Boardman, "Managing Conflict: Policy and Research Implications," *Journal of Social Issues* 50. 1 (1994): 197-212.

THREE

DISENTANGLING DISPUTES: CONFLICT IN THE INTERNATIONAL ARENA

ALEX MORRISON[1]

A. Introduction

When people hear the phrase "peace and conflict", they often think of war – or more generally, of conflict among nations. While, as has already been seen, this is not the whole of the concern of Peace Studies, it is an important part. This chapter offers a description and analysis of such conflict and of the international organizations that deal with it. Taking both theoretical and practical innovations and applications into account, it recommends further changes which must be made to acclimatize our international institutions to a post-Cold War world, and to maximize the effectiveness of their peace-seeking efforts.

Three fundamental arguments will be made, in support of the following claims:

- Sovereignty must be ceded by individuals and governments in the cause of achieving the best possible common good.

- Conflict resolution must be approached from a very broad perspective; it must involve many disciplines and organizations.

- The maintenance of international peace and security must be conducted within the framework of the United Nations and in accordance with its Charter responsibilities.

There is a growing recognition and acceptance that there must be an umbrella framework for international conflict resolution. It ought to be centred in the United Nations and supported by civil/military cooperation. Such a broad and unified force for peace, as will be seen, offers more beneficial results than separate efforts ever could.

The idea of international organization and cooperation is not new. Each of the two major international conflicts of the twentieth century gave rise to a separate international organization dedicated to the protection of peace.

The end of World War I brought about the League of Nations and hopes that various national ideals of government and inter-state connections could somehow be combined to form one grand scheme of international relations. Of course, individual national proponents advocated the adoption, in the main, of their own currently-existing forms of government. This lack of open-mindedness, combined with the failure of the United States to join the League (which had been brought into being largely through the efforts of its president, Woodrow Wilson) and the inability of League members to agree on enforcement measures to deal with a breach of the covenant, meant that it was doomed to founder on the shoals of international crises. Founder it did, due in large part to the inability of member states to deal with the 1935 Abyssinian situation.[2] A Canadian senator may have best summed up the attitude of the isolationist powers of the time when he justified disinterest in international affairs by saying that Canada was a "fireproof house, far from the sources of conflagration."[3] (Lester Pearson's view is that the failure in 1935 of the members of the League of Nations, including Canada, to stand up to a single aggressor, had much to do with the start of World War II in 1939.[4])

The outbreak of World War II in 1939 ended any lingering hopes that the League of Nations could serve as a protector of international peace. Another organization had to be devised to confront conflict in a more effective manner. Within two years of the start of the war, the allies had adopted the London Declaration, which proclaimed that they were looking forward to and would put into place a "world in which, relieved of the menace of aggression, all may enjoy economic and social security."[5]

Just as the League of Nations emerged from the wreckage of World

War I, so did the second world conflict of the twentieth century give rise to another international organization on which hopes for international peace, security, and stability would be based – the United Nations. Following the successful allied invasion of Nazi-occupied Europe in 1944, the Dumbarton Oaks "conversations" took place at the estate of that name just outside Washington, D.C. Those meetings, presented as informal gatherings, brought together in one session the USA, UK, and USSR, and in another, the USA, UK, and China. They produced the outline and much of the detail of the United Nations Charter.[6] The San Francisco Conference of April-June 1945 enhanced the work which had been carried out at Dumbarton Oaks and concluded with the signing of the UN Charter on June 26 by representatives of 54 countries.

B. Understanding the United Nations

The UN was established "to save succeeding generations from the scourge of war…"[7] Its name was derived from that of the war-time alliance among Russia, Britain, and the United States. It was American President Franklin Delano Roosevelt who insisted on retaining the name for the post-war organization, defending his vision of the UN as an extension of the cooperative arrangements utilized by the Allies in quest of a permanent peace over the objections of the Soviets, who didn't like the title.

It is important to understand the purposes and structure of the UN in order to assess its effectiveness and its political will to continue as the one international body representing virtually all countries of the world. Article 1 of the Charter sets out clearly and directly that the purposes of the UN are:

1. To maintain international peace and security, and to that end: take effective collective measures for the prevention and removal of threats to the peace, and for the suppression of acts of aggression or other breaches of the peace, and to bring about by peaceful means, and in conformity with the principles of justice and international law, adjustment or settlement of international disputes or situations which might lead to a breach of the peace;

2. To develop friendly relations among nations based on respect for the principle of equal rights and self-determination of peoples, and to take other appropriate measures to strengthen universal peace;

3. To achieve international co-operation in solving international problems of an economic, social, cultural, or humanitarian character, and in promoting and encouraging respect for human rights and for fundamental freedoms for all without distinction as to race, sex, language, or religion; and

4. To be a centre for harmonizing the actions of nations and in the attainment of these common ends.[8]

The UN's principal organs are the General Assembly, the Security Council, the Economic and Social Council (ECOSOC), the Trusteeship Council, the International Court of Justice (ICJ or 'World Court'), and the Secretariat. A brief explanation of each follows.

The General Assembly (GA) is composed of all member states and is the main deliberative body of the UN. It can discuss virtually any subject (provided the Security Council is not treating the issue), makes recommendations, and takes decisions. Each member of the GA has one vote, and majority voting prevails except in the case of "important questions," which require a two-thirds majority.[9] These include, but are not limited to:

- making recommendations with respect to the maintenance of international peace and security;

- electing the non-permanent members of the Security Council and the other principal organs;

- approving the admission of new members to the United Nations;

- censuring the membership and expelling them if need be;

- handling questions relating to the operation of the trusteeship system and budgetary questions.

Decisions of the GA are not binding on UN member states; however they often serve as strong indicators of the thinking of a majority of UN countries. Recent years have seen increased calls for a "People's General Assembly" to serve as a parallel instrument, representing groups of people in the same way that the GA represents governments.

The Security Council (SC) is composed of fifteen members, five of them having permanent seats (P-5): China, France, Russia, UK, and USA.

The remaining ten, non-permanent, members are elected for two-year terms with due regard supposedly being specially paid, in the first instance, to the contribution of candidate members to the maintenance of international peace and security and to the fulfilment of other purposes of the organization. Secondary consideration is given to achieving an equitable geographical distribution for the SC membership.[10] However, a close examination of SC membership elections would no doubt reveal that much more attention is paid to geography than to the first criterion noted above.

The SC has "primary responsibility for the maintenance of international peace and security," and its decisions are binding on all member states. These two Charter provisions place great authority in the hands of SC members. Whatever they declare to be a threat to international peace and security is, *ipso facto*, a threat to international peace and security. Such latitude must be used maturely or there would be a risk of loss of credibility. An SC resolution can be adopted by a positive vote of nine of its members. However, if one of the permanent members votes against the resolution, it is lost, no matter how many positive votes were cast. This additional power over the SC's affairs entrusted to the P-5 is known as the "veto."

The Economic and Social Council (ECOSOC) is composed of 54 member states and co-ordinates the economic and social work of the UN. In doing so, ECOSOC operates within a wide array of jurisdictions, including "international economic, social, cultural, educational, health and related matters,"[11] while also "promoting respect for, and observance of, human rights and fundamental freedoms for all."[12]

The Trusteeship Council (TC) is composed of member states which administer "Trust Territories," together with permanent members of the SC that do not have such territories as well as certain other members of the UN, so as to ensure a balance between administering and non-administering countries.

The International Court of Justice (ICJ) is "the principal judicial organ of the United Nations." While the other five principal UN organs sit in New York, the World Court has its office in The Hague (Netherlands). A recent significant international legal development has been the adoption in July 1998 in Rome of a statute to create a permanent International Criminal Court (ICC), by a vote of 120-7, with 20 abstentions. Once the accord is ratified by 60 states, it will enter into force and the ICC can begin trying cases. The founding of a permanent court of this type hopefully will ensure that, in the future, war crimes are not investigated only when the victor is seeking to punish the vanquished further. The ICC will hold all sides to the same standard whether they seek such scrutiny or not.

The UN Secretariat is composed of the Secretary-General and staff. The Secretary-General is the Chief Administrative Officer and is appointed by the General Assembly on the recommendation of the SC.

It is important to bear in mind that the UN is not a "world government." It is an organization consisting of representatives of 185 sovereign, independent countries who meet in New York and elsewhere to deliberate and take action on the basis of national policy and interests. The degree to which the UN has been successful may be judged by the degree to which member states have been willing to relinquish various aspects of national sovereignty in the interests of the international community as a whole.

C. Approaches to International Conflict Resolution

The founders of the UN envisaged that conflict would be dealt with under the general provisions of the Charter, but with specific reference to Chapters VI, VII, and VIII.

Chapter VI, *Pacific Settlement of Disputes*, in Article 33.1 provides that

> [t]he parties to any dispute, the continuance of which is likely to endanger the maintenance of international peace and security, shall, first of all, seek a solution by negotiation, enquiry, mediation, conciliation, arbitration, judicial settlement, resort to regional agencies or arrangements, or other peaceful means of their own choice.

This article is clear in its intent that differences of opinion are to be dealt with, in the first instance, outside of the UN. There has developed, however, a tendency for member states to resort directly to the UN by calling for regular emergency meetings of the SC to deal with their disputes. Nations are aware of the prestige, high responsibility, and authority of the Council. Many feel that if their concerns are dealt with by means other than SC consideration, they will not receive the attention they are due. Additionally, nations often receive greater media notice, and thus greater international notice, when the SC is debating their situation.

Chapter VII, *Action With Respect to Threats to the Peace, Breaches of the Peace, and Acts of Aggression*, deals with situations in which the SC decides that there is a threat to international peace and security and that action must be taken. It deals with intrusive methods of conflict resolution.

Chapter VIII, *Regional Arrangements*, provides that regional agreements for dealing with conflicts are not at variance with the UN Charter. It also sets out that "no enforcement action shall be taken under regional arrangements or by regional agencies without the authorization of the Security Council." It should be noted here that the North Atlantic Treaty Organization (NATO) does not consider itself to be a regional organization. This interpretation, of course, ensures that NATO does not have to obtain authorization from the SC for its actions under Article 5 of the North Atlantic Treaty, which outlines the right of individual or collective self-defence.[13] NATO's role in conflict resolution will be discussed in greater detail later in this essay.

The intention of those who drafted the UN Charter "to save succeeding generations from the scourge of war" was that this would be accomplished through the threat of the use of force, or the use of force itself. Of course, diplomatic mechanisms and modalities were to be attempted before force was used, but there was no doubt at all that the UN intended to use force if necessary. It was to have its own standing military force of over 2,000,000 personnel, hundreds of warships, and thousands of combat aircraft;[14] at one point serious consideration was given to arming this force with atomic weapons. It was to be used by the UN to prevent or deal with conflict in a timely fashion. Article 43 of the Charter outlines the undertaking of each member state to make armed forces available to the UN in accordance with that state's agreement.

To control and advise on the use of this UN force, Article 47 of the Charter established the Military Staff Committee

> to advise and assist the Security Council on all questions relating to the Security Council's military requirements for the maintenance of international peace and security, the employment and command of forces placed at its disposal, the regulation of armaments, and possible disarmament.[15]

However, the Military Staff Committee (MSC) is composed of military representatives of only the five permanent members of the SC. Thus it does not represent the whole of the Council membership, a severe drawback to its offering advice and recommendations and to it giving guidance to the other non-permanent membership. This limitation, coupled with the onset of the Cold War, rendered the MSC inoperative and, along with other reasons, meant that the UN never established a Standing Military Force. The MSC is, in the opinion of many, a non-functioning moribund body, and no member state has concluded an Article 43 agreement with the UN whereby it would undertake to make its armed forces available to the SC as defined by the Council.

In the Cold War era, ideological disagreements between the USA and the USSR were at times permitted to escalate to conflict, but only when that conflict could be engaged in by smaller, client states of the two superpowers. The use of the veto on various occasions by either the Americans or the Soviets in the SC effectively prevented any concerted, cooperative action aimed at conflict resolution.

As a result of SC deadlock, the UN turned to more modest ways of dealing with inter-state differences. In 1948, it established the UN Truce Supervision Organization (UNTSO) "to oversee the truce called for in Palestine by the Security Council."[16] Early in the following year, the UN Military Observer Group in India and Pakistan (UNMOGIP) was established to watch over the India-Pakistan cease-fire in Jammu Kashmir. Finally, in response to the invasion of the Republic of Korea by North Korea in June 1950, a UN Command was established under the terms of a Security Council Resolution.[17] The UN established each of these three operations as a separate endeavour without any unifying concept, other than that of responding to a conflict resolution imperative.

The word "peacekeeping" is not mentioned at all in the Charter. Although it did not come into common usage until the late 1950s, it is now universally associated with the First UN Emergency Force (UNEF I), established in the autumn of 1956 in response to the Suez Crisis. At that time, Lester B. Pearson, Canada's Secretary of State for External Affairs, suggested the formation of an international force which would be placed between the invading military units of the UK, France, and Israel and those of Egypt. For this invention of peacekeeping, Pearson was awarded the 1957 Nobel Peace Prize. Practically universal in terms of country participation in its activities, peacekeeping has as its true aim the saving of lives and alleviation of human suffering – tasks in which the UN has been engaged virtually since its foundations.

Although, in 1945, it was intended that the "sav(ing) of future generations from the scourge of war" was to be accomplished by the threat of the use, or the actual use, of military force by the UN, the 1956 invention of peacekeeping has proven to be the main conflict prevention instrument of the last half of the twentieth century. There is everything to indicate that this will continue well into the twenty-first century. Thus the UN, with its dream of world peace only one decade old, provided the firm foundation on which the peacekeeping edifice has been built.

Peacekeeping served the UN well during the Cold War because its non-confrontational and impartial approach worked to maintain a certain degree of stability in international relations, while not upsetting the superpower *status quo*. Generally, UN peacekeeping operations thrived when the conflict in question was not in the shadow of either superpower's direct interests, when the often "Machiavellian" trappings of international relations could be exchanged for a more constructive approach. Thus it has succeeded so far in attaining the goal set out at its conception by reining in some of the post-war violence that might have led to global conflict, thereby establishing relative stability. Moreover, when judging the UN's Cold War record it is best to keep in mind that expectations far outweighed ability. As Sir Brian Urquhart, the UN former Under Secretary-General for Special Political Affairs, commented in his memoirs:

In the optimism surrounding its birth, there was a popular impression that the United Nations would act on the international level as a government acts on the national level. For better or for worse, the UN is nothing like a government. It has no sovereignty or power of sovereign decision-making. It is an association of independent, sovereign states which depends for its effectiveness on the capacity of its members to agree and to co-operate, and on the ingenuity and dedication with which the Secretariat interprets and carries out their wishes. The capacity of governments to agree and co-operate has proved to be quite limited.[18]

Despite this fact, the innovation of peacekeeping is an example of how the UN member states and UN Secretariat have managed to create solutions to problems far beyond their perceived potential. In perhaps the most brilliant stroke of the UN during the Cold War, it managed (in part) through peacekeeping to avoid becoming involved in a polarization of the world between East and West. Largely foregoing the more decisive and volatile avenues open under Chapter VII, which would never have been allowed under the circumstances of the era, the UN opted for a more conservative approach that did not seek to agitate any great power by altering greatly the *status quo*.

With the end of the Cold War in 1989, there was much talk of the freeing of the UN from the shackles imposed by the once divided superpowers. There was much hope that the UN would operate as envisaged by the drafters of the Charter, now that the deadlock of the Security Council (best illustrated by the extravagant use of the veto) was no longer a prime limiting factor. The naive optimism of many for the UN at this time was reminiscent of post-World War II enthusiasm that had many believing the UN would be humankind's deliverance from the prospect of any type of war. The international community's swift and decisive action against Iraq's invasion of Kuwait in 1990, apparently brought about through the UN, created even greater expectations and talk of a "New World Order" which resounded around the world. However, the exact form that this new world order was to take was never clearly described.

While the UN Security Council appeared to be revitalized and successful in the wake of the Gulf War, it was still lacking in a number of respects. It did not have a working Military Staff Committee (Article 47) or any readily available troops and equipment at its disposal. The Gulf War misrepresented the UN's strength, and those not directly familiar with the details could be forgiven for thinking that it possessed much more force than was actually the case. In fact the whole operation was largely run by the US who, wisely, used the UN to construct a coalition that would ensure international support. Great pressure was placed on the US by its friends and allies to use UN mechanisms and institutions. And the fact that the US operated through the UN *was* in accordance with its responsibilities under the Charter. However, there is no doubt that the US could have "gone it alone." Once the operation was authorized, it became an almost exclusively US-led undertaking with the UN quickly relegated to the sidelines and then reintroduced in the role of peace supervisor once the war had ceased. As retired Major-General Indar Jit Rikhye, perhaps one of the foremost peacekeepers of UN history, noted: "The UN, having given the authorization for enforcement action against Iraq, was not even an actor in the implementation of the Resolution."[19]

However, with the UN apparently born again, it set out on an ambitious journey. The false sense of empowerment from the Gulf War led many to forget that the UN did not have the resources to mount large scale peacekeeping operations of any type, in particular, those authorized under Chapter VII, which almost always result in the use of force. The UN was (and is) dependent upon the willingness of member states to carry voluntarily the burden necessary to make such undertakings successful. And while the Gulf War provided clear incentives for the UN to continue to use its resources in more adventurous and more forceful military campaigns, the rash of conflicts which followed did not lend themselves to such activity. The post-Cold War era was not going to be a *Pax United Nations,* as it came with new kinds of conflict, and the UN's shortcomings, previously largely hidden by Cold War inactivity, became glaringly obvious.

D. The Face of Post-Cold War Conflict

After the fall of the Berlin Wall in the autumn of 1989, a prominent American academic, John J. Mearsheimer, published an article entitled "Why We Will Soon Miss the Cold War." While some dismissed him at the time, the farther the world travels into the post-Cold War era, the more sense Mearsheimer's assertions seem to make. At the heart of his stance is the belief that there is nothing more stable than a bipolar balance of power since multiple and unipolar balances are open to fluid alliance formation with the aim of toppling or rivalling the hegemonic power. As Mearsheimer wrote in his introduction:

> We may, however, wake up one day lamenting the loss of the order that the Cold War gave to the anarchy of international relations. For untamed anarchy is what Europe knew in the forty-five years of this century before the Cold War, and untamed anarchy — Hobbes's war of all against all — is a prime cause of armed conflict. Those who think that armed conflicts among European states are now out of the question, that the two world wars burned all the war out of Europe, are projecting unwarranted optimism onto the future.[20]

In a bipolar arrangement, power is distributed to a point of near equity; each party realizes that dislodging the other is not a practical policy and that any move to prevail over the rival will be matched. The resulting balance lends itself to prolonged periods of stability, accented only occasionally by brief periods of instability, examples of which are the U_2 incident and the Cuban Missile Crisis. In many ways the bipolar balance of the Cold War was a Faustian bargain. In exchange for general stability between the great powers, the world only had to endure the possibility of the nuclear annihilation of humanity. To ensure that no one upset the nuclear apple cart, the *status quo* was imposed upon states through super-power-sponsored or -tolerated repressive regimes which kept a check on conflict between various ethnic and political groups. Ethnic political ambitions, in particular, were not to be tolerated as they constituted a potential threat to the territorial integrity of the state and, as a result, to the overall stability of the international system. State disintegration can quickly lead to opposing superpowers escalating actions to armed conflict as a result of mutual intervention. The classic example of this dynamic was the breakdown of the Austro-Hungarian Empire in 1914, which quickly moved from a regional to a European and finally to a world-wide war.

With the end of the Cold War bipolar balance, the stakes in maintaining international stability were greatly reduced as the threat of nuclear war between the superpowers subsided. In addition, the collapse of the Soviet Union and its many client regimes around the globe, coupled with America's withdrawal from its support of various military dictatorships in the developing world, meant that the forces of repression were greatly weakened. Russia was no longer a superpower and thus could no longer continue the global "chess match" that had seen each superpower intervene and intrigue against the other in some of the most insignificant states for the simple reason of denying their opponents a victory. Russia was in no position to act globally, and so the US likewise had no reason to interfere in the internal affairs of sovereign states. As a result, their previous repressive client governments lost their key backers. While this was seen as a great advancement for freedom, democracy, and human rights, it also let loose many ethnic rivalries that had been put on hold for the duration of the Cold War. One expert summed up the post-Cold War realities thus: "Today there is neither the danger of great power wars nor the relative tranquillity once imposed by each great power within its own sphere of influence."[21] People unaccustomed to and unschooled in freedom and democracy and ingrained with a distrust of their central government due to the actions of previous regimes reverted to tribal or ethnic mentalities, electing extreme nationalist governments and reviving old prejudices. The result was that conflict shifted from the traditional inter-state form, which the UN was founded to prevent, to intra-state conflict, where the scope of the UN's authority was not well defined.

The primary problem facing the UN in intra-state conflict is the issue of sovereignty: does it have the right to intervene in the affairs of a sovereign state? The short answer is yes. Under its Chapter VII powers the UN can declare war on or otherwise enter a sovereign state (such as Iraq or North Korea), yet it has generally been assumed that these powers would be exercised only in cases of aggression by one state against another. Many suppose that for the UN to intervene in what a sovereign state describes as its internal matters would lead the organization down a very slippery slope. But the post-Cold War paradigm is one of increasing political turbulence and eroding state sovereignty, and the UN has to walk a very fine line.[22] Secretary-General Boutros Boutros-Ghali, in his distinguished work, *An Agenda for Peace*, wrote with regard to the changing nature of sovereignty:

> The foundation-stone of this work (internationalism) is and must be the state. Respect for its fundamental sovereignty and integrity are crucial to any common international progress. The time of absolute and exclusive sovereignty, however, has passed; its theory was never matched by reality.[23]

It is important to recall that it was in part comments like this that brought about an early end to the tenure of Boutros-Ghali. Although the Secretary-General's observations were practically true, they were politically unacceptable to some member states. As the UN's work depends on the cooperation of a collection of sovereign states, infringements on the tenets of sovereignty must be carefully gauged and undertaken with extreme caution, lest it estrange itself from its clientele.

In response to this dilemma, the UN has had to opt for a "middle of the road" approach, pursuing intervention with the non-confrontational and impartial instruments of traditional peacekeeping. It has, with one notable exception (aside from the Gulf War), not actually resorted to full Chapter VII powers of forced intervention; that exception was in Somalia. Rather, Chapter VII powers have been dealt out in a piecemeal fashion by allowing some actions but not others. Some of these attempts to graft the practices of Cold War peacekeeping onto post-Cold War conflicts have not been as successful as had been hoped.

In the case of a state's disintegration or "Balkanization," a country of two or more definable groups coalesces into opposing factions, with the minority(ies) often seeking some political and territorial autonomy from the majority group. The political dialogue between such groups can run from the civilized and cordial discussion of the Czechoslovakian "Velvet Revolution" to the bloody civil wars of the Balkans. The problems that such a situation presents for the UN are several:

- Does the UN wait to be invited into the state, or does it seize the initiative and intervene?

- Does the UN work to maintain the integrity of the state or facilitate its division?

- If a section of the state opts for secession, does the UN recognize it, and move then to protect it?

- If one group is being attacked, does the UN fight off the aggressor?

There are no easy answers to these questions as the UN contemplates becoming involved in intra-state conflict. This was not the case with traditional inter-state war; having the UN intervene between two belligerents was often welcomed, as it ensured that while nobody won the war, nobody lost it either. A classic example of this sort of dynamic was evident in the first official peacekeeping mission, (UNEF I), in which the UN intervention enabled all parties to back down without losing too much face. However, in intra-state conflict, any intervention will likely have a negative impact on the side seeking to preserve the integrity of the state, as their goal requires maintaining the *status quo*. The presence of the UN means the injection of a new actor who will invariably impede the return to the pre-war *status quo* by protecting the breakaway faction. As a result of this, factions within an intra-state struggle often do not behave as do those in an inter-state conflict. They can often include such non-state actors as warlords, criminal syndicates, and ethnic militias. Further, intra-state conflict often destroys governmental institutions, thereby increasing the impact of the conflict on civilians while weakening the international community's ability to contain the situation because there is no recognizable centre of power with which to negotiate. Somalia is a prime example. It is precisely because of the confused and intractable nature of these internal struggles that the international community seeks to avoid entanglement – a lesson that the UN learned the hard way in the Congo in 1960, where it became embroiled in the civil war brought about by the secession of Katanga province. In the Congo, the UN took sides and fought a largely conventional war against the insurrectionists under Chapter VII. However, the international community did not have the stomach for such an operation then and clearly does not now; hence, the determined wish to stick by the traditional peacekeeping "rules" (impartiality, restrictions on the use of force, etc.) when confronted with cases such as Bosnia and Rwanda. Canadian Major-General John A. MacInnis wrote of his experience in the former Yugoslavia as United Nations Protection Force (UNPROFOR) deputy commander:

The international community, for the foreseeable future, will continue to have difficulty in dealing with this type of conflict. Prevented on the one hand by public opinion from doing nothing and on the other from imposing a military solution, the UN will continue to search for some middle ground in which it can "do something."[24]

The reasons why the UN experienced difficulty in its post-Cold War operations are multifaceted. At the risk of overgeneralization, the major problem facing the UN in its security endeavours in the early 1990s was dealing with post-Cold War conflict with Cold War doctrine and strategy. In many ways, the UN quickly found itself "yesterday's man" in Yugoslavia and its like. While it was in the post-Cold War world, its mind-set and expectations were still very much of the Cold War era. Expecting respect and restraint from actors in a conflict, the UN found itself instead in the middle of a conflict over which it had almost no control. Much of this was due to the middle-of-the-road approach or the grafting of traditional peacekeeping onto situations where it was neither effective nor prudent. As Major-General MacInnis's comments indicate, the UN was truly in a bind during this period when public expectations and public will were grossly out of balance.

Nowhere was this more evident than in Somalia where American public opinion, driven by the US media, prompted both US intervention under Chapter VII with the Unified Task Forces' (UNITAF) "Operation Restore Hope," as well as its withdrawal, due largely to the pictures of the failed US Special Forces raid in which 18 Americans were killed.[25] The view of the Americans in light of this event was summed up by the Secretary-General's Special Representative, Jonathan T. Howe (an American), when he lamented that "the rescue of the Somali people was deemed unworthy of another American Life."[26] The withdrawal of the world's foremost military power after suffering what was tantamount to a bloody nose revealed its public's lack of will to take risks for peace, which was as great a loss to the cause of the UN as it was an unintended boost to those seeking to circumvent its principles. This pattern of behaviour is hardly endemic solely to the US; however, the US is perhaps the most extreme and visible case.

The Somalia debacle, precipitated by the loss of 18 US soldiers, and the Haiti fiasco, caused by the fear that a handful of US troops might be killed while defeating that country's military dictatorship, sufficiently exposed the current unreality of the great power

concept. In pride or shame, America might dispute any wider conclusion from those events. They would like to reserve for themselves the special sensitivity that forces policy to change completely
because 18 professional soldiers are killed (soldiers, one might add,
who come from a country in which gun-related deaths were last
clocked at one every 14 minutes).[27]

If the member states of the United Nations have shown weakness in
the post-Cold War world, they have also shown a growing willingness to
adapt themselves to these new times with innovations. An emerging
doctrine, presently being tested in the operational theatre, which
emphasizes internal revisions and a new way of thinking regarding security operations as well as firmer partnerships with other bodies such as
NATO and the Organization for African Unity (OAU), is receiving
increased attention. However, before looking at various innovations in
UN security operations, it must first be established what role the UN
should play.

E. Reevaluating and Reinventing the UN in the Post-Cold War World

1. The Task at Hand

A four-fold task is faced by the UN both now and in the years ahead:

- maintaining its position as the frame of reference for conflict resolution

- ensuring that it retains its peacekeeping expertise in a time of decreasing
  activity

- responding to the call of the international community

- co-operating with individual states and other international and regional
  organizations in conflict resolution missions

a) Maintaining its position as the frame of reference for conflict resolution
The UN is now the only international organization of any type to have
universal legitimacy in the field of conflict resolution. Its Security Council, with "primary responsibility for the maintenance of international
peace and security," and Secretary-General, whose office has come to be
associated with a more activist approach, have international attention

and serve as focus points. Its post-World War II mandate to save succeeding generations from the scourge of war has resulted in the development of peacekeeping, in all its forms, as the conflict resolution instrument of choice. The UN has thus emerged as the natural frame of reference for any international action to prevent or defuse a crisis.

This single frame of reference makes possible the development of guiding principles or discussion points to be used both within and outside the UN. A striking example is *An Agenda for Peace*, submitted to the Security Council by Secretary-General Boutros Boutros-Ghali in June 1992. A challenge to the Secretary-General to reflect on the future of peacekeeping had been initiated by the SC's first ever meeting of heads of state in January of that year. The document broke new ground, and while it has not won universal acceptance, it and its supplement continue to serve as the frame of reference for peacekeeping.

Individual citizens, individual states, groups of countries, and regional organizations look to the UN for solutions to their conflict problems and challenges. Member states realize more and more that it is much easier to advance international action in conflict resolution when such action is carried out under terms authorized by SC resolutions.

b) Ensuring that it keeps its peacekeeping expertise in a time of decreasing activity
The dramatic expansion in the number of peacekeeping missions, the number of personnel involved in each and in total, and the types of tasks assigned to the military and civilian peacekeepers have all combined to force a reorganization of the UN Secretariat. This reorganization has resulted in the creation of a Department of Peacekeeping Operations (DPKO) with a vast increase in the number of civilian and military professionals employed at UN Headquarters (UNHQ). The increase in employees was brought about in two ways: by hiring more personnel paid out of the peacekeeping budget and by accepting more officers whose expenses were funded by their individual national governments. Those nationally-funded personnel and the whole idea of member states paying directly the wages of those who function as international civil servants attracted much negative attention, notwithstanding the UN's need for their services.

On a regular basis, the General Assembly must approve the number of personnel in UNHQ. This severely hampers the long-range planning processes so important to peacekeeping. Additionally, the number of DPKO employees is governed by the number of missions extant in the field: the greater the number of missions and the greater the number of peacekeepers, the greater the number of employees authorized for DPKO, and *vice versa*.

For as long as the UN conducts peacekeeping operations there will be a continuing need for expertise in DPKO. This expertise must be retained at a certain level, regardless of the number of operational missions. The UN member states will need to accept this principle and be more realistic in approving employee numbers.

The pressure to maintain resident expertise is increased by the fact that the current Secretary-General, with the agreement of many member states, has undertaken to do away with the national provisional funding of officials. This is being done for two reasons. The first is a fear that affluent nations, in virtue of their considerable financial resources, will be able to control the agenda in UN peacekeeping affairs. Secondly, it is felt that if the UN Secretariat needs a certain number of officials to manage current operations and to plan for the future, then they should be provided and funded according to normal procedures.

c) Responding to the call of the international community

UN peacekeeping operations are, at present, in something of a dormant stage. The number of persons assigned to missions has decreased. Some member states are not in favour of establishing new missions. Their leaders feel that if their military forces are deployed abroad in dangerous situations where fatalities are suffered, then the government will not be re-elected. Other member states must continue to bring pressure to bear on their UN colleagues to take a broader, less selfish, and more universal view.

The UN also must continue to be innovative in its approaches to international conflict resolution. Such measures as the increased use of, and authority for, the Special Representative of the Secretary-General, the furthering of the UN "vanguard system" together with the establishment of the nucleus of a stand-by force headquarters in New York, progress towards a Stand-by High Readiness Brigade (SHIRBRIG), and the continuing use of "Peacekeeping by Proxy"(see below) all combine to indicate that the UN is not standing still in its response to contemporary and future challenges. Such innovations are key as the international community expects solutions to security challenges and a UN capable of responding in a timely and efficient manner.

d) Co-operating with individual countries and other international and regional organizations in conflict resolution situations

Over the years, there have been instances in which the UN *qua* UN has been unable or unwilling to act and has passed the task to others. Some examples are the Multinational Force and Observers in the Sinai, the Italian-led operation in Albania, and, of course, the UN-authorized, NATO-led operation in the former Yugoslavia.

These are all instances of what the Pearson Peacekeeping Centre describes as "Peacekeeping by Proxy." In such situations, the UN "hands off" or "contracts" out important tasks to individual member states, groups of states, or other organizations to accomplish the mission. The UN action in the Gulf War may not be regarded by all as peacekeeping, but it, and its virtually identical predecessor, the UN action in the Korean War, are other examples of the UN extending its proxy in international conflict resolution situations.

The benefits of this partnership are not exclusively for the UN. In the case of the Gulf War, it was much easier for the US and its allies to forge a virtually unanimous international consensus because they proceeded according to the UN Charter. As member states of the UN will continue to demand action, it is up to the UN to be able to cooperate with other actors when it cannot orchestrate a response independently.

2. Getting the Job Done

In order to reach its goals in a post-Cold War world, the UN has developed and applied various new conflict resolution concepts and strategies, many of which involve closer relationships with other agencies. Consider first a number of variations on the theme of peacekeeping:

- Peacemaking

- Peacebuilding

- Preventative Deployment

The following table gives fuller information for each of these.

Peacemaking is perhaps the broadest of the new variations on peacekeeping; it ranges from peaceful to forceful means in moving states towards conflict resolution. As defined in *An Agenda for Peace*, peacemaking is "action to bring hostile parties to agreement, essentially through such

	Preventative Deployment	Peacekeeping	Peacemaking		Peacebuilding
			Peacemaking (peaceful means)	Peace Enforcement	
Chapter of the UN Charter	Chapter VI	Chapter VI (also Chapter VII)	Chapter VI	Article 40, Chapter VI	Chapter VI
Consent required from the parties	Request of the Government of All parties or with their consent (Paragraph 28)	"hitherto with consent" (Paragraph 20)	"Seek a solution" to differences. (Paragraph 34)		Cooperate in "construction of a new environment" (Paragraph 57)
Typical Mandate	Deploy on both sides or one side of border; provide humanitarian aid; maintain security. (Paragraph 29)	Provide presence to prevent conflict or to make peace. (Paragraph 20)	Bring hostile parties to agreement essentially through peaceful means. (Paragraph 20)	"Respond to outright aggression, imminent or actual". (Paragraph 44)	Disarm parties; restore order; repatriate refugees; train security personnel; monitor elections; protect human rights; reform governmental institutions. (Paragraph 55)

Taken from Bruce R Pirnie and Wiliam E. Simons, *Soldiers for Peace, An Operational Typology* (Santa Monica, LA: 1996) 78.

peaceful means as those foreseen in Chapter VI of the Charter of the United Nations."[28] However, as the table above indicates, peacemaking can include what is referred to as peace enforcement: the use of military force to counter an act of aggression, two classic cases of which are Korea (1950) and Kuwait (1990). There have also been more limited uses of force in recent UN activities, such as the Unified Task Force on Somalia (Operation Restore Hope) (UNITAF) and the second UN Operation in Somalia, 1993-1995 (UNOSOM II). While the success of UNITAF is difficult to assess due to its rapid withdrawal from Somalia and hand-over to the unprepared UNOSOM II, it did save a great number of lives by helping force aid through to starving people. However, UNITAF had a problem — it was almost completely separate from the UN mission. Its chain of command did not include the UNOSOM force commander, so in essence two agendas were pursued in isolation from each other.

> Heretofore the United Nations authorities have believed and main-
> tained that when a country agrees to contribute troops to a peace-
> keeping mission, it places those troops under the commander of
> the particular peacekeeping force. However, that UN position has
> not always been honoured. National contingent commanders
> habitually deploy to the field with rear link communications to
> their national capitals.[29]

The unwillingness of states to put their contingents under UN command is part of a vicious circle that weakens both the UN and its contingents in the field. The UN is unable to launch coordinated operations without lengthy delay because contingent commanders must seek permission from their political masters at home before committing themselves. As a result, if one contingent were to find itself in harm's way, relief might be slow in coming as the same dynamic prevents the UN commander from launching an immediate rescue. This helps explain the disaster of the downing and ambush of the US Rangers en route to an arrest in Somalia in October 1994. The forces with the required heavy armour which could extract the embattled US troops were under the UN chain of command, but that same command had no prior knowledge of the US operation and thus, quite understandably, responded slowly.

Perhaps a key difference between the classic peace enforcement ideal as used in Korea and modern peace enforcement is that the latter may be contracted out to one or a few states who carry out the task independently of UN control – Peacekeeping by Proxy. More recent examples include the US presence in Haiti and France in Rwanda. While the UN may not have as much control as it would like in these operations, it does garner support much more easily for them than for others since it only taxes the resources of states willing to volunteer. In these peace enforcement operations a single state or a small number of states intervene with military force to quell the conflict; traditional UN troops relieve them once open hostilities have ceased. However, such operations carry inherent risks for the UN as will be outlined when Peacekeeping by Proxy is examined more fully later on.

In addition to military action, peacemaking may include economic and political sanctions. Examples include the sanctions imposed on South Africa and Rhodesia during their apartheid eras, and more recently, those imposed on Iraq.

On the Chapter VI side of peacemaking are the non-coercive means used to push the parties in a conflict to seek settlement through "negotiation, inquiry, mediation, conciliation, arbitration, judicial settlement, resort to regional agencies or arrangements, or other peaceful means of their own choice."[30] Chapter VI does provide the UN with investigative powers over conflicts, however, short of Chapter VII powers, the UN is dependent on the will of the belligerents to co-operate.

Peacebuilding is a blanket term used to describe post-conflict activities designed to sustain and entrench the peace settlement. The activities involved in peacebuilding can involve:

- disarming former belligerents

- holding or destroying surrendered weapons

- supervising the repatriation of refugees and prisoners

- training new security personnel (police, etc.)

- setting up and monitoring free elections

- entrenching human rights

- re-strengthening government and its institutions[31]

Peacebuilding has been one of the success stories of the UN's post-

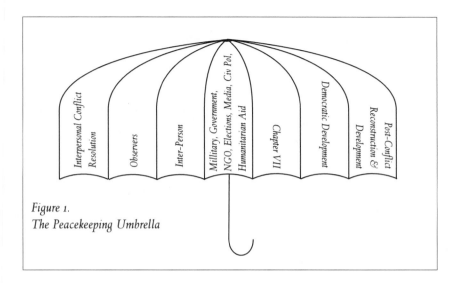

Figure 1.
The Peacekeeping Umbrella

Cold War activities. Operations in El Salvador, Mozambique, and Haiti have all shown that the UN can play a significant role in helping to get a state back onto its feet. While some might challenge the UN's claim of success in its peacebuilding activities, it is important to focus on reasonable expectations of the mission and the organization, especially in states that have no history of either a democratic or a human rights regime.

Peacebuilding can often follow a Chapter VII-sanctioned intervention and restoration of stability, as was the case in Haiti. Here the US led an intervention, which it in turn handed over to a UN peacekeeping force designed to secure the peace. Haiti has now moved towards peacebuilding with a UN-sponsored program of police training for Haitians.

Preventative deployment is perhaps the most important development in post-Cold War UN security operations as it addresses the fundamental *raison d'être* for the UN's existence – the prevention of war. There has been but one case of preventative deployment – the United Nations Preventative Deployment Force (UNPREDEP) in Macedonia – and it may claim credit for keeping Macedonia out of the quagmire of conflict in the former Yugoslavia.

The logic and appeal of preventative deployment is obvious: a conflict is much easier to contain if checked either before war erupts or at its outset, and before a conflict has festered and the actors become intransigent. Upon deployment between two possible combatants, the UN could establish a Demilitarized Zone (DMZ) on the conflict frontier and, by reducing the immediate tensions of otherwise imminent war, could allow for a meaningful diplomatic dialogue between the two (or more) rival parties.

Along with these three new innovations in peacekeeping doctrine, the spectrum of peacekeeping activities has itself been rethought. The Pearson Peacekeeping Centre in Nova Scotia, Canada grounds all of its research, education, and training activities on three basic concepts.[32] The first is a much *broader concept of peacekeeping* than we have assumed so far, which can be defined as follows: "actions designed to enhance international peace, security, and stability, which are authorized by competent national and international organizations and which are undertaken cooperatively or individually by military, humanitarian, good governance, civilian, police, and other interested agencies and groups." As can be seen, this definition encompasses everything from interpersonal conflict resolution in war-torn areas to post-conflict reconstruction and development. It is meant to include the widest possible range of relevant activities.

Next is the related idea of a *peacekeeping umbrella*. It is designed to depict graphically the larger inclusion of peacekeeping activities and sources of definition. The range of activities covers monitoring, training, and aid as much as it does military action and policing. The focus is as much on economic and political development and interpersonal reconciliation as it is on classic Chapter VII definitions.

Finally, there is the (again, related) concept of the *new peacekeeping partnership*, the term applied to those organizations and individuals that work together to improve the effectiveness of modern peacekeeping operations. It includes the military, civil police, government and non-government agencies dealing with human rights and humanitarian assistance, diplomats, the media, and organizations sponsoring development and democratization programmes.

Those who advocate a new peacekeeping partnership recognize that peacekeeping is not, and never has been, a purely military undertaking. It is a professional, cooperative undertaking best accomplished within a framework of tolerance and patience. Never has the need for this been greater. For example, many of the post-Cold War UN security operations have been launched in theatres where humanitarian concerns are a significant factor. This has meant that UN troops have had to be prepared to assist in the administration of aid. But UN military and humanitarian organizations involved in the same operation do not always see their roles the same way. This has led in some cases to an internecine dynamic, with each side undercutting the other and thus weakening the operation as a whole. The new type of post-Cold War conflict management is particularly susceptible to this since intra-state warfare often cripples a state's ability to feed and maintain its people. As a former UN official with UNPROFOR stated: "Inability to adapt to the rapidly changing environment in which military and civilian personnel have to operate will reduce chances of success in the mission and increase exposure to risk and causalities."[33]

In response to such problems, UN Secretary-General Kofi Annan on July 14, 1997 announced a plan to establish what he called the *UN House*, a single, central structure to unify the efforts of all the UN agencies participating in an operation.[34] This, it is hoped, will erode the tendency of these otherwise largely autonomous organizations to plan and operate without consideration for each other and so help to bring the new peacekeeping partnership into being.[35]

The UN is not only learning to develop cooperation between its own agencies, but to function in tandem with other international actors. The classic example of this new form of partnership is *peacekeeping by proxy*. Peacekeeping by proxy is a very important innovation for the UN as it overcomes its two primary weaknesses: its lack of political will and the lack of its own military resources. Peacekeeping by proxy allows the UN to hand over the often dangerous and divisive work of Chapter VII peacekeeping to a regional organization such as the OAU or NATO. Those in favour of such arrangements argue that allowing regional bodies to take over the handling of a military operation sanctioned by the UN creates a win-win situation. Regional states and organizations are more likely to have an interest in ending local instability, and such operations will not tax the resources of uninterested states that may have been resistant to a traditional UN effort because of the potential personnel and financial costs. On the other side, however, many argue that while regional states are most likely to have an interest, they are also most likely to pursue an agenda contrary to the purpose of the mission. A recent example of this fear arose when Russia was authorized as the sole state to constitute the peacekeeping contingent in Georgia, one of its former republics. As one observer noted:

[T]he idea of Russia as peacekeeper is hard for many to swallow, coming so soon after the collapse of the Soviet empire. Many are suspicious of Russia as a "neutral" force, fearful that its peacekeeping is an attempt to reassume an old Russian role – that of an imperial arbiter of the fate of the many nationalities that lie along and even within its vast borders.[36]

Sometimes peacekeeping by proxy involves NATO. A recent example is NATO/IFOR (Implementation Force), established in the former Yugoslavia in December 1995 by Security Council Resolution 1031 (1991) and acting under Chapter VII of the Charter. IFOR was the outgrowth of the Dayton Peace Agreement, which was concluded in one month. UNPROFOR had been plagued throughout its duration by an ambiguous and shifting mandate as well as the problems of command and control already outlined in this chapter. Contrary to the common interpretation, UNPROFOR was not a Peace Enforcement Operation, in spite of some of the references to Chapter VII in its related resolution. UNPROFOR was not designed to end the war in the former Yugoslavia. Rather it had three primary roles: 1) to provide humanitarian relief, 2) to contain the conflict, and 3) to promote a diplomatic settlement. Given the numerous cease fires that came and went, when Dayton was concluded through the assistance of NATO air power, NATO was also drafted to enforce the peace agreement. NATO had the advantage in that, with its superior command and control system, it could plan and orchestrate operations with the knowledge that its membership would comply. When it took over command, IFOR was composed of all NATO and 16 non-NATO states. With a much stronger mandate and heavy weaponry, IFOR maintained the peace in former Yugoslavia. IFOR and its successor, SFOR (Stabilization Force), are excellent examples of Peacekeeping by Proxy because they so clearly filled in a gap where the UN could not operate. For reasons already outlined, member states are extremely reluctant to place their contingents under UN command. NATO, however, already had a firmly established chain of command that made its members, as well as non-NATO states, comfortable in entrusting their troops.

The principles of Peacekeeping by Proxy have come under scrutiny with the recent military action taken by NATO in Yugoslavia in response to that state's brutal repression in Kosovo. NATO proceeded without the consent of the United Nations, and without consulting it. Many worry that this established a precedent for the international community and critically undermined the credibility of the UN. According to its Charter the UN is charged with the maintenance of international peace and security [Chapter I, Article I, Section 1]. As Secretary-General Kofi Annan stated at the outset of the NATO action:

In helping to maintain international peace and security, Chapter VIII of the United Nations assigns an important role to regional organizations. But as Secretary-General I have many times pointed out, not just in relation to Kosovo, that under the Charter the Security Council has primary responsibility for maintaining international peace and security and this is explicitly acknowledged in the North Atlantic Treaty. Therefore the Council should be involved in any decision to resort to the use of force. [SG/SM/6938]

Now it may be that NATO does not consider itself to be a regional organization under terms of Chapter VIII of the UN Charter but that takes nothing away from the point made here in support of the view that the UN Security Council should have been consulted.

The debate over the NATO action in Kosovo will likely carry on well into the future. Those in the NATO camp argue that a Security Council resolution would never have been achieved with Russia and China stating they would veto any resolution. Thus the Alliance had to act unilaterally to save lives. Those opposed argue that NATO ought not to ignore the international community (in the form of the UN Security Council) whenever UN actions do not coincide with its own desires. Further, they propose that the precedent NATO has set, at the expense of the UN, will mean a proliferation of non-UN interventions around the world that could destabilize the international community.

The case of Kosovo demonstrates both the UN's strengths and weakness. On the one hand, the possession of the veto by the P5 ensures that the Security Council will always have a fundamental flaw that prevents it from being a truly effective international security actor. On the other hand, the unique inclusiveness of the UN's international composition means that it is the only institution that represents the whole of the international community.

The new peacekeeping partnership also involves cooperation between the UN and (non-UN) *Non-Governmental Organizations*. These can range from large, international groups such as *Medicins sans Frontières* (Doctors Without Borders) and the International Committee of the Red Cross (ICRC), to national bodies of international umbrella organizations such as CARE and small agencies commonly referred to as "mom and pop" NGOs. While there are several thousand NGOs in existence, the bulk of governmental and international funding is given to approximately three dozen. While these latter undoubtedly accomplish the most, the work of a majority of the smaller NGOs is of high quality as well. Recently there has been much discussion within NGO circles as to where the money should go.

The UN has a long established relationship with NGOs, going back to its founding and the inclusion of Article 71 in the Charter which gave ECOSOC the mandate to establish relations with them. The UN-NGO relationship has become more important in recent years as the UN struggles to become a more effective and representative organization. As Secretary-General Javier Pérez de Cuéllar stated:

> If the hopes and aspirations which the peoples of the United Nations enshrined in the Charter are to be fulfilled, multilateralism, as embodied in the United Nations, needs its champions; they must speak more boldly and knowledgeably ... I wish, in this connection, to refer specifically to the many non-governmental organizations which share the goals, and in many instances, the work of the United Nations. I am convinced that, in the coming years, the United Nations will need to place even greater emphasis on close communications and co-operation with these organizations. They constitute an essential extension of the capacity of the United Nations to reach its global constituency.[37]

One of the important roles that NGOs can play in improving international security is that of advocate for those suffering from abuse of all types. In giving voice to those who cannot speak for themselves due to active conflict or a repressive government, the NGO makes the world aware of their plight and helps to generate a response to relieve their suffering. Some have argued that to make the UN a truly effective and democratic organization there ought to be a parallel body to that of the General Assembly in order for NGOs to have a greatly increased influence in UN activities. Proponents argue that this would significantly increase the accountability of the UN and its membership to citizens around the world. They feel that if the NGO assembly were there to act as the conscience of the UN, the tragic and purposeful neglect of crises such as Rwanda would never happen again.

Since today's human rights violations are the seeds of tomorrow's conflicts, the role of NGOs in publicizing these violations should be viewed as advance warnings of impending trouble. NGOs carry out this task more effectively than state actors, as NGOs rarely have ulterior motives (such as trade interests, security arrangements, etc.) that might inhibit them from drawing international attention to the illegal actions of states. Of course, the Office of the UN High Commissioner for Refugees, and the UN High Commission for Human Rights play equally important roles. However, NGOs often lead the way in exposing human rights violations, and as a result can compel an embarrassed UN membership into action.

At the theatre of operations level, UN organizations and NGOs possess two key advantages. First, they have been in the region where the conflict has been taking place, often long before the arrival of the UN military force. They generally possess much useful information. They know which actors speak for what group and the general intentions of each actor. This is invaluable information/intelligence because the mistaken inclusion or exclusion of an actor can make or break an operation from the start. This is a particular concern in the post-Cold War paradigm of conflict, where there are often more than two actors involved. The second, related, advantage is that the long-term presence of NGOs in the conflict zone may be seen by the actors in a conflict as providing an impartial conduit between themselves and soldiers.

Another avenue of conflict resolution recently opened up to the international community was the adoption of a statute in Rome in July 1998, which will lead to the establishment of an *International Criminal Court* (ICC). The work of the UN in some areas will be considerably facilitated by relationship with this new institution. It may be appropriate to quote at length the preamble to the Rome Statute to gain an understanding of the purpose of such an institution and how it can work to bring about greater international security.

> **Conscious** that all peoples are united by common bonds, their cultures pieced together in a shared heritage, and concerned that this delicate mosaic may be shattered at any time,

> **Mindful** that during this century millions of children, women and men have been victims of unimaginable atrocities that deeply shock the conscience of humanity,

> **Recognising** that such grave crimes threaten the peace, security and well-being of the world,

> **Affirming** that the most serious crimes of concern to the international community as a whole must not go unpunished and that their effective prosecution must be ensured by taking measures at

the national level and by enhancing international cooperation,

Determined to put an end to impunity for the perpetrators of these crimes and thus to contribute to the prevention of such crimes,

Recalling that it is the duty of every State to exercise its criminal jurisdiction over those responsible for international crime,

Reaffirming the Purpose and Principles of the Charter of the United Nations, and in particular that all States shall refrain from the threat or use of force against the territorial integrity or political independence of any State, or in the internal affairs of any State,

Emphasizing in this connection that nothing in this Statute shall be taken as authorizing any State Party to intervene in an armed conflict in the internal affairs of any State,

Determined to these ends and for the sake of present and future generations, to establish an independent permanent International Criminal Court in relationship with the United Nations system, with jurisdiction over the most serious crimes of concern to the international community as a whole,

Emphasizing that the International Criminal Court established under this Statute shall be complementary to national criminal jurisdiction,

Resolved to guarantee lasting respect for the enforcement of international justice.

Perhaps the first major innovation of the ICC is the fact that it will be a permanent institution rather than an *ad hoc* affair as in the case of the Yugoslavia War Tribunal. The ICC has a narrow mandate in that it will examine only four kinds of crime: those concerning genocide, crimes against humanity, war crime, and crimes of aggression. Another major advance that the ICC offers is the fact that whenever state violence takes place, there will be an investigative and judicial body to ensure that any violations are addressed. And perhaps most importantly, all actors in the conflict will be held to the same standard, rather than the victors trying the vanquished as has been the case in the past. Furthermore, states are obligated to cooperate with the ICC (Article 186), and while the ICC may not have an international police force to enforce cooperation, other states under the direction of the UN or other organizations such as NATO may enable the ICC to enforce and arrest by proxy. The case of the British making two arrests of Serb war criminals (one suspect was killed in the process) and of the Dutch making another in July 1997, and the recent ruling in Britain that Chilean dictator General Augusto Pinochet may not be entitled to legal immunity, indicate that the ICC may not require a military/police force of its own to be effective. The ICC has a long way to go before its performance can be judged, but should it prove effective, it will serve as a strong impediment to both the blatant disregard for the laws of war and flagrant defiance of human rights so common among actors in the "new wars."

It is important to bear in mind that the ICC has its opponents, particularly the US, one of just a handful of nations to vote against its creation. Nevertheless, the wide international support for the ICC may enable it to rise above this resistance to become an established bulwark of the international system.

F. Moving into the Next Millennium: Charting a Course Between Scylla and Charybdis

Greek mythology presents a classic predicament that describes the state of the UN as it moves beyond the Cold War and into the new century, one commonly referred to as the Scylla and Charybdis dilemma. Scylla and Charybdis were the monstrous daughters of Poseidon and Gaia who lived in caves on the opposite sides of the Strait of Messina. Odysseus had to negotiate his ship between these two destructive forces; in moving to avoid one, he brought himself closer to the other. Indeed, Scylla devoured six of Odysseus's companions when they ventured too close to that side of the strait.

The UN shares Odysseus's dilemma in this way: if it allows states to continue with unrestricted sovereignty, this will most assuredly lead to more inter-state rivalry, in direct contradiction of its *raison d'être.* On the other hand, if the UN moves too quickly and openly to curb abuse by states, it may risk a backlash from its members that could destroy its very credibility and effectiveness. This too would lead to war and suffering as it becomes estranged from its members and loses its political leverage. Thus the UN has to plot an arduous course to avoid becoming prey to either of these two ominous obstacles. Should it manage to stay the course through these transitional times, it will be well-positioned to take the world into a new era of peace and prosperity.

In the introduction to this chapter it was stated that sovereignty must be ceded to the UN by the member states and that the UN must be the primary framework through which international action towards curbing conflict is co-ordinated. Bearing in mind the Scylla and Charybdis dilemma, it is easy to see how carefully these two goals must be approached. The slump in UN peacekeeping activity since its height in 1995 has had much to do with the fact that many member states believed the UN was going too far, too quickly. While the UN must always try to be prescient in its disposition towards global conflict, it must do so with the tact acquired from a firm understanding of its members' mentalities.

Many of the recent innovations to complement classic peacekeeping, such as the new peacekeeping partnership and peacekeeping by proxy, seek to advance the UN's mission by improving its operational abilities, yet not at the expense of member sensitivities. Portions of a state's sovereignty must be entrusted to the UN of its own volition, not wrested from its hands. Here the former Yugoslavia serves as a good example. The US would never have allowed its troops to go to the former Yugoslavia under the command of the UN. The UN would never have been able to bring the Bosnian crisis under control without the aid of American military might. The solution, peacekeeping by proxy, was a compromise. While the UN may not control the operation, it is a partner with some significant input, and so long as NATO/SFOR keeps the peace in the former Yugoslavia, it is an excellent arrangement for the UN. But we need only consider the situation in Kosovo to see the limits of NATO's effectiveness, at least from the air.

The UN must develop new working relationships, not only with its member states through an innovation like peacekeeping by proxy, but also with the NGO community. While some may be reluctant parties in such future arrangements, it can be argued that NGOs and other non-UN actors could do much worse than increase cooperation and coordination with the world body given that body's responsibility for international peace and security.

While there is no general agreement as to the effectiveness of NGOs in influencing government policy during the Cold War, it appears that, in this era of increased peacekeeping and innovative approaches to international conflict resolution, they figure prominently in government calculations. For their part, NGOs are learning to trust and network with governments. They are realizing that government/NGO cooperation can accomplish much, as was evidenced in the cooperative effort of the landmines ban.

Just as countries act in their own best interests, so do NGOs. Oftentimes those interests can be advanced faster and be a benefit to greater numbers if adequate funding is available. Some democratic countries, including Canada, have a long and honourable history of providing financial support to NGOs – even in some cases where the money is used to oppose existing government policy. In a 1997 presentation to the Oslo NGO Forum on banning anti-personnel mines, Canadian Foreign Minister Lloyd Axworthy spoke of the role of NGOs:

> Clearly, one can no longer relegate NGOs to simple advisory or advocacy roles in this [land mines] process. They are now part of the way decisions have to be made. They have been the voice saying that governments belong to the people, and must respond to the people's hopes, demands and ideals.[38]

In a variety of ways, therefore, sovereignty is gradually being entrusted to the UN by its member states, for the purposes of peace and human security. The UN needs patience enough to wait for its work to reach fruition and, in the meantime, to carry on its precarious yet inventive balancing act, guiding the organization between Scylla and Charybdis: a task it has accomplished without significant incident since 1945. It is important to remember that, despite all the horrendous problems in our world, we are living in the longest period of great power peace since the Roman Empire. For this at least the UN deserves substantial credit.

Notes

1 I would like to thank Daniel Neysmith and Christine Dodge of the Pearson Peacekeeping Centre for their assistance in drafting this chapter.

2 The Abyssinian crisis arose in 1935 when Italy, under the leadership of the fascist dictator Benito Mussolini, invaded Abyssinia (now Ethiopia). The naked aggression of Italy shocked the international community. The League of Nations was paralyzed by inaction and enfeeblement due to some key members' interest in maintaining Mussolini as a possible ally against a re-emerging Germany. As a result, the League sanctions against Italy were halfhearted and did not include key resources for the Italian war machine, such as oil.

3 Raoul Dandurand, *The Canadian Encyclopedia Plus*, CD-ROM (Toronto: McClelland & Stewart, 1995).

4 Lester B. Pearson, *The Memoirs of the Right Honourable Lester B. Pearson*, vol. 1 (Toronto:

University of Toronto Press, 1972) 101.

5 Escott Reid, *On Duty: A Canadian at the Making of the United Nations, 1945-1946* (Toronto: McClelland and Stewart, 1953) xix.

6 France was not represented at Dumbarton Oaks since at the time it did not have an internationally recognized government.

7 Preamble to the United Nations Charter.

8 Charter of the United Nations, Chapter I, Article 1.

9 Chapter IV, Article 18, Paragraph 3 reads: "Decisions on other questions, including the determination of additional categories of questions to be decided by a two-thirds majority, shall be made by a majority of the members present and voting."

10 Charter, Chapter V, Article 23.

11 Charter, Article 55, Section B.

12 Charter, Article 55, Section C.

13 NATO, *NATO Handbook* (Brussels: NATO Office of Information and Press, 1995), 233.

14 The US Department of State produced, in 1945, a film entitled "Watchtower Over Tomorrow." It was designed to explain how the UN would work. One sequence illustrates how the standing Military Force would be called into operation.

15 Charter, Chapter VII, Article 47, Paragraph 1.

16 United Nations, *The Blue Helmets: A Review of United Nations Peacekeeping*, 3rd ed. (New York: UN Dept of Public Affairs, 1996) 17.

17 The SC action essentially sanctioned the American action, which had already been undertaken. The military forces of 36 countries carried out the operation. However the predominant force was provided by the Americans, who also contributed the command and control mechanism. The action came at a time when the USSR had absented itself from the Council, hence eliminating its veto option.

18 Brian Urquhart, *A Life in Peace and War* (New York: W.W. Norton and Co., 1997) 108.

19 Indar Jit Rikhye, *The United Nations and the Aftermath of the Gulf War* (Toronto: The John W. Holmes Memorial Lecture, Editions du GREF, 1991) 40.

20 John H. Mearsheimer, "Why We Will Soon Miss the Cold War," *The Atlantic Monthly* August 1990: 35-50.

21 Edward N. Luttwak, "Where Are the Great Powers?, At Home with the Kids," *Foreign Affairs* 73. 4 (July/August 1994): 23.

22 22. William Malet, "Peacekeeping and Peacemaking," *A Crisis of Expectations: UN Peacekeeping in the 1990s*, ed. Ramesh Thakur and Carlyle A. Thayer (Colorado: Westview Press, 1995) 237.

23 Boutros Boutros-Ghali, *An Agenda for Peace*, 2nd ed. (New York: United Nations Publications, 1995) 44.

24 John A. MacInnis (Major-General), "Lessons from UNPROFOR: Peacekeeping

from a Force Commander's Perspective," *The New Peacekeeping Partnership*, ed. Alex Morrison (Cornwallis, NS: Canadian Peacekeeping Press, 1995) 186.

25 It must be mentioned that the conventional wisdom in the US is that ineffectual UN leadership was responsible for the American deaths. In fact, they were under American command, not that of the UN.

26 Jonathan T. Howe, "Somalia: Frustration in a Failed Nation," *Soldiers for Peace*, ed. Barbara Benton (New York: Facts on File, 1996) 177.

27 Luttwak 23.

28 Boutros-Ghali 45.

29 Alex Morrison, "Command and Control," *Peacekeeping and International Relations* 22. 4 (July/August 1993): 1.

30 Charter, Chapter VII, Article 33, Paragraph II.

31 Boutros-Ghali 61.

32 The Pearson Peacekeeping Centre in Nova Scotia Canada has built its international and multi-disciplinary programs and activities on these three components. The PPC has the task of enhancing the Canadian contribution to such an understanding of international peacekeeping, and its courses are recognized for credit by both Canadian and American universities.

33 Andrew Blair, "The Changing Nature of Civil-Military Operations in Peacekeeeping," Morrison, 65.

34 *Renewing the United Nations: A Program for Reform*, A/51/950, July 14, 1997.

35 The Secretary-General has recently succeeded in coordinating the activities of UN agencies and organizations to a degree not heretofore achieved. If they do not, or only reluctantly, recognize his power, they have at least agreed to meet with him and his senior officials on a regular basis to coordinate activities.

36 Laura Neack, "UN Peacekeeping: In the Interest of Community or Self?," *Journal of Peace Research* 32. 2 (May 1995): 182.

37 Keith D. Suter, "The United Nations and Non-Governmental Organizations," *Building a More Democratic United Nations*, Proceedings of CAMDUN-1, ed. Frank Barnaby, (London: Frank Cass and Co., 1991) 12.

38 David A. Lenarcic, *Knight-Errant? Canada and the Crusade to Control Anti-Personnel Land Mines*, Contemporary Affairs No. 2 (Toronto: Irwin Publishing — Canadian Institute of International Relations, 1998) 100.

FOUR

NONVIOLENCE: A ROAD LESS TRAVELLED

JO VELLACOTT

A. General Introduction

1. Outline of Chapter

In this chapter we will look at nonviolent action as an agent of social change and at the broader concept of nonviolence. Accounts of a variety of situations of conflict or wished-for change in which nonviolent methods have been used will form the core of our discussion. Some examples illustrate the use of nonviolent techniques in seeking to bring about social change. Others raise the possibility of nonviolence as a way of life, which might preempt the causes of conflict rather than merely solving existing crises, thus providing a route by which to move closer to positive peace – that is, towards the freeing of the potential of all.

Following the case studies, we will look briefly at the thinking of some of those who have influenced nonviolent practice and theory in the twentieth century. Keeping the case studies in mind, as well as events experienced personally, or discussed in contemporary media, readers are invited to consider in what conditions and to what extent nonviolent action can take the place of violence in bringing about change. Students should not be content merely to discover the ideas of this or that proponent of nonviolent action, but should apply their own critical thinking and make up their own minds as to where they stand. For this reason, although many questions are asked in this chapter, few are answered.

2. Motivation for Nonviolent Action, and Some Terms

When the actions of some authority or power place us in a situation that we consider unfair or harmful or when we see other people caught in such a situation, we respond in a number of possible ways. We may simply decide that the situation is not serious enough to warrant interference and must be tolerated, or we may think that, bad as it is, there is nothing we can do about it. If the situation is really felt to be intolerable, we may turn to violence as a way of forcing change.

Nonviolent action lies between the two extremes of doing nothing and having recourse to violence and may be chosen either because of conviction or because it seems to be the only option available. The term "nonviolent action" covers a wide range of behaviour, but what is true of almost all such action is that it is undertaken openly to make a public statement. The term "nonviolence" goes deeper, generally implying "refraining from violence on grounds of principle."[1] Adam Curle defines nonviolence (in part) as "achieving without harm to ourselves or others, things that are normally thought to be attainable only through violence." He goes on to say that nonviolence is both an attitude and an action.[2]

The uses of nonviolent action familiar to most of us are nonviolent protests against measures introduced by the government or some other authority and unpopular with a particular segment of the population — for example, marches against hikes in student tuition fees, the 1997 protests against the Ontario government's megacity bill, demonstrations by First Nations peoples in support of their land rights, and picketing by environmental groups. We are all also familiar with the strike, a form of nonviolent action that has been around long enough to have garnered its own government-approved rules of procedure.

Beyond our borders, we hear of demonstrations against non-democratic regimes; one of the best-remembered is the student demonstration in Tienanmen Square, together with the harsh response of the Chinese government; or we may have taken part in the boycott of South African products that preceded the end of legalized apartheid and the introduction of majority rule in that country.

3. Introduction to Case Studies

Nonviolent action has a history going back more than two millennia. Our case studies are all taken from the twentieth century and are given in roughly chronological order.

Nonviolent action may be used in a good cause or a bad one, and if used in a good cause, it may still be used inappropriately. Our examples will be of instances where, at the very least, a case can be made for the justice of the cause, but as a technique, nonviolent action is not the monopoly of the politically correct or spiritually inspired. It has, for instance, been used on both sides of the free choice/anti-abortion conflict.

Our narratives focus on the actions, with only brief explanations of the background. They are all written to some extent from the point of view of the participants in the action described – that is to say, they are based on sympathetic accounts. It is hoped that enough information is included for readers to project themselves into some of these situations and to form their own opinions as to the effectiveness and appropriateness of nonviolent action. In other words, what would you have done?

4. Food for Thought

Some of the questions raised by the case studies may be: What were the prior conditions to be met before nonviolent action was undertaken? Were alternatives explored? Was nonviolence chosen on principle, or as the most effective strategy available? What, if any, was the role of charismatic leadership? How were decisions made by the participants? Was the aim of any particular action coercion or conversion? Are both objectives legitimate? Must there be an achievable external goal, or may there be times when the need to witness publicly is a sufficient motive – the need to refuse complicity, for instance, in some government measure or action? What was the nature of preparation for the action? Were the methods consistent with the objectives? If nonviolent action leads to or provokes violence does this render it invalid? Is nonviolent protest in danger of crossing the line into violent action unless it is informed by thought-out principle? What was the effect on the participants? on the opponents? on public opinion? on later long-term developments? What is the role of secondary participants – for example, supporters of a boycott? How would you measure success in nonviolent action?

Some broader questions may be: Is there a dimension to nonviolent practice which goes deeper than its use as a strategy? Is there a quality to be found in participants in some nonviolent campaigns that suggests a component of internal strength? Can this be consciously developed? What bearing does its presence or absence have on an action or campaign? Can nonviolence be a way of life?

Answers to these questions will vary from individual to individual and, to some extent, from situation to situation. It will be useful to have the questions in mind as you read the case studies.

B. The Case Studies

1. The Campaign for Women's Suffrage in Britain (1905-1918): Towards Political Equality

Two different techniques were used in the early twentieth century by two different groups of British women in order to obtain the right to vote; they provide a useful comparison.

a) The Women's Social and Political Union (WSPU — Known as Suffragettes)[4]
The best-known story has long been that of the so-called militants or suffragettes, under the leadership of the Pankhurst family, and the organization they developed, the Women's Social and Political Union (WSPU). They began from 1905 to use nonviolent means of making their voices heard, by interrupting political meetings with unwelcome questions, organizing mass marches, picketing at elections, and sending large delegations to the House of Commons, outside which they also demonstrated, in some instances chaining themselves to railings. When the government failed to respond to their demands, they escalated their attempts to gain attention by damage to property, throwing stones through store windows on the main streets of London's West End, and setting fires in mail boxes. Imprisoned, a number refused food and were forcibly fed.

From time to time, when a bill offering some measure of franchise for women was under discussion, the WSPU declared a truce, renewing their militancy with fresh vigour when it failed to go forward. By 1913, with much of the leadership in prison or fled abroad, a handful of individual militants turned to more extreme methods, committing arson or bombings at several houses and making threats and symbolic attacks on the persons of anti-suffrage politicians. No one was injured in these attacks, though one politician was hurt in a brawl outside the prime minister's residence; the casualties of the militant campaign were among the women themselves, some few of whom suffered permanent damage to their health from force-feeding. Some, too, were injured on "Black Friday," when the contingent of London police assigned to control the demonstration delayed making arrests, leaving the women exposed to assault and sexual molestation from a hostile crowd and from the police themselves.[5]

When war broke out in August 1914 the suffragette leaders renounced militancy and were released from prison. The WSPU's lack of an internal democratic process makes it impossible to assess opinion within that organization, but Christabel and her mother Emmeline Pankhurst whole-heartedly supported the war effort.

b) The National Union of Women's Suffrage Societies (NU — Known as Suffragists)[6]
Much less well remembered than the "militants," the NU's methods were described by themselves as "constitutional" (that is, as always within the law), which puts them on the conservative end of any spectrum of nonviolent action. However, a comparison of their contribution with that of the WSPU is thought-provoking.

Undoubtedly, in the first decade of the twentieth century, the NU, a much older organization, benefited considerably from the publicity gained by the activities of the Pankhursts and their followers. Women flocked to join the NU, which grew rapidly. Among its leaders were many women whose commitment to peaceful and conciliatory methods was based on principle and a sense of strategy. Put briefly, the NU's leaders held to the view that the basis of government must be the consent of the governed and that women must be represented on the same basis as men.

To use force to attain the vote seemed illogical and impractical to many in the NU. The alternative was to persuade the men who sat in parliament to grant the vote; persuasion could be by conversion, by the arousal of voter interest, or by forms of political pressure. Catherine Marshall (1880-1961), above all others, brought the art of political pressure to new heights.

The methods of the NU included many standard nonviolent techniques. Like the WSPU, they held marches, mass demonstrations, and big public meetings. More systematically than the WSPU, the NU made use of the press, writing letters and articles and whenever possible working to gain the understanding and sympathy of journalists and editors. They campaigned vigorously at by-elections and general elections, attempting not to disrupt but to educate the voters and convert the candidates. Locally in the constituencies and centrally in the corridors of parliament, the NU sounded out politicians one by one, exerting pressure whenever they could, and keeping in particularly close touch with any senior members, of whatever party, who had expressed support.

Increasingly, the NU leaders discovered where party political interest lay and how it could be brought to bear on their cause. There were, for example, many working men who still did not have the vote, and others who were deprived of its exercise by constraints of residence and registration. Gradually, by patient behind-the-scenes lobbying, the NU brought the support of the trade unions behind women's suffrage. By 1912 they had built a working arrangement with the Labour Party (the third party in the British Commons). In return for a party commitment to vote against any franchise measure that did not include women, Labour candidates could receive substantial financial and organizational help from the NU in the lead-up to elections.

During 1914 the NU was beginning to exploit the emergence in both major parties (Liberal and Unionist) of a perception that women's suffrage (or adult suffrage) was inevitably coming and that, in the event of a big increase in the electorate, it was better to be seen as the party to be thanked for granting the vote rather than as the party obstinately opposing it.

Although mythology has favoured the WSPU, the NU was very largely responsible for the fact that by the outbreak of the World War I the campaign for the extension of the vote to women was headed for success. Their campaign was a blend of persuasion and pressure, making use of one-on-one conversion and of political coercion by marshalling public opinion, self-interest or party interest. They had also steadily built the image – and the self-image – of women as fit for public responsibility, meanwhile training themselves through the formal democratic processes of their own organization. When the WSPU turned to violence (even if mainly against property), NU members found themselves often hampered, and even physically attacked, because of hostility to the suffragettes. Aggressive tactics also enabled fainthearted or devious supporters to claim that women were not fit for the vote, or that it would be unprincipled to give in to violence.

Because of the war, the general election of 1915 did not take place, so no direct outcome of the suffragists' political strategies can be documented. But in 1918 women over 28 were enfranchised.

The foregoing account looks at the women's suffrage campaign in Britain in terms of its expressed objectives – that is, as a campaign to obtain the vote for women. There is, of course, another whole way of telling the history of the British suffrage movement. Apart from its role in gaining the vote, the WSPU, far more than the NU, has been eulogized for its role in sexual politics. Undoubtedly, individual suffragettes found liberation from the stifling conventions of their time in defying the canons of respectability, taking risks, and exhibiting extraordinary physical courage. The numbers involved in actual violence against property were inevitably quite limited, but a healthy sense of rebellion certainly rubbed off on their wider following. The NU displayed a keen feminist awareness on all sorts of topics, but the WSPU, better served by its own historians, has continued to be the subject of women's liberation mythology. The present writer is uncomfortable with the credibility this lends to the use of methods more extreme than are called for and with the devaluation of the remarkable and effective political work of the NU.

2. Gandhi: Towards Indian National Independence (1915-1947)[7]

Mohandas K. Gandhi (1869-1948) was born in India, educated as a lawyer in Britain, and spent twenty years in South Africa, where he took up the cause of the civil rights of the Indian community there. By the time he returned to India in 1914 to work for the betterment of his people, he had developed both a powerful philosophy of nonviolence and the techniques of nonviolent action. We will look at some of the elements in his thinking below; here, the focus is on his actions.

Gandhi's first initiative on his return to India was to establish an ashram, where he trained those who would work alongside him to help expose and ameliorate some of the worst exploitation of indigo workers, peasants, and mill-workers. For Gandhi, the training of followers involved the internalization of a commitment to nonviolence even in the face of extreme violence from opponents.

In 1918, at the end of World War I, when the British government made cosmetic changes to Indian provincial constitutions, but failed to yield any real power, Gandhi gathered a national following and became the leader of the Indian National Congress party. Disturbances in 1919 led to the Amritsar massacre, when General Dyer, the local British commander, opened fire on an unarmed crowd, killing 379 and wounding 1,200. Gandhi served on the investigation committee, making sure that there was no cover-up.

From this time, the goal of independence took precedence, subject only to Gandhi's overriding conviction that it must be brought about without violence. In 1920, he launched his first mass non-cooperation campaign, boycotting all British colonial institutions such as schools, courts, and legislative councils, and moving on to boycott imported goods. Two years later, when he was unable to prevent some violent incidents, Gandhi suspended the campaign. This remained his practice whenever violence erupted in a cause in which he was engaged.

Sentenced to six years in prison, Gandhi was released after two years for health reasons: he abstained from political action for the remainder of his sentence, using the time to work on social issues.

While the British government continued to delay the granting of full independence, Gandhi's moral leadership grew steadily. At the end of 1929 the Indian Congress declared independence, and shortly after, Gandhi renewed the civil disobedience campaign. Choosing the highly symbolic focus of the government monopoly on salt, he set out with 78 trained followers to march 240 miles to the salt-pans by the sea at Dandi. Thousands joined him; hundreds withstood severe beating by the bamboo canes (lathis) of the police, until beaten down and carried away on stretchers. An eyewitness reported, "I saw and heard hundreds of blows inflicted by the police, but saw not a single blow returned by the volunteers. So far as I could observe the volunteers implicitly obeyed Gandhi's creed of nonviolence. In no case did I see a volunteer even raise an arm to deflect the blows from lathis." The same observer reported that some of the police "seemed reluctant to strike," and slackened off when the officers were occupied at the other end of the line.[8]

At the salt-pans and elsewhere that year, Gandhi and 60,000 other men and women were arrested, but his credibility was now so high that the government could not ignore him. Released from prison, he attended the second session of the Round Table Conference on the Indian Constitution in 1931, and was also involved in one-on-one negotiations with the British viceroy of India. Nevertheless, successive British governments still dragged their feet, and tension between Muslims and Hindus made the design of a constitution genuinely difficult.

Gandhi's programmes combined political with social objectives. His promotion of simple technologies aimed to make the poor less vulnerable to victimization by landowners and manufacturers and to make India no longer dependent on imports. His campaigns for the Untouchables (in one of which he fasted almost to the point of death while imprisoned) were also part of his vision of the future of an independent India. Public awareness was raised both in India and in Britain. Coarse cotton cloth, handspun and handwoven, came to be worn by all in India; it was spun with a little handspinner by Gandhi himself and by thousands of his followers.

The outbreak of World War II led to the renewal of the independence movement, and Gandhi was jailed again from 1942-1944 for his part in the "Quit India" campaign. In 1947, after 26 years of nonviolent struggle, India gained independence.

Sadly, the creation of a partition between the Muslim state of Pakistan and the rest of India, deplored by Gandhi, was followed by serious violence against the minorities now left in each of the two nations. Gandhi had lost some of his support, and there were many who could not rise to his vision of nonviolence. In 1947 he walked through some of the most disturbed regions and had local successes in quelling violence, but in January 1948 after moving to New Delhi, a city filling with refugees, he was assassinated.

3. The Ruhrkampf, 1923:[9] Civilian Resistance to Invasion

After World War I the victorious Allies decreed, in the Treaty of Versailles, that Germany should accept blame for causing the war and pay reparations for all the damages suffered by the Allied populations.

Immediately after the war, Germany had undergone a revolution and become a republic, with a fragile democratic constitution. Germans found the terms of the imposed treaty harsh and humiliating, and many particularly resented the reparations clauses, which French statesmen saw as a way to keep Germany economically and militarily weak.

Reparations and inflation hit the German economy hard, and she soon began to default on payments. In January 1923 France and Belgium occupied the Ruhr, the major German industrial zone, from which German troops were excluded by the Treaty. A body of officials and engineers, called the *Mission Interalliée de Contrôle des Usines et des Mines* (MICUM), was sent in to control the German authorities and the industries, and a large body of troops (totalling 90,000 by June 1923) was sent to protect the commissioners.

Despite constant previous threats from the Allies, the German government prepared for the invasion only in the last two or three days before it occurred. Of the spectrum of possible responses, military resistance was out of the question given the weak and confused state of German forces, and submission politically dangerous because of the strength of feeling against the Treaty, let alone against the invasion. In between lay various forms of violent resistance (e.g., sabotage, assassinations, and rioting), active nonviolent resistance (such as physically blocking the movement of troops or supplies), or passive resistance (boycotts, non-cooperation, refusal to work).

The German government, located in Berlin — well outside the occupied area — after consulting the trade unions and the employers' organizations, ordered and orchestrated a campaign of passive resistance. (This was a strategy, in no way a matter of belief in nonviolence.) Support was widespread, and communications between the occupied and unoccupied regions were never effectively cut (indeed, the post office had managed to set up a secret telephone system with connections to Berlin), so the government remained able to give some direction to the resisters.

Because of the economic motive behind the Ruhr invasion, the event lent itself specifically to the development of economic means of resistance. The invaders found the centre of the city of Essen almost deserted when they marched in, with no one at work in the public buildings. The trade unions and the employers planned to continue work as usual except that whenever an order was given by any invader, it would not be obeyed. Strikes, boycotts, and demonstrations of various kinds were also organized or occurred spontaneously. For weeks, the invaders had little success in breaking up this uncommon agreement between employers and workers.

The refusal of the mine owners to deliver coal to the French and Belgian authorities, and indeed the German government's decision to stop what reparations payments it had been making, gave encouragement to others, and the growing harshness of the sentences handed down by the court martials hardened feeling against the occupancy force. Within a few weeks, civil servants, transport workers, shopkeepers, restaurant workers, and the general public were refusing to respond to any demands of the invading troops and administrators, refusing to serve them, refusing to sell to them, refusing to stay in any bar or restaurant where they entered.

The press, too, remained solid; and the refusal of editors, publishers, and printers to print what the invaders wished and to refrain from printing what they did not led first to temporary bans and then to heavy reprisals, followed by the appearance of underground news-sheets, with volunteers risking prison sentences to distribute them.

As the weeks wore on, requisitions of private property and billeting of troops were carried out with great brutality, culminating in an incident at the Krupp works where French soldiers were ordered to shoot into a crowd of workers, killing thirteen people. The violent element in the resistance also grew. In June, a railway bridge was blown up by saboteurs, killing ten Belgian soldiers and wounding many more, leading to savage reprisals against innocent people who happened to be nearby.

The defeat of the resisters came about mainly through an economic disaster. Even before the invasion, Germany had been suffering from inflation. Added to the economic impact of the invasion, the efforts of the German government to finance the resistance, to compensate industrialists for their losses, and to send food into the densely populated

Ruhr completed the devastation of the German economy. Through the summer of 1923, inflation rose astronomically, with banknotes being churned out not only by the government, but by Ruhr banks as well.[10] In September a visitor reported that a cab fare registering three marks on the meter was officially charged at nine million in the morning and rose to fifteen million by the afternoon.[11] The cost of necessities similarly soared, with a sense that everything was out of control. Bread riots occurred, violent crime shot up. Extremists on the right and on the left (some secretly encouraged by the occupiers) staged uprisings; Russian Communists anticipated the extension of their revolution to Germany; fascist groups saw success as just around the corner; paramilitary units of dubious loyalties abounded; people in the street spoke of a dictatorship as the only solution.

The resistance had made the Ruhr virtually ungovernable, but had failed to drive the invaders out. In August the German government resigned, and the new administration under Gustav Streseman capitulated the following month, putting an unconditional end to the government-directed civilian nonviolent resistance.

However, this was not all the effect the resistance had. As much as the invasion itself, the resistance and finally the collapse of the German economy had attracted international attention, with public opinion running heavily against France, where the government also lost much support. The German government struggled painfully back to relative political and economic stability. An international commission put together a package, the Dawes Plan, which set more realistic reparations payments, provided Germany with a loan to meet her first payments, and required France to withdraw from the Ruhr. In the medium term, the Weimar Republic survived, and the peace of Europe was saved.

At the time, the Ruhrkampf attracted great interest among those who were looking for alternatives to war. Among the international public, the nonviolent resistance attracted sympathy; acts of sabotage weakened support from outside.

The tension between nonviolent and violent resistance in the Ruhr attracted the attention of some peace organizations interested in the concept of nonviolence. The Women's International League for Peace and Freedom sent envoys (including British, French, and German WILPF members) to meet with statesmen in France and in Germany, hoping, by explaining each to the other, to encourage the opening of negotiations. They also sent "missioners" to the Ruhr to support those they identified as true nonviolent resisters, who found themselves under constant pressure not only from the French occupation forces but from German militarist nationalists who had no principled objection to the use of violence. Some of the workers saw their resistance as a spontaneous defence of the dignity of free labour and a better route than violence.[12] Some, particularly in the trade unions, saw the resistance as a challenge to exert a power, in the hands of the people, which could replace war.

Given the slender choice of options, it is of interest to identify ways in which the resistance might have been more effective. In hindsight, of course, preplanning and education might have made a big difference. Equally significantly, there was a limited understanding of nonviolence. Even tactically, the Germans would have benefited if they could have found "the right mixture ... of friendliness towards the soldiers as fellow human beings on the one hand, and resistance against them as instruments of foreign and unjust domination on the other."[13] The hatred between France and Germany left by the war was only deepened on both sides in the experience of invasion and resistance. In addition, the invasion had further polarized factions in Germany, weakening democracy and encouraging extremism of the left and of the right. All these factors helped manure the seedbed of Nazism and pave the way for World War II. But it is still probable that a more violent response would have had even worse effects.

This example also raises the wider question as to whether a country could mount an effective defence against an invasion, if it had chosen nonviolent civilian resistance in advance and had prepared and trained the population appropriately.

4. Rosa Parks and Martin Luther King: The Struggle for Civil Rights[14]

On December 1, 1955, in Montgomery, Alabama, Rosa Parks, a seamstress at a department store, refused to give up her seat in a bus to a white passenger. The front few rows were reserved for whites, the back rows for blacks, but if the "white" seats were full, it was customary for black passengers to yield their seats without any argument. This time, the operator told four passengers to move; the other three complied, but Rosa Parks quietly refused. The driver called the police and had her arrested for violating the city's segregation by-law.

As Martin Luther King later wrote, Rosa Parks's stand was no part of a planned campaign or test case, but "her own intrepid affirmation that she had had enough.... She was not 'planted' there by the NAACP [National Association for Advancement of Coloured People], or any other organization; she was planted there by her personal sense of dignity and self-respect."[15]

No one could have predicted the extent of the effect of this simple action, which triggered reservoirs of pent-up resentment and at the same time gave the African Americans of Montgomery a way to demonstrate their solidarity and self-respect. Leaders of the black churches and of other community groups called for a one-day boycott, which was totally observed, and at a mass meeting that night, it was agreed to continue the boycott until the bus company made important concessions and guaranteed courteous service. The same day, Rosa Parks was fined and appealed to a higher court.

Martin Luther King, a young black minister, was chosen as president of a newly formed organization, the Montgomery Improvement Association. King had been influenced already by his reading of Thoreau and by Gandhi's campaigns and writings, and he now took advice also from some who had experience with nonviolent action. Other black ministers – and only one white minister – were the principal leaders of the campaign that rapidly developed.

Instead of soon petering out, the bus boycott remained rock solid, although it was impossible to organize alternative transport for everyone, and many had to walk long distances. Attempts by the city council to break the boycott by any possible means failed.

The spirit behind the boycott was kept alive by twice-weekly meetings in one or another of the black churches, at which singing and praying alternated with reports on progress and workshops given by Dr King and other leaders not only on the philosophy of nonviolent resistance, but on how to react when confronted by violence. When King was arrested for allegedly speeding in his car, such a large crowd gathered at the jail that the officer in charge released him, although the crowd had made no threats.

The Ku Klux Klan, and probably others, began to send anonymous letters and threatening phone calls to King and the other leaders, and at the end of January 1956, a bomb was thrown on to the porch of King's house. This time the crowd of African Americans who gathered was angry and was calmed only by King's own pleading.

As the world became aware of what was going on, support, financial and moral, poured in. Meanwhile, the leaders were arrested and charged with conspiracy "to prevent the operation of a lawful business." King was fined $500 and appealed, but counter-appeals kept the case going, and the boycott had to continue, until finally, at the end of 1956, the Supreme Court supported the earlier decision that segregation of buses was unconstitutional – a huge victory.

When the people returned to the buses after the boycott of over a year, they were well prepared to meet possible violence with conciliation, but in the main they were not harassed at first. White anger spilled over a few days later in random shootings at the buses and in serious bombings of churches and ministers' houses. City leaders and businessmen, however, now realized that nothing but harm could come by allowing violence to continue and offered a reward for information leading to the conviction of those who were responsible. Seven were arrested and charged, and although the white jury would not convict them the bombings came to an end, and the people rode the desegregated buses in peace.

5. Cesar Chavez and the California Grape Workers:[16] Claiming Labour's Right to Organize

Through a combination of reasons, farmworkers in California have long been exceptionally vulnerable to exploitation and for almost as long have struggled for justice. For more than 100 years, the landowners have been able to play one group of workers off against another, often on a racial basis – indigenous people, Chinese, Japanese, Mexican, European, Middle Eastern, and Asiatic immigrants and refugees have all been imported from time to time.

In the 1930s, landowning senators from the South succeeded in having farm workers excluded from the benefits and protections of what passed into law as the National Labor Relations Act (1936). Consequently the owners had been able to enlist the forces of law – the police and the courts – on their side against agricultural workers and to prevent the formation of effective unions.

In California, a very few huge corporations came to control the land, farming, and local government. Hiring was largely done through labour contractors, middlemen who supplied workers for a job, controlling their wages and making sure that any thought to be trouble-makers never got work.

From about 1914 to 1934, the readiest supply of labour came across the border illegally from Mexico; the authorities turned a blind eye except to turn on any who stepped out of line. In the 1930s the drought and the Depression sent masses of desperate unemployed citizens west in search of work, and Mexicans were temporarily pushed back over the border,[17] until World War II created a huge demand and led to enormous growth in the agribusiness industry.

From time to time, groups of California farm workers from all over the world struggled to better their lot – for example, staging an isolated strike when wages were forced down, or attempting to protest about appalling living conditions, exposure to chemical pesticide spraying, or child labour. But nothing lasting could be achieved without united action. This came only when Cesar Chavez, with the support and vision of many others to back him, provided the leadership.

Chavez, a Chicano (Mexican-American), grew up as a migrant worker after his father lost his Arizona farm in the Depression. In his twenties he helped to raise community consciousness among the Chicanos. In 1962, Chavez moved into the grape-growing region to address the root problems of working conditions.

Beginning with the formation of a union mainly of Chicanos, Chavez managed in 1965 to merge his union with a group of Filipino workers to form the United Farm Workers. No longer would the growers be able to play one batch of workers off against another. In September of that year, as harvest began, the UFW embarked on its first strike, after the owners refused their requests for collective bargaining rights. The strike lasted five years. Picketing was kept up in the face of the violent response of the growers, who used armed guards and were backed by local and state police. The police watched complacently while all kinds of violence and intimidation were used, scarcely ever laying charges against those on the owners' side. Chavez believed passionately that a total commitment to nonviolence had to be at the centre of the workers' resistance and saw the constant harassment to which they were exposed on the picket lines as providing a training and a test of each worker's commitment. Public attention was drawn to the conflict when Chavez enlisted the sympathy of church people to join in some of the protests.

Two major steps were soon taken. The UFW affiliated with the AFL-CIO (American Federation of Labour-Congress of Industrial Organizations), gaining support and a sense of solidarity with the wider trade union movement.

Second, the UFW initiated a boycott of California grapes to bring pressure to bear on the growers, capitalize on growing international sympathy, and further educate the public. The striking workers went in twos and threes all over the United States and Canada, holding meetings and setting up committees to continue the work of leafleting, holding vigils at supermarkets, and being available for meetings. AFL-CIO unions helped with funding, transportation, accommodation, and food. Churches, students, and the general public as well as workers took up the cause; not only were individuals refusing to buy California grapes, but supermarket chains found themselves under pressure not to stock them. Support came even from overseas.

Chavez, with a large majority of the grape workers, was a Roman

Catholic, and substantial public support came from the Roman Catholic Church, especially from a group of California Catholic bishops, and at the other end of the scale, from Dorothy Day and the Catholic Worker movement. Again, Chavez's vision led to the breaking down of old barriers; he played an active role in drawing together workers and supporters from different and formerly hostile Christian denominations and other faith groups.

When a Senate sub-committee, co-chaired by the sympathetic Senator Robert Kennedy, was set up to look at the whole issue of migratory labour, the extraordinary feudal attitudes of the growers and some of the police were exposed to public light through their own testimony.

By the spring of 1967, some but not all growers expressed a willingness to negotiate a contract, especially after a widely publicized march to the California state capital, Sacramento. Movement continued to be very slow, and some of the workers believed things could be speeded up by the use of threats and sabotage. Chavez took a personal spiritual responsibility for acts of violence committed by protesting farm workers; on several occasions he fasted for prolonged periods as an act of penance. For him, the march to Sacramento had been as much an atonement for past violence as it had been a triumphant demonstration of solidarity.

After five years of strike and boycott, the UFW won contracts with all the major grape-growers in California and Arizona. The contracts included basic workers' rights and a number of provisions for such things as an education fund for workers' children, into which owners had to pay, and health insurance, both controlled by the UFW. Hiring halls under union direction replaced the labour contractor system, and child labour was prohibited. The UFW began to branch out to enrol workers employed on other crops and elsewhere.

Three years later, when the first contracts expired, the growers adopted a new tactic, calling in the Teamsters' Union, which – without taking any vote or holding public meetings – declared itself representative of the farm workers and signed contracts with the owners, wiping out all the concessions the UFW had gained. The workers again went on strike, and this time picketers suffered terrible violence from both the growers and their new henchmen, the Teamsters. Over 300 UFW members were hospitalized after being injured on the picket line, and eventually two were killed. Chavez's life was threatened, and in an era when Martin Luther King and Robert Kennedy had both been gunned down, the menace was real. Meanwhile, the police, once more cooperating with the growers, arrested over 3,000 UFW members for peaceful picketing.

Chavez wanted martyrdom for his followers no more than he would tolerate violence against their opponents, and remarkably his followers held loyal to his vision. Indeed, the role of innumerable followers who kept the democratically run UFW dedicated to nonviolence was at least as important as Chavez's leadership. The UFW withdrew the picket lines and, again with the support of the AFL-CIO, turned all their efforts towards a renewal of the boycott. The effectiveness was even more widespread than before; for instance, the US National Board of Rabbis declared that grapes harvested by exploited workers were not kosher, and European dockers refused to unload grapes not marked with the UFW mark.

Again, a large measure of victory ensued. One outcome of the renewed struggle was that California passed a state law in 1975 mandating the right of farm workers to decide by a formal vote under state supervision whether they wanted a union, and which union they wanted. The Teamsters had to concede defeat and leave farm labour to the UFW.

What we have covered here is only the first two of the UFW's campaigns. The huge agribusiness corporations have not lain down and accepted the need for humane practices, and in California and elsewhere other campaigns have been or have yet to be waged.

6. Greenham Common: Protesting Nuclear Armaments[18]

In August, 1981, in response to the news that American nuclear weapons (Cruise missiles) would be stationed at Greenham Common near Newbury, Berkshire, in the south of England, a group of 36 women and four men expressed their outrage by walking to Greenham from Cardiff in Wales, a journey of about nine days; some brought their children with them, others were old enough to be grandparents. The outcome went far beyond anything they had had in mind. The Women's Peace Camp remained at Greenham Common without intermission for many years, until the Cruise missiles were finally removed from the site following the end of the Cold War.

Initially the women were seen as no more than a passing embarrassment to the military. But more came intending to stay, so that by the end of 1981 the campers had set up a semi-permanent camp, were issuing regular newsletters, had blocked an attempt to lay sewer pipes that would increase the capacity of the military camp, and had been threatened with eviction by Newbury District Council.

Greenham, originally common land, had been expropriated during World War II, and later leased to the United States Air Force (USAF), who were now preparing it to receive the missiles. The site was surrounded by a wire fence nine miles in circumference and eight feet high, which would later be raised higher to withstand the women. Those who flocked there in protest camped on the fringe of common land outside the fence, at first close to the main gate and later at other gates around the perimeter.

Many of the women were at Greenham because of what they saw as the intolerable threat to their children posed by nuclear arms; others saw their protest as a strong feminist statement against patriarchal militarism; others had reasons ranging from a lifelong commitment to pacifism to a hostility to the American presence on land seen as belonging to the people.

The first major controversy which the participants had to resolve was whether Greenham should be an all-women camp. Not easily and not without hurt and the loss of some women, it was decided – after many weeks – that men could visit by day, but not remain overnight. Many other things had to be worked out – the commitment to nonviolence and its definition and limits, how to communicate with the media, and whether to try to talk with the military personnel.

Sharpened by the conflict over the role of men and made more challenging by the diversity of those present, much early work of the participants centred on the development of a non-hierarchical decision-making process. A number had had negative experiences in other organizations, where forceful individuals (often men) dominated, and the opinions of some were never heard; some had had positive experience in consensus decision-making or with the Quakers, who similarly seek unity without use of voting.

No one name, nor even a handful of names, is commonly identified with leadership of the prolonged witness at Greenham, and this may be a testimony to the success of the feminist women who gave, in fact, a great deal of guidance in a direction which would ensure that neither they nor any others would become dominant. Notes made by Dr. Rosalie Bertell when she visited Greenham show how the process ensured that all were heard, and all had a free choice as to the extent of their personal participation in a planned action. The option of standing aside was available, but if any woman felt certain that the action should not proceed, it would not do so. The process dealt with central issues only; friction over peripheral issues was lessened by a sort of natural separation for daily living into groups who shared a common lifestyle or beliefs.[19]

Of course, the camp was never without internal arguments, many of them passionate.[20] Women came to Greenham from varied religious as well as political backgrounds, or from none. Many would have rejected the word "religious," but their visual, spoken, and sung symbolism was rife with spiritual imagery, whether it was expressed in traditional Christian terms, or in terms of a feminist goddess, through "embracing the base", through covering the fence with such signs of life as flowers and photos of children, or through the song that became almost an anthem of the camp: "You can't kill the spirit/She is like a mountain/ Old and strong/She goes on and on and on."

The camp was controversial in both the wider peace and anti-nuclear movements and among feminists (some of whom saw it as a "motherhood" exercise), though it drew increasing support in both areas.

Throughout 1982 and 1983,[21] the Greenham women were constantly involved in direct actions, blockading at the gates to stop the movement of supplies or the entrance of workers, cutting the wire or rushing the gate to invade the base, weaving woollen webs across the gates, making their presence visible when important visitors came to the base, extending their range to protest against the Falklands War (October, 1982), bringing the media in whenever they could, and enlisting the help of sympathetic experts to testify to the effects of nuclear war at the trials which resulted from some actions.

The response of the authorities hardened. The whole camp was forcibly evicted again and again by police and bailiffs, who often used bulldozers. Thereafter the women lived in "benders," frail structures of plastic stretched over wire or branches. Those who resisted eviction were arrested, and, if they refused to be bound over "to keep the peace," they were sent to prison, as were some of those charged following the actions; some continued their non-cooperation in prison.

One of the most dramatic and symbolic actions occurred when, after months of planning and spreading the word, an estimated 30,000 women came and held hands to form a ring around the USAF base. In another action just before dawn on New Year's Day, 1983, 44 women climbed over the fence (using carpet to cover the barbed wire on the top) and danced for an hour on one of the silos housing the Cruise missiles before the police arrived to arrest them.

Despite escalating popular protest throughout the NATO nations the missiles arrived (by air) in November 1983. But by this time there were many other peace camps and demonstrations at other sites of the Cruise and Pershing missiles, throughout the British and European deployment area and in the United States. Fear of bringing more of this latent support into open opposition, or of making martyrs, may account for the fact that the heaviest possible charges were not laid against the women demonstrators, although they were constantly harassed and underwent a great deal of hardship.[22]

After the arrival of the missiles the Greenham women, working with the Campaign for Nuclear Disarmament (CND), added to their activities that of helping to keep track of practice exercises – supposedly secret – in which the missiles were taken out of the base at night and deployed temporarily at other locations. Greenham women also travelled, in Britain and around the world, sometimes to protest at other missile bases and sometimes as speakers. A number of women called Greenham home for years.

As the Cold War began to wind down in 1987, the USA and the USSR signed an agreement to get rid of the Cruise and some other missiles. After they were removed the Greenham camp diminished to a very small presence but did not completely disappear for many more months; the women made the point that the missiles and the warheads had not ceased to be a menace.

The reasons for Greenham's persistence as a women-only initiative, and the effect of this decision, are worthy of discussion, but should not be the only focus of consideration. The Greenham experience had elements in common with other nonviolent actions, and some that were unique. The extent to which it was not planned in advance has contributed an unusual degree of transparency to our eyes of its development and processes and of the growth in understanding, or conversely the disillusion, of individual participants.

7. Osijek, 1992-1995:[23] *Transforming the Legacy of War*

The background to this story is complex, as anyone who has followed developments in the 1990s since the disintegration of the former Yugoslavia will realize. The scene will be set here only in general terms.[24]

The Balkans, in the southeast of Europe, have seen centuries of ethnic and religious hostilities, of wars and oppression. After World War I, a number of small previously antagonistic states were combined to form Yugoslavia. In each region there might be a predominant ethnic group (Serb, Croat, Slovene, Hungarian, Albanian), religion (Catholic, Orthodox, Muslim), and culture, but in every region there are also substantial minorities from the other groups.

During World War II, Yugoslavia was coveted for strategic reasons by both sides, leading to renewed fighting between ethnic and cultural groups. After the war Tito gained ascendancy as the President of

Yugoslavia, and the lid stayed on the volatile mix, more or less, until after his death in 1980 and the shifting of the pattern in eastern Europe as the Cold War came to an end.

Dormant nationalisms and prejudices were easily re-aroused when an old dream resurfaced – a dream of a Greater Serbia taking in all areas where Serbs lived. War shortly broke out, engulfing large areas of Croatia and the whole of Bosnia during the next several years. By the beginning of 1992 the Serb army had succeeded in gaining control of nearly 30 per cent of Croatia. This situation was frozen by the United Nations in January 1992, and the area has since been administered by Serb authorities and the UN Protection Force.

Osijek is a town in northern Croatia that never fell to the Serbs, but suffered almost continuous bombardment, diminishing but not ending when the UN cease-fire took hold. Osijek was left as almost an island, surrounded by Serb-occupied areas under UN control. Osijek's own population of just over 100,000 is mixed, with a majority of (mainly Catholic) Croats, but with about 20 per cent Serbs, together with a number of Hungarians and some Muslims. In addition, during the war about 30,000 refugees from the surrounding country poured in and remained.

Constant shelling or sniper fire, about 11,000 casualties including over 1,000 dead, complete destruction of many buildings and damage to virtually all, a shortage of food and of all goods and services, the added burden and bitterness of the refugees, a great increase in crime, the evacuation of all the children to safer areas, unemployment, the loss of large tracts of food-growing land to the Serbs, the uncertain future – no wonder that fear and bitter anger engulfed most residents.

The material distress served to harden attitudes and feed hostilities. There were many internal dissensions and mistrusts among the people of Osijek, but they were almost all united in hatred and demonization of the Serbs and a clamour for vengeance. Those Serbs who had remained in Osijek lost friends, jobs, and property.

Yet there were some in Osijek, as elsewhere throughout Yugoslavia, who clung to a belief that violence begat only violence and alienation and who were convinced that there had to be a better way. Some were troubled even more profoundly by the deepening climate of fear and hatred and its psychological effects than they were by the appalling physical conditions, although they wanted also to find a way to help refugees and other distressed people.

Some of those looking for a way out were in touch with Vesna Terselic, a Croatian woman from Zagreb, who had courageously set up an anti-war campaign (Anti Ratna Kampgne, ARK), and early in 1992 they planned to set up a branch of ARK in Osijek, despite the prevailing climate of active hostility towards those who spoke of peace.

In Osijek a woman and a man, Katarina Kruhonja and Krunoslav Sukic, planned a five-day workshop to take place in June, and invited Adam Curle, a British peacemaker, to lead it. Curle's role as a lifelong peacemaker has largely been behind the scenes, working as an educator and as a mediator in conflict situations, speaking to the humanity in leaders on both sides, trying to open the way to negotiation.

The situation in Osijek was a novel one. The people asking for help were not political leaders, nor had they any contact with the Serb occupiers, cut off as the latter were behind UN protective lines. Neither mediation nor nonviolent action, in the usual sense, was appropriate. Nevertheless, a move towards nonviolence might be possible.

Adam Curle has recorded the story, but wants it made clear that "the main power house of both thought and action is Katarina." The form taken by the workshop derived from Krohonja's thinking and from Curle's own underlying philosophy. For Krohonja nonviolence "does not just mean acting harmlessly, but to promote the well-being of all involved in any particular situation; not just not hurting or hitting your 'enemy,' but doing all you can to help him escape the compulsion, anger, fear, etc. that is driving him."[25]

Faced with the Osijek situation Curle, in his own words, "tried to understand what would be most useful to help a group of ... people ... who were facing almost any imaginable exigency, to function best both as individuals and as members of a team," and concluded that

> what is needed, and is always needed by all of us, is the fullest possible development of our humanity, our potential as human beings. This means becoming able to escape from the mindless automatism that governs so much of our lives, from senseless worries and fears, from prejudice, from ego cherishing and irritability, from vanity, from illusions of guilt and badness, from belief in separate existence. These and all other negative emotions are like a fist tightly closed around the heart. They imprison our consciousness within the narrow confines of the self. But to be fully human our consciousness must expand, gradually embracing all others with whom we share the planet. It means losing the lonely sense of separation. It means to be rather than to do.

So Curle went into the workshop not to help plan any concrete action, nor to train people in the methods of nonviolence. Instead, the workshop would be used "for sharing and mutual help; the learning would come from all of us, rather than from any formal instruction." He took it as his responsibility to give some structure to the process and to set the work on the basis of a belief that if we expect the best of people it will bring out their better nature (and the reverse). About twenty people attended (some part time); few had known each other well before this. Beginning with quite personal sharing, and making use of awareness and listening exercises, they explored what raised their own defences and what were their blind spots, prejudices, anxieties, "things that could impair our judgement and our relations with colleagues and others." They considered the interconnectedness of all humanity and of all life, and what this did to concepts of "self and other, friend and enemy."

From this the group – now beginning to have a cohesiveness and to use the term "we" – moved into consideration of violent situations, devising appropriate role plays and exercises as they went, focusing particularly on the traumas most affecting Osijek; they came at last to learn "something of the basic principles and practices of nonviolent protest and conflict resolution and ... their application in particular situations." By the end of the five days, Curle reports, "... everyone had reached an unspoken agreement that we formed the nucleus of a group which would do the things we had been discussing."

The Osijek residents who had attended the workshop formed a Centre for Peace and Nonviolence. Initially the main work was expected to be educational, helping to meet the needs of refugee children and to introduce peace education both in the schools and to the public. But when the Centre was flooded with reports of human rights violations, the workers set themselves to address them as best they might and soon changed the title to Centre for Peace, Nonviolence and Human Rights, seeing these as inseparable.

The complaints received came mostly from members of the Serb minority, who were constantly evicted from their apartments, often with violence, to make room for Croatian soldiers. Though illegal, the action was initiated by a judge and sanctioned by the local courts, leaving the Serbs with nowhere to turn. Centre members, working in teams, offered nonviolent protection to threatened families, reasoning with the soldiers who came to carry out evictions, and frequently succeeding in at least delaying the evictions. But the hostility of the military grew, and the judge accused Krohonja and Sukie of being traitors and in effect refused to offer them any protection against the anger of the soldiers.

They did not drop the work of helping those whose rights were being violated, but set about to widen their basis of support, "appealing to responsible people locally and internationally, reporting and monitoring breaches of human rights, enlisting the help of the clergy, and initiating a national debate on the issue." On this they were able to build a well-organized and eventually well-respected human rights programme, with a full-time lawyer, a training course for human rights officers, and links with other national and international groups.

The Centre has also followed through on its educational plans, conducting training in nonviolent action for social change, and supplying courses to meet the needs of specific groups, such as health workers and teachers (including those who have been themselves displaced and need to be able to heal themselves and help their students to heal), as well as members of the general public. Much of this is "training for trainers" and is spread further throughout the community by workshops given in turn by the participants. An important task is to bring together young people from different backgrounds.

Another major focus of the Centre is on refugees and displaced persons, fostering work in the camps by (for example) providing glasshouses for market gardening and courses in sewing and tailoring and then helping with the marketing of what is produced. More ambitious still is a project for the future resettlement of a destroyed village in the UN zone, involving both material help and preparation for living again as neighbours with the Serbs who drove them out. By the time Adam Curle's account was written (1995), the Centre's work had gone far towards changing the climate in a region where one might have said everything was against it.

8. Postscript: 1995-1999

Meanwhile, unfortunately, President Milosevic continued to pursue his dream of Serbian hegemony, while in response some regional ethnic groups militantly renewed the struggle for independence from Serbian domination. By early 1999 many Kosovars (the majority ethnic group in Kosovo province) were subjected to severe oppression and brutality at the hands of Milosevic's forces. Many were driven from their homes and out of the country while support grew for the Kosovo Liberation Army (KLA).

Milosevic constantly disregarded attempts to bring this situation to an end by negotiation, and ignored also escalating threats from Western powers. In March 1999, NATO, led by the United States and Britain, and supported by other NATO countries including Canada, began to bomb military targets in the former Yugoslavia. At the time of writing the bombing had continued without intermission for three months and targets had been widened to include many (notably the country's power grids) whose destruction brought death to some civilians, undermined the country's economy, and made life of the whole population scarcely bearable. NATO was divided on the question of whether to send in a massive ground force. There are two issues in the Kosovo crisis which are set outside of the mandate of this chapter. These are the questions of NATO's sidestepping both international law and United Nations process, and the linked question of whether more could have been done to cut off arms supplies to both sides (it could be argued that only arms traders and a few politicians were benefitting from the conflict, and the Kosovars were the heaviest losers).

For a student of nonviolence many other questions arise. Granted that unacceptable oppression and human rights violations were taking place, was the route taken by NATO the only possible one? What have been its effects? What will be the long term effect?

The root cause of the troubles in the Balkans lies in longstanding tensions and misunderstandings between groups of people of different ethnic, cultural or religious backgrounds which provide a fertile field for any demagogue who wishes to whip up fear and hatred. Milosevic's immediate (and surely predictable) response to the bombing was to remove any remaining restraints in the attack on the Kosovars, killing thousands and driving hundreds of thousands out as refugees. For the long term the bombing and Milosevic's response have laid down a whole new layer in the history of remembered suffering and blame, making even harder the resolution of underlying causes of conflict.

What alternatives were there? Such initiatives as that of the peace Centre at Osijek can surely be seen as the most hopeful route towards removing the underlying causes of war. The process can only be a slow one but much had been achieved before NATO's intervention. The work at the Osijek Centre, from the start, relied on and contributed to the development of a network of connections with people of good will elsewhere, both internationally and in other parts of the former Yugoslavia. Groups have emerged among people on previously opposing sides who want to address the historic tensions between people of different religions and ethnicity. Locally-run projects have made real progress and have benefitted from communication with each other, although often faced with hostility from the government and from others less far along the road. Bosnian, Croatian and Serbian groups have worked on conflict resolution training, peace education, human rights issues, helped with refugee resettlement and reintegration, counselling and legal advice. With the help of international peace workers (for example from the British Quaker Peace and Service) young people from different ethnic backgrounds have been brought together from all over Bosnia for training weekends, for work towards not only a more tolerant society but also towards a "civil society," where more activity would be self-directed and locally led, and less would be government controlled. Similar initiatives have been taking place all over the former Yugoslavia.

The recent events in Kosovo have inevitably been a severe setback to progress towards laying the foundation of a sustainable peace but have not ended it. Outside peace workers kept in touch with the continuing activity of the Balkan Peace Team (a coalition of seven peace groups) with Catholic Relief Service and with the Centre for Protection of Women and Children in Pristina. Local initiatives continued to try to counter human rights violations and to assist refugees, many of these efforts built on the network of non-governmental groups already established.

The NATO bombing has been represented as a "just war" and as the only way to put an end to atrocities, few even know of the achievements of those practising the more fundamental approach to peacemaking described here. Such efforts to remove the causes of war are seldom reported internationally, and even less blessed by official approval or financial support although we can find money for bombs and a high moral tone to justify dropping them. Yet, notably, while bombing tends to increase support for an embattled government, a political side effect of building greater tolerance and understanding is to lessen support for a regime that practices gross intolerance.

C. Nonviolence: Theory and Analysis[26]

We have, with some exceptions, left discussion of theories of nonviolence out of our case studies, hoping that this will lead to more rather than less thought about what could underlie actions and campaigns of the kinds described. What follows now is a brief account of some threads in twentieth-century thinking about nonviolence and of how some of the threads interweave or develop from one another, while some seem at odds with each other. All of course, have connections with earlier streams of thought which we have not space to trace here.

1. Henry David Thoreau (1817-1862), United States: The Duty of Conscientious Disobedience

Thoreau's contribution to nonviolence theory resides in one essay, "Civil Disobedience" (1848). In the twentieth century, this essay has become a classic of the literature of nonviolence. Thoreau's central point is the overriding obligation of everyone to act according to conscience, even when this means disobeying the law.

Government, in Thoreau's view, is a convenience until we can learn to do better without it. The decision of the majority does not absolve individuals from following their consciences. He declares: "It is not desirable to cultivate a respect for the law, so much as for the right. The only obligation which I have a right to assume, is to do at any time what I think right."

His personal protest took the form of tax refusal, for which he went briefly to prison. In demanding tax from him, Thoreau saw government as ordering him to violate his conscience – that is, to support the Massachusetts slaveholding policy and the Mexican war, to both of which he was opposed.

Besides this central theme, Thoreau reflects in the essay on his belief in simple living and a relationship with nature. Relevant to nonviolence theory is his contention that ownership of property makes us dependent on the protection of the state, more reluctant to take risks, and able to shrug off our responsibility to refuse complicity in wrong done.

2. Leo Tolstoy (1828-1910), Russia: Christian Anarchism and Passive Non-resistance.

Already a writer of renown and a wealthy man, Leo Tolstoy was over fifty when he developed his radical philosophy of Christian anarchism. While rejecting all institutions based on violence – that is, governments, law courts, the police, armies, private property, and money – he believed that we are commanded not to resist even these evils by force.

Passive non-resistance to evil is the doctrine most clearly associated with Tolstoyan thought. The practice of non-resistance may mean non-cooperation, and has included conscientious objection to military service and to taking part in other force-based functions of government. Tolstoyan nonviolence, however, does not include attempting to influence government or improve it, since government is by its nature evil.

On the positive side Tolstoy's social philosophy strives towards a vision of "society based on a maximum of consent ... social life reorganized on the basis of voluntary consent."[27] In his society all would labour for the necessities of life, but without hierarchical compulsion.

Tolstoy is remembered for his intellectual analysis and his wide influence rather than for involvement in personal action, although he would have been glad to have been held responsible when the Doukhoubor peasants refused military service and suffered harsh retribution.

3. Mohandas K. Gandhi (1869-1948), India: Active Nonviolent Resistance; Satyagraha, Ahimsa

Mohandas K. Gandhi was better known as Mahatma Gandhi, meaning "Great Soul." Scholars continue to debate the extent of his debt to Western or Eastern influences. A second area of debate arises from Gene Sharp's emphasis (see below) on Gandhi's political genius rather than on his spiritual force.[28]

Gandhi admired Tolstoy for his condemnation of violence and for his social doctrines, which condemned the idleness and luxury of the rich as the direct cause of poverty and advocated "bread labour" for all. Gandhi made these part of his own life.

But the two saw nonviolence very differently. Gandhi was no anarchist, but constantly interacted with the state and worked to transform it through active nonviolent resistance. He named the concept *Satyagraha*, or truth-force, deeper in meaning than the English negative, "nonviolence." A related concept is that of *ahimsa*, embodying complete courage and complete freedom from any urge to violent response. Gandhi preferred courageous violent resistance to wrongs to a nonviolence based only on cowardice.[29]

As our case study showed, Gandhi had a profound understanding of the dynamics which would contribute to success. For such action, training was surely important. A person's own convictions must determine whether one accepts Sharp's contention (see below) that the courage and even more the restraint shown, for example, at the saltpans, was based predominantly on a rational estimate of the chances of success, or whether the most essential element in training had to be spiritual, towards the internalization of *ahimsa*, rather than technical or intellectually political.

As Parliamentary Secretary to the NU, Catherine Marshall more than any other developed the National Union of Women's Suffrage Societies into the remarkable political pressure group described above. Meanwhile, well educated and well read, she developed a philosophy beyond the immediate cause. Nonviolence became to her not only the best strategy in the circumstances, but a principle to live by.

Much of Marshall's thinking has to be extrapolated from her actions, but it became more transparent when she was faced with the challenge of World War I.[30] She did not commonly use the term "nonviolence," but spoke more of "anti-militarism." Her insight derived from several related sources. As a suffragist she had had frequently to counter the argument of anti-suffragists who claimed that the basis of government was force, and that women did not fight and therefore could not vote. On the other side she had had to defend the choice made by the NU to campaign for the vote by nonviolent means.

Marshall, along with many feminists, saw the war as in large part the result of male monopoly of power. She never advocated that a matriarchy should replace the patriarchy, but she thought it essential for national and international peace and justice that women should share power. She believed in equality; she thought women could change things; she sidestepped the argument that has run through so much recent feminist writing as to whether the difference between men and women was by nature or by nurture. She did not see the difference as in any way absolute; experience taught her that there were militarist women and anti-militarist men, and she spent as much time during the war years working with male conscientious objectors to compulsory military service as she did working with the newly-formed Women's International League for Peace and Freedom.

The term "militarism" for Marshall encompassed patriarchy, hierarchical rule, the concept of domination, colonialism and the perpetuation of social injustice. "Anti-militarism," close to some definitions of "nonviolence," involved gender equality, social justice, and political power for the common people. More importantly, she saw it as embodying an attitude which respected the humanity in all, refusing to demonize the opponent, and which approached conflict resolution, whether between individuals or nations, as something to be negotiated with the interests of both sides taken into consideration. This theme of "positive peace" recurs among exponents of nonviolence.

5. Dorothy Day (1897-1980), United States: Catholic Nonviolent Action for Social Justice

Dorothy Day's career as a journalist began with extensive work for various Marxist and socialist publications. She opposed World War I primarily as a capitalist war waged at the expense of the poor. Later she became a convinced Catholic, and her advocacy combined Christian nonviolence with communist idealism. She founded an influential paper, the *Catholic Worker*, in which she expounded radical antiwar views and in connection with which there emerged a strong Catholic grassroots movement for peace and social justice.

For Day, as for Thoreau, the citizen has the right and obligation to refuse cooperation with laws which conflict with conscience. The causes she espoused included women's suffrage, opposition to fascism, support for the unemployed and homeless in the Depression, conscientious objection to war service, Chavez's campaign to unionize farm workers, reconciliation between the USA and Cuba, opposition to the Vietnam War, and support for nuclear disarmament.

Day's influence, exerted through her journalism and personal example, had a significant effect in liberating Catholics to become politically involved in causes more radical than had traditionally been supported or indeed sanctioned by the Church.

6. Martin Luther King, Jr. (1929-1968), United States: Nonviolent Direct Action, Christian Love

Although Martin Luther King admired Gandhi and sometimes quoted Thoreau, his nonviolent philosophy and practice were the product of his own beliefs and of his own times. An outstanding orator and a charismatic leader, he also had a sophisticated education in philosophy and theology that enabled him to present the intellectual arguments against segregation and for nonviolence to a wider audience.

Propelled into leadership by the bus boycott in Montgomery, Alabama (outlined above), King studied and adopted the practice of nonviolent resistance and infused into it his own deeply-held religious commitment to Christian love. We have again the combination of inspiration and strategic skill.

King's Christian love in no way condoned racial injustice, and he challenged the long-held view that time must be allowed for slow change. King's approach, in contrast, was to lead aggressive nonviolent direct action. In 1963 King wrote a powerful "Letter from Birmingham City Jail," where he was being held for his part in demonstrations. Addressing his fellow clergy, both black and white, he articulated the constant outrage to which black Americans were subjected and described how it could be addressed. When attempts to negotiate change fail or are betrayed (as they had been in Birmingham), the oppressed must move to "self-purification" before undertaking direct action. By this King meant a process of self-examination, to reach certainty of the justice of the cause, and internalization of Christian love, so that the commitment to nonviolence will not crumble in the face of violence and abuse. Workshop training was also part of the preparation.

Criticized for actions which provoked a violent response, King made it plain that he saw conflict as an inevitable part of the struggle. Freedom, he thought, was never voluntarily granted by the oppressor, but must be demanded.

Like many exponents of nonviolence, King's vision went beyond a mere change of laws or treatment: "The present tension in the South," he wrote, "is merely a necessary phase of the transition from an obnoxious negative peace, where the Negro passively accepted his unjust plight, to a substance-filled positive peace, where all men will respect the dignity and worth of human personality."[31]

Martin Luther King, Jr. was assassinated in Memphis, Tennessee on April 4, 1968.

7. Gene Sharp: Nonviolent Action — Its Politics, Methods, Dynamics

Gene Sharp's three-volume work (*The Politics of Nonviolent Action*) is probably the most comprehensive study of nonviolence, covering theory, methods, and dynamics.

Sharp's analysis of political power takes as its premise that government rests at bottom not on force but on cooperation. Consequently, nonviolent action is a potentially effective alternative to violence as an agent of change.

Sharp classifies the methods of nonviolent action into three broad groups: nonviolent protest and persuasion, non-cooperation (social, economic, and political) and nonviolent intervention. In the third volume, he goes into more detail on the actual operation of the technique, describing the moves towards its use; specific preparation; initial impact; the response to be expected; the need for perseverance; and the effect on participants, opponents, and public opinion. He categorizes the potential outcomes as conversion (rare), accommodation (that is, a negotiated change), or nonviolent coercion, when "even an oppressive system" may be unable to function without conceding the demands of the resisters.

The struggle for the independence of India is a material example of Sharp's premise that government rests on the consent of the governed, and he gives Gandhi credit for the most significant contribution of any individual to the development of the technique – the strategy and tactics – of nonviolence. Sharp argues that the main engines of Gandhi's campaign were his understanding of this theory of power and his ability to convince his followers that nonviolent non-cooperation was the most effective way forward. Gandhi fully understood what it meant to "cease to play the part of the ruled."[32]

Sharp downplays spiritual inspiration in the leadership of Gandhi, Chavez, King, and other of the examples treated here, preferring to emphasize that the actions were those of "ordinary people, not pacifists or saints, struggling imperfectly for their diverse causes."[33] Nonviolent action, however, may be a force for improvement of the human condition; the empowerment of people through its use can contribute to beneficial social change by redistributing power on a wider basis.

8. Ursula Franklin, Canada: Violence as Resourcelessness

Ursula Franklin is a professor emeritus of engineering at the University of Toronto, a founding member of the Voice of Women, and a speaker and writer on a wide range of social and political concerns. Central to her thinking is that violence is never acceptable, never provides the better solution to a conflict. When response to any situation starts from this premise, she holds, a nonviolent way will be found. Violence she defines as "resourcelessness,"[34] a definition that bears thinking about; try it on some of the countless acts of violence, from war to mugging, that clutter our news media. Refusal to make use of violence does not imply inaction, but the obligation to look for creative solutions or ways to move forward.

Dr Franklin argues that only the moral solution is truly practical. It is not the way of nonviolence, ecology, and caring that threatens the world; the evils in our present situation, in her view, are brought about by those who have rejected the moral way for what they have touted as the realistic way.[35]

No women have achieved the reputation as exponents of nonviolence of such writers as Tolstoy or of such leaders as Gandhi and Martin Luther King, though the case studies have shown that plenty of women have been involved in the practice of principled nonviolence. Reasons for their lack of fame may be found both in history and in the writing of history, but also more positively in the nature of their contribution, which has often explicitly encouraged shared leadership.

Feminist nonviolence has made particular contributions in three areas, all of which have been touched on in the case studies.

a) Creative Methods

Feminists have consciously sought new ways to put their message across, often combining a practical application with the message, at other times using humour. Greenham women's actions provide many examples. Campaigning against the Vietnam War, the Voice of Women touched a painful chord when it set people to making garments for Vietnamese babies and emphasized that they must be knitted in dark colours so that they would not be visible to strafers and napalm bombers. Similarly, in protest against nuclear arms testing, the VOW orchestrated the collection of children's baby teeth in order to measure widespread strontium deposit, both a practical scientific exercise and a frightening comment on the possible effects of testing. Karen Ridd, a Canadian worker with Peace Brigades International, once worked her way out of an ugly situation in El Salvador by assuming a clown persona (she is in fact a professional clown) and making animal figures from balloons for the hostile guards – not a mere diversionary tactic, but a way of establishing human interaction. Lighter examples can be found currently in the humorous appearance and social protest songs of the "Raging Grannies."[36]

b) Addressing the Causes of Violence

Throughout the twentieth century, feminist pacifists as well as some who would not accept the name, have put an emphasis on removing the causes of conflict, rather than either binding the wounds or trying to stop violence once it has begun. There are many examples, large- and small-scale. We have only space for one. From its beginnings at the international women's conference held at The Hague in 1915, WILPF maintained transnational relations, both during and after the bitter war of 1914 to 1918, refusing to accept the concept of "enemy." Between the wars, they engaged in the issues seen as most threatening to peace, advocating treaty revision, economic justice, and the development of structures which would enable the voice of common people to be heard. When they could not avoid the palliative work often considered appropriate for women, they turned it to political advantage, as, for instance, when they provided rubber teats to facilitate the feeding of starving babies in Germany in 1919 and made sure the campaign served as publicity against the Allied blockade.[37]

c) Nonviolent Group Process
Implicit in Gandhian nonviolence and explicit, for instance,in the work in Osijek is an understanding that nonviolence is not just something to be pulled out in extreme situations. Rather it is the practice of certain principles which define a way of living and relating.

From time to time groups working on nonviolent action have come to recognize that their decision-making has not been free of systemic violence. The peace and civil rights movements of the 1960s and 1970s were one of the important seedbeds of modern feminism, in part because some of the women engaged in them became aware that the principles of respect for all people were only too obviously not always present in interpersonal dealings within the movements. Women were often expected to take traditional roles, typing, copying, providing food, doing the dishes, even at times providing sexual service. They should not complain, as the importance of the cause was overriding, and the charismatic male leaders put themselves on the line in their chosen roles. Decisions were made hierarchically, and most often the leadership was dominated by men.

As women's consciousness rose, several distinct responses developed. Many active movement women became disillusioned about working with men and chose to work only with other women. Some turned away from the peace movement and focused all their energy on women's rights. Others became active in the women's peace movement.

One group which specifically addressed group process was the Movement for a New Society, a Philadelphia-based group involving both men and women, which worked on community nonviolence and civil rights issues. The first stage was to recognize men's habit of dominance; the second to accept that the problem could not be addressed simply by leaving it to the women. Attempts to do without structure altogether, far from ensuring equal participation, were found to facilitate domination by an individual or a clique. From these insights, MNS moved to identify behaviours in group interaction that needed to be changed and to develop genuinely consensual group processes to enable and encourage full participation of all members of a group.[38]

While the problem being addressed was initially, in many cases, one of gender roles within groups, it should be no surprise that all-women groups and all-men groups are not free of the familiar pattern of the dominant and the compliant, the vocal and the seldom-heard. The process of course has to be adapted for differing circumstances; its rough outlines are similar to that described as in use by the Greenham Common women. Attention is also paid to good listening skills, the ability to understand uncritically what others are saying.[39]

D. Themes and Conclusions

A wide range of nonviolent thinking and action has been outlined here. Some themes recur overtly or subtly: the power of nonviolence to effect change; the role of conviction; group interaction among participants; the need for self-discipline and training; a possible tension between charismatic leadership and group process; the variety of methods that may be employed; consistency or otherwise of methods with aims and circumstances; the value or danger of martyrdom; and the effect on those who take part and on those whose behaviour, it is hoped, will change.

I have, as I explained at the beginning of the chapter, deliberately left many questions open, believing that each reader has a right and obligation to form her/his own opinion, but as a postscript I will outline my own thinking, which has of course influenced my choice and interpretation of material.

I have given a good deal of space to examples and ideas which raise the question of the underlying spirit informing much nonviolent action. I strongly recommend Gene Sharp's comprehensive description of nonviolence in action, but I question that part of his analysis that downplays the spiritual component of, for instance, Gandhi's campaigns.

Where nonviolent action has been most effective, the participants have often undergone something of a transformative experience either in training or during the action; many have been aware of a strong spiritual component in their empowerment. The term "spiritual" should not be confused with "religious" as commonly used, much less with specific doctrines of Christianity or any other religion, though the experience may have come through one or other religious channel in a particular instance.

The case studies are arranged chronologically, but it is fitting that they conclude with the work at Osijek. The Osijek story focuses on the power of nonviolence as a way of life, something which is implicit in much of the theory and practice we have looked at. Like our other stories it deals with a way of making change in a particular – and violent – context. But it may also raise questions in the mind of the reader about whether the concept of living nonviolently is more generally applicable. Some, but not all, of us will find ourselves challenged at some stage to initiate or take part in a nonviolent protest or action. In my view, that does not permit the rest of us comfortably to relegate the issue of nonviolence to purely academic study. If nonviolence is a way of being, we may want to examine how we deal with gender, race, and intergenerational relations; with privilege; with group interaction; with competitive situations; with our use of natural resources; with the source and use of our income – make your own list.

The need for caution and for wide criteria in assessing success or failure leads to thought about the less obvious effects of the choices we make. No action is without consequence. When we choose to submit to serious injustice or ignore injustice against others, we affect our own future responses and may set an example to others. When we choose to force a solution on others, whether physically or psychologically, that action has a ripple effect on those who witness it; some may be disempowered by it, some may see it as the way to behave. When we attempt a nonviolent solution, we affirm and reinforce our own internal strength and may leave an impression beyond what is immediately visible. Whether or not we gain our objective, our choice of a violent or nonviolent approach will leave ourselves, our opponents, and others in or around the situation altered in one way or another.

Notes

1 *Chambers Twentieth-Century Dictionary*, 1972-3.
2 Adam Curle, *Tools for Transformation* (Stroud, UK: Hawthorn Press, 1990) 145.
3 It is an interesting imaginative exercise to rewrite (or perhaps roleplay) some of the case studies from the viewpoint of those who were in some sense the object of the actions or were bystanders, simulating, for example, the confidential report of the military police, the story given to his/her spouse or partner by a police constable, an official government report, a discussion by the Cabinet behind closed doors, columns in a right-wing and in a left-wing newspaper, or a conversation between two workers affected by a blockade.

4 Andrew Rosen, *Rise Up, Women!* (London: Routledge, 1974) and Sylvia Pankhurst, *The Suffragette Movement* (reprint; London: Virago, 1977).

5 Nov. 18, 1910. See Rosen, 138-43, 198-201. Emily Wilding Davison was killed when she threw herself in front of the King's horse as it ran in the Derby Races on June 3, 1913.

6 Jo Vellacott, *From Liberal to Labour with Women's Suffrage: The Story of Catherine Marshall* (Montreal: McGill-Queen's University Press, 1993); Sandra Holton, *Feminism and Democracy: Women's Suffrage and Reform Politics in Britain* (Cambridge: Cambridge University Press, 1986); Leslie Parker Hume, *The National Union of Women's Suffrage Societies* (New York and London: Garland, 1982).

7 Articles by Klostermaier, Amore, Hunt, and Hay in *The Pacifist Impulse in Historical Perspective*, ed. Harvey L. Dyck (Toronto: U of T Press, 1996); Gene Sharp, *The Politics of Nonviolent Action*, 3 vols. (Boston: Porter Sargent, 1973), 82-7; Mulford Q. Sibley, *The Quiet Battle* (Boston: Beacon, 1963) chap. 5; Richard Gregg, *The Power of Non-Violence*, (Ahmedabad: Navajivan Press, 1960); *Biographical Dictionary of Modern Peace Leaders*, ed. Harold Josephson (Westport and London: Greenwood, 1985). For a feminist critique of Gandhi, from two points of view, see articles by Costello and Shivers in *Reweaving the Web of Life: Feminism and Nonviolence*, ed. Pam McAllister (Philadelphia: New Society Publishers, 1982).

8 W. Miller, UP special correspondent, in the *New York Telegram*, 22 May 1930, quoted in Gregg.

9 Wolfgang Sternstein "The Ruhrkampf of 1923: Economic Problems of Civilian Defence," and other sources in *Civilian Resistance as a National Defence*, ed. Adam Roberts (Harmondsworth: Pelican, 1969); A.J.Nicholls, *Weimar and the Rise of Hitler*, 2nd ed. (London: Macmillan, 1979); Raymond J. Sontag, *A Broken World: 1919-1939* (New York: Harper and Row, 1971); Lisa Foley, "The Search for Non-Nuclear Alternatives," and Myrtle Solomon, "Nonviolent Struggle and Peace Building," *Over Our Dead Bodies*, ed. Dorothy Thompson (London: Virago, 1983). Some details have been added from documents in the Women's International League papers in the British Library of Political and Economic Science, and Women's International League for Peace and Freedom papers at the Swarthmore College Peace Collection and at the University of Colorado at Boulder. I appreciate the use of these collections.

10 Historians have debated whether inflation was a deliberate policy to avoid payment of reparations; here we are concerned only with its effects.

11 Typed draft of report, amended in Marshall's handwriting, 9 September 1923; Gertrud Baer to Marshall, 23 September 1923. WIL papers, British Library of Political and Economic Science.

12 WIL papers (esp. WIL/4/9) include a number of reports, British Library of Political and Economic Science. Others who investigated included Edith Pye, on behalf of

the Society of Friends (Quakers); her report, based on observations conducted from 12-31 March 1923, describes well-substantiated cases of cruelty by the occupying forces. Report in WILPF collection, Swarthmore College Peace Collection.

13 Sternstein 156.

14 Gregg. See also Josephson and Rosa Parks, *Rosa Parks: My Story* (New York: Dial Books, 1992).

15 M.L. King, *In Their Own Words*, quoted by Carol Hymowitz and Michaele Weissman, *A History of Women in America* (New York: Bantam, 1978) 339-40.

16 Christopher Child, *The California Crusade of Cesar Chavez* (London: Quaker Peace and Service, 1980).

17 John Steinbeck's novel *The Grapes of Wrath* and the film made from it are recommended reading and viewing for a sense of what the 1930s were like for many. Some of Woody Guthrie's songs also relate.

18 Barbara Harford and Sarah Hopkins, eds., *Greenham Common: Women at the Wire* (London: Women's Press, 1984); Jill Liddington, *The Long Road to Greenham* (London: Virago, 1980); Ann Snitow, "Holding the Line at Greenham Common: Being Joyously Political in Dangerous Times," *Women on War*, ed. Daniela Gioseffi (New York: Simon and Schuster, 1988), 344-57. For a vivid account of the early days (and good illustrations) see L. Jones, "On Common Ground," *Keeping the Peace*, ed. Lynne Jones (London: The Women's Press, 1983).

19 Rosalie Bertell's unpublished notes. My own visits to Greenham Common were each for less than a day, in 1985 and 1987. A non-hierarchical process is at least as dependent on the consent of the participants as any autocracy is on the consent of the governed; by my second visit in 1987, difficulty was being experienced because of the takeover of a camp at one gate by a group with its own motivation (perhaps legitimate, but having little to do with the primary aim of the camp), its own agenda, its own more hierarchical methods (which did not include any commitment to nonviolence), and its unwillingness to buy into the process which had been established. See also Liddington 283. For a discussion of women-only actions, see Barbara Deming, *Prisons That Would Not Hold* (San Francisco: Spinsters Ink, 1985) 189-215.

20 Rebecca Johnson, quoted by Liddington 283. Johnson also commented that the attempt to avoid [hierarchical] structure made it hard to get after people who shirked their share of the chores.

21 For a personal account of the action of 21 March 1982, see Maggie Lowry, "A Voice from the Peace Camps," Thompson.

22 Liddington 268, 280-2.

23 Adam Curle, *Another Way: Positive Response to Contemporary Violence* (Oxford: Carpenter, 1995). For Adam Curle's general approach to nonviolence, see Adam Curle, *Tools for Transformation* (Stroud, UK: Hawthorn Press, 1990) and Adam Curle, *True*

Justice: Quaker Peace Makers and Peace Making (London: Quaker Home Service, 1981).

24 A relatively simple account is given in Adam Curle's *Another Way*, 111-115. This has been my source in this case study along with comments on a first draft of this section from Adam Curle, for which I am most grateful.

25 Adam Curle to Jo Vellacott, 1 August 1997.

26 Useful sources include: Peter Brock, *Pacifism in Europe to 1914* (Princeton: Princeton UP, 1972) and his *Twentieth-Century Pacifism* (New York: van Nostrand Reinhold, 1970); see also his work updated in Peter Brock and Nigel Young, *Pacifism in the 20th Century* (Syracuse, NY: Syracuse University Press, 1999) and Peter Brock, *Varieties of Pacifism: A Survey from Antiquity to the Outbreak of the 20th Century* (Syracuse, NY: Syracuse U. P., 1999); plus Harvey L. Dyck, ed., *The Pacifist Impulse in Historical Perspective* (Toronto: U of T Press, 1996); Arthur and Lila Weinberg, eds., *Instead of Violence* (Boston: Beacon, 1968); Phillips P. Moulton, *Violence or Aggressive Nonviolent Resistance* (Pendle Hall Pamphlet, 1971); Hugo Adam Bedau, ed., *Civil Disobedience: Theory and Practice* (New York: Pegasus, 1969); Gregg; McAllister; Josephson. Two valuable Canadian sources are George Woodcock, *Civil Disobedience* (Toronto: CBC, 1966) and Thomas P. Socknat, *Witness Against War: Pacifism in Canada, 1900-1945* (Toronto: University of Toronto Press, 1987).

27 Peter Brock, *Pacifism in Europe to 1914* (Princeton: Princeton UP, 1972) 459.

28 Sharp I, 82-7.

29 Hay and Klostermaier, Dyck, 278-80, 285; and 229-20.

30 For two of Marshall's few published essays, see "Women and War" and "The Future of Women in Politics," *Militarism Versus Feminism: Writings on Women and War* eds. Margaret Kamester and Jo Vellacott (London: Virago, 1987) 37-42 and 45-52.

31 Reprinted *inter alia* in Bedau 72-89.

32 Gandhi, quoted by Sharp I, 84.

33 Sharp. The outline on the inside front cover of Volume One is a model of clarity and presents a succinct overview of the three volumes.

34 Ursula Franklin first gave me this definition about twenty years ago, in a private conversation.

35 Ursula Franklin, "Technology and Pacifism," lectures in the Bertrand Russell series at McMaster University, February 1995.

36 For the Karen Ridd story, and many more examples see Jack Ross, *Nonviolence for Elfin Spirits* (Argenta, BC: Argenta Friends Press, 1992). Other feminist writing on nonviolence include McAllister and *Feminism and Nonviolence Study Group: Piecing It Together: Feminism and Nonviolence* (Buckleigh, Devon: 1983).

37 For WILPF, see Gertrude Bussey and Margaret Tims, *Women's International League for Peace and Freedom* (London: Allen & Unwin, 1965), and Jo Vellacott, "Transnationalism in the Early WILPF," Dyck.

38 See David H. Albert, *People Power: Applying Nonviolence Theory* (Philadelphia: New

Society, 1985); Virginia Coover et al, *Resource Manual for a Living Revolution* (Philadelphia: New Society, 1982); Barbara Deming, *Two Essays: On Anger; New Men, New Women* (Philadelphia: New Society, 1982); Bruce Kokopeli and George Lakey, *Off Their Backs ... and On Our Own Two Feet* (Philadelphia: New Society pamphlet, 1983); and Berit Lakey, *Meeting Facilitation: The No Magic Method* (Philadelphia: New Society leaflet, n.d.).

39 Many students can recall being in a seminar where the discussion was dominated by one or two, or in a working group where there was little chance to share ideas or make new suggestions. Peace Studies students may want to give thought to what may be done to avoid this kind of situation and to set up instead a climate in which participants are genuinely listening to and learning from one another.

FIVE

FROM PROTEST TO CULTURAL CREATIVITY: PEACE MOVEMENTS IDENTIFIED AND REVISITED

NIGEL YOUNG

A. Distinguishing Study and Action

A central part of peace and conflict research is the study of those social movements called *peace* movements. One way to begin a discussion of this area of study (arguably a good way, because of the confusion that often arises here) is to note that Peace Studies is not itself a peace movement. It might seem to be otherwise. It might be claimed, for example, that peace education (to all appearances a part of Peace Studies) did for a while constitute something of a social movement when its advocates became a substantial lobby among teachers in schools – for example, in the early 1980s. But while peace educators may at times combine peace study and peace action, Peace Studies is by definition an intellectual endeavour, not a social movement. Though, like some other disciplines (e.g., sociology), it springs from deeply rooted social concerns and pragmatism, it is part of a project that goes beyond movements and parties, pressure groups and campaigns. While peace movements are phenomena concerned with political action or protest, Peace Studies, by definition, involves theory, analysis, and explanation and is not as such an agent or instigator of political change.

Peace Studies as a field has developed separately, in different conditions, and at different times from the peace movements, but, like them, in a context of growing peace concerns – especially during the "nuclear age." Clearly, specific peace movements and traditions have had an orga- nizational impact in developing, motivating, and funding the field. At times the agenda of Peace Studies has been altered by the history of peace ideas, and the agendas of the movements. Equally, some findings of peace research and study have filtered into peace movements – especially fac- tual information for policy campaigns – and through them into political decisions.

But while such factors sometimes lead students, activists, and antago- nists of Peace Studies to confuse and conflate them, peace study or research and peace action remain conceptually distinct. Peace Studies is an academic phenomenon, a truth-seeking – even if not a narrowly scientific – enterprise. And it seeks truths in a way that is different from, say, Gandhian nonviolence and its experiments with truth, or any seek- ing of "truth" through action and change. (Sometimes, indeed, peace movements have shunned truth in search of change.)

B. Why Study Peace Movements?

Studying the failures and successes, however defined, of the peace action movements enables us to sharpen our knowledge of the interaction of states and society, ideals and realities, of ideology and utopia.[1] It illumi- nates the links between theory and practice, research and action, analysis and "publicism" – the latter perhaps serving as a euphemism for propa- ganda.

In my view, new forms of social movement have become an emergent expression or an external dimension of *all social life*. Political systems or states left to themselves may be incapable of creative human change – indeed, they are often the main obstacle to it. If this is the case then human change has to come from outside and from below, from the non- state sector or so-called *civil society*, especially non-governmental organizations. Comparatively researching these processes, and the role of peace movements within them, thus becomes a crucial part of our intellectual responsibility in the new millennium.

Insofar as inherited systems fail to represent adequately new forces and aspirations, social movements – some benign, and others proble- matic or pathological – emerge and become a central focus of attention. Such movements exist throughout the world and are a key fact of mod- ern transnational life. They are a dominant factor in a multiplicity of global communities. Both overt and covert movements working within institutions, states, churches, and at the grassroots level see globalism or transnationalism as a fundamental part of their identity. Issues they raise – issues of culture, identity, and not least, language – clearly ought to be addressed by any attempt to understand the ways and means of peace.

C. The Origins of Peace Movements

What is clear is that many of the present movements and movement organizations have their roots in the universalist ideas of the enlightenment and in the first peace societies after 1815. Advocacy for what we today call negative peace can be recognized in opposition to the kind of butchery seen in the Napoleonic Wars between 1793 and 1815. But an emphasis on *positive* peace also emerged in the form of enlightenment principles, as support for peace linked to social and human rights and justice, as well as visions of social harmony and schemes of universal co-operation, principles, and utopias.

Modern public protest arose in the eighteenth century and as the labour movement truly established the idea of a modern social movement. Along with other forms of political agitation from the late eighteenth century onwards, the problem of war became an issue attracting public gatherings and protest. There were popular peace organizations often rooted in Western, usually Anglo-Saxon, and usually Protestant, radicalism. These organizations were particularly linked to nonconformist Christianity and to the emergent idea of the role of the democratic political *lobby* or public pressure group or campaign, such as Chartism in England.

The particular issue of compulsory military service, an institution which was spreading rapidly and globally throughout the nineteenth century, also became a focal point for protest. It precipitated substantial migrations to non-conscripting countries, especially in the Americas. By the second half of the nineteenth century, the first social opposition to specific wars and atrocities took to the streets and the public halls. Notable orators from a range of traditions began to denounce war, the arms race, and national chauvinisms, already predicting by the 1890s the catastrophe of 1914 – and initiating what is really the first peace movement, properly so-called.

An interesting element of this movement was the way in which notable figures spoke out to large gatherings in a number of countries. Women like Rosa Luxemburg on the left, or Berta von Suttner, a conservative liberal, and men like Keir Hardie, leader of the Labour Party, and Jean Jaures, the great French Internationalist and anti-militarist, all spoke against the arms race, national chauvinisms, and the possibility of war. Each represented a different tradition, as did the young Bertrand Russell or as had Leo Tolstoy. Yet they all shared a sense of the scourge of war, years before Emperor Franz Josef signed the warrant at his desk in Bad Ischl and the German army entered Luxembourg. Indeed, Hardie embarked on world speaking tours in the preceding years. By 1914 four of these six were dead, and Luxemburg, a prisoner during the war, was to be murdered early in 1919. Russell, despite incarceration, survived to participate in five subsequent, significant phases of the increasingly international twentieth-century peace movement.

D. The Nature of Peace Movements

Some points relevant to the nature of peace movements have already been made. Here I want to enter a little more fully into that discussion. Perhaps the first thing to note is that, if we wish to be most accurate, we *do* need to speak in the plural: while writers (including the present writer) sometimes refer loosely to "the" peace movement, in most periods and in many countries, "the" movement has been made up of a disparate set of organizations and movements. Some of these agencies had a general following, and others specific memberships. Many, like the anti-nuclear and anti-Vietnam War movements, have had both specific memberships and public manifestations. Their numbers expand and contract by the hundreds of thousands, even millions, within a few years. Moreover, there are a number of distinct approaches: religious and secular movements, political and ethical movements, single issue and multi-issue movements. They adopt diverse programs and address various constituencies in different areas and countries. Individuals join and rejoin; their priorities and ideologies change. Since these movements rise and fall at different times, and at a different *pace*, in various societies and even on the same issue, it is difficult to discern *one continuous social movement for peace* over the past century.

Recognizing that there are really many peace movements, and noticing certain general features they share (e.g., some form of mass activity on peace issues over some period of time), we still face the question whether a more precise definition can be fashioned: What exactly *makes* a peace movement a peace movement? It is an important, though difficult, question. And it is not just theoretically, but practically, important. We can see this when we consider how the issue of "official" and "unofficial" Vietnamese Buddhists arose to divide peace movements in the context of the Vietnam War. The independent, non-sponsored, essentially oppositional peace organizations emerging in Eastern and Central Europe by the 1980s raised similar issues. They were unofficial, often illegal, banned or underground. One had the situation of international peace movement conferences where debate arose as to whether to seat the delegates of official or of unofficial (dissident) peace movements or organizations or both. In these situations, sometimes both were represented, sometimes a painful or tactical choice was made, or empty chairs were symbolically left. The question of what is a *real* peace movement is not just academic. Certainly by the 1980s it was also highly charged, strategic, and political!

Academics have attempted to clarify the issue. April Carter proposes the following criteria as a litmus test by which to judge whether a movement is a peace movement: 1) its oppositional autonomy from a state or party, 2) its critical nonalignment with any state or military alliance, and 3) its adherence to nonviolence as a methodology of action or protest.[2] As a student of Eastern European resistance and change it is perhaps no accident that Carter should settle on these points. For her, the symmetric relationship between independent, nonaligned, and nonviolent peace groups critical of governments, both East and West, is obvious. This is true even though their agendas greatly differed.

But while helpful, provocative, and likely to be influential, Carter's scheme faces certain problems. A movement could after all be autonomous, nonaligned, and nonviolent and yet not seek *peace* in any recognized sense. (This is perhaps why Gandhi's movement and that of his successors like Vinoba Bhave are sometimes not seen as peace movements.) Without defining peace goals or aims, the Carter criteria seem insufficient as a defining statement.

Let us consider this in a little greater detail. The anti-Vietnam War coalitions of 1964-73, for example, included absolute and relative pacifists, as well as non-pacifists. It included those opposed to war as an institution, those opposed to this war in particular, those opposed to specific acts (bombing the north, invading Cambodia), those opposing military service (the draft), those supporting the Buddhists, those supporting wars of national liberation, those campaigning against specific weapons (e.g., napalm), those supporting the counter-culture and nonviolent revolution, and, finally, those supporting anti-imperialist class struggle and revolution. Clearly some of these goals fall outside the peace movement as Carter would define it.[3] Some of the groups mentioned would use violence, were state- or party-sponsored, or were aligned; and some would not legitimately have been part of the peace movement of the time even if they had joined meetings and demonstrations. (I have argued at length that this confusion of identity in the New Left brought about a loss of its identity and its collapse and disintegration.[4])

The Hague peace conferences of 1899 and 1909, and many international organizations since then, were in part state-sponsored. A visit to the Peace Palace at the Hague, later to be home of the International Court of Justice, quickly reveals the degree to which this was not only an organization of state representatives. In addition to the private benefactors such as Carnegie, state gifts were also an important part of the enterprise. The irony of World War I's outbreak shortly after the completion of the palace, suggests the limitations of that episode. Like the *Palais des Nations* in Geneva it stands as a monument to one of the frustrated phases of liberal internationalism.

Communist internationalism, or *cominternationalism,* as I have termed it, was also born in the light of internationalist principles, however distorted they may have become in practice. Like liberal internationalism, cominternationalism was prepared to use force if necessary, and revolutionary force in particular, to abolish the perceived causes of war – which were notably capitalism and imperialism. The ideas of uniting the working people who lacked any fatherland, the abolition of the arms industries, and the eventual withering away of the state were not so far from the ideals of peace movements. In practice, Communist internationalism after Lenin became a pragmatic extension of the foreign policy exigencies of the USSR. It used "entrism" into existing peace movements, or created its own peace fronts, which were ostensibly coalitions under party control. But one cannot deny the genuine idealism of many of those who joined such groups.

Even liberal democracies have found it convenient at times to use "peace" as a public relations term. The Strategic Air Command, for example, announced that "peace is our profession," and several right wing "peace through strength" groups emerged. Why should we not include these under our definition of twentieth-century peace movements? They certainly were not overtly "pro-war" groups in the sense of some fascist or militarist movements. Nor did they share the irrationalist glorification of war prevalent amongst some intellectual and artistic groups at the outset of the 1914 war (e.g., Futurism). They simply believed the classical dictum: "If you want peace, prepare for war."

Thus it seems that Carter's definition is incomplete. What we can learn from it is that if we wish to be accurate and properly inclusive we need to also make some mention, in our definition, of *peace* as the goal of any social movement properly called by that name, while at the same time recognizing that views as to the nature of peace and how best to pursue it vary enormously. (More on this later.) Given the great diversity we face here, it seems that a precise and *convincing* analysis or definition of "peace movement," though perhaps desirable for some purposes, is difficult to attain.

E. Classifying Peace Movements

Similar difficulties attend the attempt to provide a precise way of *distinguishing* peace movements one from another. A number of classifications and typologies have been put forward. For example, Bob Overy, in a pioneering effort, develops the initially plausible idea that it should be possible to classify peace movements according to their ends or goals – are they against all wars, against some wars, against some aspects of wars or weapons?[5] But since movements and their members pursue so many different goals, often shifting priorities within their groups in the process, the typology seems problematic. They also often pursue overlapping goals. For example, many movements have had as a central goal the *prevention* of a war (Overy seems to miss this in his typology) – most notably, between 1918 and 1989, a major war between the West and the Soviet Union.[6] The same preventative goal existed with respect to wars in Central America, and, early in peace movement history, with respect to a potential war between Norway and Sweden at the time of Norway's secession.

Let us develop the first of these points a little more fully. Most peace movements have included multiple goals and issues. I will give two examples. First, we have the anti-Vietnam War coalitions of 1964-1973, mentioned earlier, in which *all* of Overy's goals are apparent. Another example is the nuclear disarmament movement after 1958, which also pursued multiple goals. Despite its adherence to unilateral nuclear disarmament (in Europe at least), the ND coalition in fact campaigned for multilateral goals, agreements to ban nuclear tests, and later, nuclear-free zones. Many of its organizations and groups opposed all nuclear weapons East and West; some just certain missiles such as Thor, or weapons like Polaris, or US bases. Some opposed deterrence or the threat of using nuclear weapons, while others did not. There were some who campaigned against manufacture as well as testing and use and linked this with economic conversion. Later on, others fused this together in opposition to nuclear power. By the 1980s the campaigns had involved feminist and ecological issues. Some adhered to civil disobedience, others did not. In the early years this was as divisive an issue as pacifism or political alignment. In the 1980s, feminism became contentious, especially in a separatist camp like Greenham. Nuclear disarmament became linked to issues as diverse as human rights or world hunger. In the 1960s the movement campaigned for prison reform and against the Greek military junta, and in the 1980s for the Helsinki process in Eastern Europe and the autonomy of Pacific islands.

It becomes clear, therefore, that to distinguish peace movements by goals is inappropriate. The problem is the same problem Max Weber found in defining the state by its ends: there are few ends or goals which peace movements, like states, do *not* pursue. Consequently, defining the means specific to them and their relations with states – as April Carter also stresses – become more significant.[7] Peace movements are part of society and culture. In terms of goals, what I would argue (and will develop more fully later on) is that the unifying idea of creating a peace culture or consciousness at a global level has become a latent, if not always manifest, goal and function of these social movements. But, as suggested, this is a goal that unifies (or may unify) peace movements, not one that enables us to distinguish between them.

It should be noted that Overy has also distinguished in his scheme between (a) movements which are lobbies or pressure groups, (b) movements which are mass movements, and (c) movements which are revolutionary (violent or nonviolent), and (d) the permanent or prophetic *minorities* which may aspire to become (b) or (c).[8] But while useful for some purposes, this scheme also fails to do justice to the complexity of the facts. In fact, movements usually involve elements from all of (a) to (d). For example, one of the best forms of creating leverage for a political lobby is to back it with mass protest. In England the Campaign for Nuclear Disarmament (CND) was envisaged in 1958 as a short, sharp pressuring lobby. Ideally it would be led by political and intellectual elites, not the grassroots mass *movement* of public protest which did in fact evolve spontaneously in the next three years. Indeed many of the CND leaders were dismayed by the populist turn of events, especially when this Frankenstein monster demanded democratic structures for its campaign and was also permissive towards its direct action wing.

How then should peace movements be classified? A chronological approach which I have used, and which has been developed further by other scholars, particularly for the Japanese and European movements, is called *periodization*. This scheme chronicles the phases when a *mass* peace movement existed and others when it did not. The phases are measured by the degree of support, of mass activity on peace issues. It is an attempt to establish periods (though these are admittedly difficult to delimit).

For example: certainly a widespread, if diffuse and nationally separated, surge of support for peace developed in the two decades before 1915. This movement arose simultaneously and in the face of the opposing rise of a militarist-nationalist and imperialist groundswell. It arose again in reaction to World War I and its aftermath, in the 1920s. Mass peace protest emerged once more, though deeply divided, in the face of the arms race and war-fears of the 1930s and again in the late 1950s, lasting into the 1960s. This latter resurfacing encompassed two overlapping (but in many ways separate) peace movements and shifting issues and (to some extent) memberships in the mid-1960s. The latter, anti-Vietnam War protest, faded during the early 1970s. And then again a peace movement developed, initiated late in the decade, drawing on the same prophetic minorities and growing to a peak in North America and Western Europe in the early 1980s and in Eastern/Central Europe in the later 1980s.

If one concludes — and I believe one should — that the great nonviolent campaigns are peace movements, then the Gandhian movement of 1917-21, in the 1930s, and again in the 1940s should be included. So should the Civil Rights movement in the USA (1956-65) and the "people's power" movements of resistance in Eastern Europe in the 1980s — and there are countless other examples.

As can be seen, periodization emphasises ebb and flow of support in its classification of peace movements. One should not, however, infer from these very real distinctions that participation in peace movements is entirely discontinuous. Indeed, studies like Sidney Tarrow's have shown the recidivism of activists in several different movements — even on the same issues, even in different countries.[9] In the discussion of "why peace movements fail," too little is made of the issue of *political generations*. There are, as we might say, cycles of protest. It is only a few remarkable individuals who can sustain high levels of movement activity over more than a few years, especially if imprisonment, injury or failure to achieve immediate goals occur. Social involvement tends therefore to have life-cycles, possibly three to five years long when participation is intense. Peace movements are no exception, which creates problems in sustaining an ongoing collective identity for such a movement. Nevertheless, there is plenty of evidence that people return to movement activity, albeit in a different way. For example, someone may be active in her or his student years (16-24), when ties and responsibilities are few. They may return in their mid-40s or 50s when middle life security has been achieved. And they may return yet again when retirement liberates them from regular work routines. To call these episodic involvements *failures*, as some do, is perhaps to miss the point that social movements do not encompass all of life.

We must expect peace movements to arise in different forms, in different places, and at different times. The anti-atomic survivors in Japan – the *Hibakusha* – were active earlier than the anti-nuclear testing lobbies of the later 1950s in the West and elsewhere. Moreover, even where the collapse of a peace movement is most dramatically evident, prophetic minorities remain. Within a few years of the 1914 debacle, for example, important new peace organizations like the War Resisters' International (WRI), the Women's International League for Peace and Freedom (WILPF), and others had been created. In 1940 the story was different and more surprising. The peace or pacifist movement did not collapse, even in the face of fascism and what appeared to many to be a "just war." Indeed, outside the dictatorships, and against all predictions – and contrary to many accounts by historians – the pacifist movement maintained considerable strength. From 1940-45 there were many more COs (Conscientious Objectors) than in 1914-18, and important voices spoke out against the bombing of mass civilian targets. By 1945, however, this movement had dissipated, and except among some scientists and religious leaders, it took some years for a public outcry against nuclear arms to emerge. Only the permanent minorities or peace sects or prophetic individuals tended to maintain a peace stance or witness in the post-war and post-holocaust wreckage of 1945. It seemed that peace, like poetry, had been dealt an almost mortal blow by World War II and the Holocaust.

F. Peace Movements, Peace Traditions, Peace Coalitions

Recognizing that peace movements begin and end, ebb and flow, we can not only distinguish them one from another, but distinguish the notion of a peace movement from that of peace traditions.[10] Peace traditions in themselves are not movements. I have argued that most traditions, unlike movements, survive over time and are cumulative and evolutionary. They are often connected to particular issues – compulsory military service, for example – or outstanding individuals like Thoreau, Cobden, Tolstoy, Gandhi, and Rolland. They may be linked to ideas or political ideologies, such as *anarchism,* or to particular constituencies: the peace mobilization of women provides the major example since 1915, but the Japanese *Hibakusha* would be another. Though they are not movements as such, peace traditions may develop strong organizational expressions and engage in public activity. Sometimes these organizational manifestations are ephemeral, at other times long lasting.

The first peace societies, while certainly linked to traditions, cannot properly be called social movements. This is so even though they generally supported abolitionism and in some cases supported the issues of liberal, labour, and anarchist movements. Like the peace churches, they may be described as prophetic minorities. They have tended to survive the ebb and flow of larger public supported, mass peace movements and organizations. This has been so even in the face of appalling or daunting persecution, not least in the USA, from 1917-21.

Until the early twentieth century these permanent minorities were almost entirely rooted in religious faith. The Dutch leader, Domela Niewenhuis, was a Protestant pastor as well as a militant anti-war orator at the meetings of the Socialist Internationals. In later years Lord Donald Soper, a Methodist preacher, played a similar role in England, linking himself to the political left. There are countless similar examples: Dorothy Day, A.J. Muste, Martin Niemoller, the Berrigans, Bruce Kent, and indeed Gandhi and King.

Secular traditions such as internationalism in its liberal and socialist variants flowered in the later nineteenth century, having their roots in eighteenth-century cosmopolitanism and a belief in progress. Free trade, global communication, and peace institutions, including international law, characterized the liberal variant. The radical links of all working people across national boundaries and opposition to the war-making, arms-manufacturing, capitalist elites of all the imperial countries, were the bonds which linked many socialists, anarchists, and Marxists against war.

There is also a grey area in which pacifists and anti-militarists tried to synthesize these liberal, radical, and socialist ideas. However, as public movements, they rarely combined. The link between economic waste of resources in war and arms races was an issue monopolized by the left until the more recent emergence of ecological and Green movements within peace coalitions.

Eventually from the latter variant of Socialist Internationalism a Communist Internationalism emerged. At first, in 1915 and at Zimmerwald, it was anti-war, without a state base, and with Leninist and Luxemburgist variants. But after 1917, or more properly after the founding of the Comintern (the Communist International), it tried to succeed the socialist internationals broken by World War I. The Communist peace tradition then had a base in the new Soviet state. After 1945 this evolved into a new, broader-based phase – the most successful, and arguably genuine, of all Communist-inspired or initiated projects: the Stockholm Peace Appeal of the early 1950s.

Many of these traditions did not work together or even see themselves as part of a common movement. However, at different times and in different places, broad coalitions did emerge, including many mentioned above. As one would expect, they usually formed or emerged around a specific *issue or goal,* or lowest common denominator. (This is where the typology spelled out by Overy may be helpful.) Illustrations might include a specific war like Algeria or Vietnam; particular weapons such as the atomic bomb, or napalm; or an issue like opposition to the draft in the US in the 1960s.

G. Resisting War: Supporting Peace?

Anti-conscriptionism has been mentioned and is sometimes linked with peace movements, but it presents a different problem. War resistance, refusal or evasion has often been highly individualized or self-preservatory, and certainly much of it is not pacifist. In point of fact, often it is not part of a peace movement. It is frequently localized, or community-based. Refusal to serve has involved a diverse set of sects or groups from Jehovah's Witnesses to "left-wing" Leninists and Maoists and "right-wing" Libertarians. Even so it did, as in the USA in 1917, often raise important general issues of civil liberties. Moreover, in places like West Germany, where 20 per cent of the conscriptable population became conscientious objectors, a natural constituency for a peace movement was created. I am convinced this helps explain the strength of the Greens and the growth of peace culture and *memory* in Germany since the 1980s, including de-nazification at a deeper level.

Anti-conscriptionist agitation for conscientious objection as a legal right and for alternatives to military service has spread dramatically in the past three decades. Agitation around these specific issues has more often become linked with peace organizations. Eventually these linked across national borders after World War I in such bodies as the War Resisters International (in the USA, War Resisters League). Very often, however, young men (but rarely young women) have merely voted with their feet to avoid serving in a war. And they continue doing so at the time of this writing. For a whole variety of reasons they have migrated, gone underground, deserted, or voluntarily gone to jail or even execution. Establishing the boundaries of peace movement activity, when confronted with such acts of individual or communal refusal, is again problematic.

H. From Peace Movement to Peace Culture

As mentioned earlier, one way of finding, or creating, unity within the many forms of peace activity I have outlined (and as I shall go on to argue, between them and Peace Studies) involves the idea of a *peace culture or consciousness* at a global level. I would argue that emergent peace communities and networks, which are not necessarily yet a movement, are part of this project — a project that includes, but extends beyond, the opposition to war (that includes the idea of negative peace, but extends beyond it to positive peace). They make up the plural constitution of a peace culture as opposed to a war culture. This project is a conscious human endeavour with many manifestations, requiring great political will, cultural imagination, and scientific research. It demands as much funding as a war, or the preparations for war. Such an enterprise requires creating a transformatory consciousness, including a new peace history and a whole range of institutions. Many of these agencies will be in their infancy, and many others are yet to be born. In one sense such a project returns to the dreams and visions of a century ago, to images of world law, universal rights, and global institutions. It is with such an imaginative concept that I will conclude, since it relates very much to peace movement identity.

There is a convergence at the end of the twentieth century in the realm of the construction of peace culture and peace memory. Both peace action and peace theory and research are part of a slow transformation of consciousness. The so-called "just wars" of democracies against dictatorships — Spain in 1936 and Europe in 1939 — brought a new public legitimation of war. Yet one must weigh not only the cost of 80 million direct deaths as a result, but the clear and demonstrable connection between war and genocide from Armenia in 1915, through the Central European Holocaust, 1942-45, on to the Cambodian, Rwandan, and Bosnian killing fields. These horrors suggest that war has become barbarism, and that total war means more civilian than military casualties, as in World War II, Korea, Vietnam and in many of the wars of Africa. For a time it was said that anti-colonial wars of national liberation also gave a new legitimation to war or armed struggle. Yet the legacy of Algeria and Vietnam is a dubious one. Nationalism, as well as statism and alignment, have been as deeply divisive of peace culture as the use of violence, either by proxy or by protestors and activists.

At the centre of this problem is the reconstruction of historical memory. I speak here of both a war memory, which looks at the inhuman toll beyond deaths in war, and a peace memory, which sustains the idea of a new public history and with it a firmer human global identity. This creation of culture has become more of a conscious effort as the century has progressed. One can multiply the examples indefinitely, but they might include a peace museum, a Peace Studies department, a peace-keeping force of the UN, a peace park, a centre for mediating disputes, a peace education text or a manual for nonviolent action, and a peace community or peace library. Such projects sustain identity just as many movements do.

A century ago some such projects were balanced between the positive creation of globalizing institutions and communications and "negative" war-prevention activities and propaganda. Others were ameliorative in nature, like the Red Cross and its attempts to deal with the aftermath of war. Participants were divided between scepticism of existing institutions and a willingness to work through them. The issue tended to be reductionist — for example, the problem could be reduced to that of economic inequality, or the lack of international law.

In a sense we have returned to that juncture with a more holistic and plural emphasis. This has been immensely expanded in past decades by the rise of such tendencies as ecological pacifism and feminist nonviolence, linking a range of issues such as patriarchy, violence, and socialization for war. Moreover, the revolution in global communications has made transnational linkages much more practical than a century ago. While these forms can be used by terrorists as much as by nonviolent activists, the sense of a world village, and the growth of multiple forms of English as a shared world-language, strengthen the forces for a peace movement in this wider sense. It allows a peace movement to sustain an identity of its own that is flexible and evolutionary rather than orthodox and dogmatic.

In part this culture has always been an anti-war culture. The truth of this is illustrated in a novel like Remarque's *All Quiet on the Western Front*, in films like *J'Accuse*, or *Shoah*, or a poem like Owen's *Dulce et Decorum Est*. All of these works of art remain in parts of the public memory longer than the so often ephemeral peace speech or pamphlet. Some peace prose, especially by women, retains a longer lasting quality simply because it is experiential and reflective and less rooted in the heat of conflict. One thinks, for example, of Rosa Luxemburg's letters from prison, Vera Britain's "testaments," Pat Barker's late twentieth-century novels, and Virginia Wolf's essays. The peace culture is inclusive in this and many other ways. There is, in addition, a positive and often more widely accessible and *popular* peace culture. Such celebratory expressions of life and hope include John Lennon's song "Imagine," the graffiti on the Berlin Wall, the glorification of life with personal objects placed on fences of the Greenham nuclear missile base, or the woven banners of the women's peace movement. The peace symbol itself is part of this still progressing cultural change. It was designed in 1958, in part an anti-nuclear "negative symbol" – N and D in semaphore – and was adopted by the positively creative counter culture in the 1960s as part of a linking of peace and love.

One of the abiding weaknesses of this peace movement, however, is a lack of material resources. While it campaigns for the diversion of funds from the arms trade and war into peaceful production and economic development, it rarely suggests the diversion of military taxation into a massive peace tax. The building of peace culture is hampered by this under-funding of peace institutions. From the United Nations to the local peace library, this is as serious a limitation as is the failure to sustain masses in protest movements. Indeed, if the latter is seen as simply part of the episodic character of peace movements, the issue of resources becomes most crucial. Even great works of anti-war art and literature – Otto Dix's astounding 1920s war etchings and Remarque's best-selling novel are good examples – were produced and a success because they paid. There was an economic market for them, and to create such a market is in large part an educational task.

In the 1960s, the phrase "the long march through the institutions" was used, and although this remains one strategic possibility for peace, the relative failure to promote the OSCE/CSCE (Organization for Security and Cooperation in Europe) after 1989 suggests its limitations. The longer march to create the *peace* institutions and culture I have described seems to me more plausible (of course, the two may not be incompatible). The Helsinki process was an interesting example of how governmental and non-governmental strategies can complement each other. It was one of the failures of the post-Cold War era that a military alliance (NATO) should be able to claim "victory" at the end of it all. The real victors were the peoples who emerged from the shadow of nuclear threat and bureaucratic oppression, largely through peaceful means. Part of peace culture is to reclaim that history.

Notes

1 In making my arguments I wish to acknowledge the use of certain sources not otherwise noted in the following endnotes: Peter Brock, *20ᵗʰ Century Pacifism* (New

York: Van Nostrand, 1970). A revised, expanded and updated edition of this book is now available. See Peter Brock and Nigel Young, *Pacifism in the 20th Century* (Syracuse, NY: Syracuse University Press, 1999). I refer, further, to much of my research on war resistance which remains unpublished.

2 April Carter, *Peace Movements: International Protest and World Politics Since 1945* (London and New York: Longman, 1992) 14-25.

3 Carter; Bob Overy, *How Effective are Peace Movements?* (Montreal: Harvest Books, 1982).

4 R. Taylor and Nigel Young, eds., *Campaigns for Peace: British Peace Movements in the 20th Century* (Manchester, UK: Manchester University Press, 1987), Chapters 2 and 3.

5 Overy.

6 Overy.

7 Carter. See especially Chapter 1 and Conclusion.

8 Overy.

9 Sidney Tarrow's work has been released in new editions. See *Power in Movement: Social Movements, Collective Action and Politics* (Cambridge, MA: Cambridge University Press, 1998) and Sidney Tarrow and David Meyer, eds., *The Social Movement Society* (Totowa, NJ: Rowman and Littlefield, 1998).

10 See Nigel Young's chapter, *Towards a Comparative Analysis of Peace Movements*, eds. Katsuya Kodama and Unto Vesa (Brookfield, VT: Gower Publishers, 1990).

SIX

SHAPING VISIONARIES: NURTURING PEACE THROUGH EDUCATION

LARRY J. FISK

A. Education and Peace Education

In Chapter 1, Conrad Brunk spoke of Peace Studies as engaged in analyzing human conflicts in order to find the most peaceful (negatively peaceful) ways to turn less just into more just (positively peaceful) relationships. In this final chapter of the book, I explore the possibility that these "ways" include a certain sort of *education*, which contributes to peace by contributing to the creation (or formation or shaping) of resourceful and peaceful persons. Most of us already assume that the right education can make a difference in our lives. Shouldn't it be capable, as well, of helping us to arrive at freedom, harmony, and creative ways of handling disputes with one another? Perhaps – but to properly explore this possibility, we will need to be a little clearer about what we *mean* by education and what goes into its various forms. Similar comments apply to what is called *peace* education; and so I begin with some clarifications.

When I use the word "education" I think of a certain kind of process – a series of actions or procedures which, whether by design or otherwise, encourages learning in a group of citizens. Now we know a great deal about state-supported schools, and some of us know about the sort of education that is sponsored by established religious bodies or political parties. Let's follow scholarly practice and call learning that goes on in such institutionally-sponsored contexts **formal education**. (The words "institution" and "formal" here are meant to call to mind the fact that this sort of education is, as it were, woven into the social fabric — explicitly sanctioned by culture and convention.) This accepted and conventional path through structured levels of learning, whether it takes one to public school, a religious school, or university, can also be called **schooling**.

There are, however, other quite different structures, environments or settings in which much learning takes place. Most significantly, we learn to walk, talk, and handle everyday difficulties in our own families, neighbourhoods, and on the streets. We learn by our participation on sports teams, in Guides and Scouts, in volunteer agencies, and in cultural, labour and professional organizations, as well as social movements. We take for granted that there is a style of learning that takes place in social clubs, bars, while watching movies and TV, listening to CDs, and reading newspapers and web pages. These learning situations, including both those designed for learning and those that are not, can be among the most meaningful and beneficial. But of course, they are not institutionalized, designed for our learning *by societally-sanctioned authorities*. We may accordingly — remember the earlier definition of formal education — refer to them as **non-formal** locations for learning. Their style, it is important to note, may not be utterly unstructured, casual or *in*formal: what makes them non-formal is that there is no state or institutional sponsorship as there is in public schools or private religious schools.[1]

There are also various **types** of (both formal and non-formal) education. We speak of business education, technical education, moral education, and inter-cultural education. Such descriptions are typically a way of saying that we educate *for* a certain purpose. National and international organizations are established to promote particular educational ends. Every nation-state on the planet has an educational system designed to educate for citizenship in that country. Significant educational contributions have been made by civil liberties unions as well as peace and labour movements for purposes to which their names bear witness: we have, for example, the American Civil Liberties Union, Educators for Social Responsibility, the European Campaign for Nuclear Disarmament (END) and, during the 1960s, Students for a Democratic Society (SDS) in the United States and the Student Democratic Union (SDU) in Canada.

The educational field associated with peace and conflict issues is broadly termed "peace education." (Peace education includes Peace Studies programs in universities, but much else as well. This is why teachers of Peace Studies can discuss peace education without simply talking about themselves!) Peace educators talk about "educating for peace" or "educating for global responsibility" (though we will want to probe what is meant, or should be meant, by all this). Peace education can and – I shall argue – *should* cut across the distinctions made above, especially the distinction between formal and non-formal education. But before developing that idea, let's say a word about how "peace" is to be understood here.

In Chapter 1 Conrad Brunk reminded us of the important distinction between negative and positive peace, first popularized by Johan Galtung.[2] **Negative peace** refers to the absence of war or other forms of violence like terrorism. **Positive peace** represents the presence of economic, political and cultural practices which contribute to the safe, fair, and healthy living of all citizens. Positive peace as an idea or concept draws our attention to social structures which can either contribute to, or detract from, just and peaceable living. When they use the term "peace education," peace educators have both senses of peace in mind.

From this fact we can derive immediately (and this is important, since often overlooked) that peace education is *not just anti-war education*. Perhaps one of the reasons peace education is sometimes associated exclusively with negative peace or, even more narrowly, with learning about wars and their causes is that it is difficult to understand and develop learning around moral intelligence and peacemaking skills. It is considerably more demanding to develop these latter skills, or even to justify their development in formal classrooms. Here we have entered the arena of positive peace. But though positive peace may be difficult, it is also (obviously) important, and for both reasons needs to be studied. Any form of "peace education" that neglects it misunderstands its own nature and calling.

Another, related but more specific, point needs to be made here. So long as peace and peace education are associated exclusively with antiwar concerns, they are in danger of being misconstrued as associated with a specific antiwar doctrine, program or school system. When perceived in this way peace and peace education can too readily be taken to represent a particular position or nation state – one side of an argument. For example, a South African study revealed that the words "peace," "peace education," and "conflict resolution" are often tarnished in South Africa because they are seen by many to have been part of the defensive language of apartheid.[3] Another study of American peace education shows that during the Cold-War era of the 1950s and 1960s, Americans "who still wished to promote dreams of 'peace' could expect to be labelled as Communist Party sympathizers."[4] As a final example, the Soviet Union during this same period sponsored the World Peace Council and huge "peace" rallies, all with Soviet influence and funding, and thus encouraged a peace education which most Westerners could dismiss as Communist propaganda. For these reasons too, we must take pains to remember that peace education addresses both negative and positive peace and need not be undertaken from any particular political standpoint.

We've been talking about what peace education is not. To introduce our discussion of what it *is* (and can be) I offer some verbal vignettes indicating how it is represented by those who call themselves peace researchers and peace educators. James Calleja of the Mediterranean island of Malta is the former Secretary-General of the Peace Education Commission of the International Peace Research Association (IPRA). He defines peace education fairly loosely as "the study of peace in groups in an educational environment."[5] Other peace educators mention the importance of passing on knowledge and experience which provides the learner with an opportunity to choose different and better worlds to live in, but without imposing a particular view.[6] (As we'll see, it can be argued that at its best this is what all education should be about.) Ake Bjerstedt, one of the pioneers of peace education, holds that peace education should not be considered a special "school subject" at all. Instead of being just another specialized field of study, with all its disconnected ways of treating knowledge, peace education should be integrated into regular school subjects or disciplines. Such integration, says New Zealander James Collinge, would focus attention on "issues concerning student development, ways of thinking, values and the ability to act rather than being primarily a matter of an easily delimited field of knowledge."[7] The typical "subject" approach to problems can overwhelm us with a sense of powerlessness by virtue of its fragmented presentation of disparate facts. Peace education can, on the other hand, provide a holistic climate within which the sense of powerlessness or fatalism can be challenged by a focus on "toleration, gender equality, cooperative group work, broadened social imagination and social literacy skills in dealing with conflict nonviolently." In short, says Australian peace educator Frank Hutchinson, peace education should "make hope practical rather than despair convincing."[8]

What seems uniformly accepted in these definitions or descriptions of peace education is that it requires solidarity. It is not something done or experienced by individuals in isolation from each other.[9] For students of Peace Studies to fully appreciate what peace education consists of and how it can help to facilitate positive peace, they will therefore have to overcome the temptation to see it as "individual" learning. This and other of the ideas present in these descriptions will be discussed more fully later in the chapter, with special reference to the formal contexts where peace education assuredly does and must occur. Before coming to that, however, some other matters need to be considered. First, I want to highlight some important moments in the *history* of peace education, in connection with the foregoing; then, against that historical backdrop, I wish to identify and discuss another ever-present temptation that must be resisted if we are to arrive at a proper appreciation of peace education: the tendency or temptation to associate it with formal education *alone*.

B. Peace Education Is Not A New Idea

A brief look at history reveals that peace education has been around for a long time. It also confirms that our emphasis above on (what is today called) positive peace is not just some modern scholar's invention and provides ample illustration of our contention that peace education takes place both in formal and in non-formal contexts.

In the classic Greek play *Lysistrata* by Aristophanes, women refuse to grant sexual favours to their warring husbands. The ancient Romans had a practice of retiring to a "Sacred Mount" and refusing civic responsibilities until such time as protests against further warfare or violence were heard. Iroquois women around the year 1600 refused both sexual activity and the bearing of children until decisions of war and peace were surrendered to them as the bearers of future warriors.[10] Such practices are not only examples of what would today be called nonviolent action; they illustrate non-formal (yet, one would think, potentially quite effective!) educational approaches.

All of the major religions of the world have taught rules of conduct with respect to war or rules protecting civilians and limiting destruction. On close examination, the Muslim "Jihad," the Christian "just war," and the Rabbinic Jewish tradition rationalizing optional and obligatory wars are all designed to avoid unnecessary warring. There are heavy responsibilities on the followers of these traditions to seek peaceful alternatives to war. And these are not mere affirmations of belief; they constitute the teachings of prophets and priests of each religion, instructions which are to be pondered and integrated into the lives of followers.

Limitations on aggressive or militaristic impulses are quite in evidence when one considers such basic religious principles as "turning the other cheek," "He who lives by the sword perishes by the sword," and the obligation of willingly "going the second mile" when compelled to go the first. Confucianism has its principle of "jen" or human-heartedness. Jainism has its "ahimsa" or renunciation of the will or desire to harm. Christianity and Judaism have their ten commandments, which include "Thou shalt not kill." And the Arabic and Judaic "salaam" or "shalom" is a peace achieved by justice – a very early example of emphasis on positive peace and sensitivity to the importance of avoiding structural violence.[11]

The history of antiwar education and activity in Europe and North America over the past century and more indicates that women's and labour organizations, the churches, and a vast array of peace societies (50 of them following the Napoleonic Wars of 1815) have been in the forefront of such education, along with some public schools and universities. But the criticisms of dominant educational practices by great educators like Marie Montessori, Fannie Fern Andrews, and John Dewey have also shaped peace education and are only minimally associated with antiwar concerns. Montessori's work led to the development of new schools confident in the potential in children for building a just and peaceful world. John Dewey condemned the bent which schools and universities had for cultivating nationalism and militarism. For Dewey pacifism and democracy could become values built into schools and the everyday experience of children. Fannie Fern Andrews helped establish international organizations for research and resources for peace, even before women were able to vote.[12]

Finally, the long history of nonviolent movements – Gandhi's struggle for independence in India, the grape-workers nonviolent struggle for unionization and better working conditions, and all of the other cases discussed by Jo Vellacott earlier on – bear witness to the range of disciplined action for peace over the years. These, again, are not only examples of nonviolent action; they are also illustrations of extensive non-formal learning about how to live and act nonviolently.

C. The Possibility and Promise of Non-Formal Peace Education

1. Some Stories

As our brief historical survey already suggests, peace education at its best is not confined to public schools and university classrooms. Because so many of us reading this essay are students or teachers in some formal, institutional setting, or have been so at some point in our lives, I feel compelled – perhaps somewhat perversely! – to focus for a bit on the limitations of formal peace education and of formal schooling in general. The stories which follow suggest that, where peace is concerned, what goes on in formal classrooms may not be as important as what goes on outside them. Later I will make the case that some of the things we practice in public schools, colleges, or universities actually work *against* peace education.

On Sunday August 2, 1998 Rosa Louise Parks received an honourary doctorate from Mount Saint Vincent University. If you have looked at Jo Vellacott's discussion of nonviolent action you know that Rosa Parks was the department store seamstress who refused to give up her seat to a white passenger on a Montgomery, Alabama bus on December 1, 1955, as she was required to do by that city's segregation laws. She was arrested for her action, and this spawned a year-long bus boycott and campaign which gave direction, purpose, and success to the civil rights movement in the American South. There is a kind of mythology about Rosa Parks, and it includes an explanation of her action: her feet were tired after a hard day's work, and so she refused to relinquish her seat.

I thought I should write something for our local newspaper about the upcoming visit of this now 86-year-old African American legend, since I had found the truth to be rather different. Visiting two different bookstores, I had discovered two new books on people involved in the American civil rights movement. I did a bit of research standing between the bookshelves, looking up the name of Rosa Parks in the index. In the first book I discovered that she had attended the Highlander Folk School in Tennessee, run by Myles Horton, a man who had devoted his life to interracial dialogue and democratic education. So the first thing I learned was that tired feet were probably not the whole story. Rosa Parks knew what she was doing. She had received some civil rights education in the tranquil Cumberland mountains of Tennessee in the months preceding that critical day in December 1955.

In the second bookstore, again standing and searching the index to another new book, I learned more about Myles Horton and his alternative school for helping the poor and "uneducated" recognize their rights and for organizing and training the leadership for school desegregation. At an early stage the school had been supported by Eleanor Roosevelt, wife of President Franklin Delano Roosevelt (and, many would say, the heart and soul of his administration); Walter Reuther, one of America's most powerful labour leaders; Norman Thomas, a leading pacifist-socialist writer and one of the founders of the American Civil Liberties Union; and Reinhold Niebuhr, one of the most politically influential theologians in the world at that time.[13]

So, what might we conclude from these bits of information? 1) The action of Rosa Parks on December 1, 1955 was not just a spontaneous reaction without a significant context. What lay behind it was the resolve of a disciplined and intelligent woman. 2) Effective education can come from a learning environment quite different from that of ordinary public schools and classrooms. Highlander had a lot to do with Rosa Parks's action, but Highlander is a very unique place in locale, structure, and purpose. It is certainly not a place of formal education. 3) Very influential people gave their time and money to create places of civil rights training like Highlander. Highlander flourished, not by accident, but because of the careful and deliberate efforts of a number of dedicated and prominent people, although other high-placed individuals tried to close it down. 4) It is doubtful whether Rosa Parks would have learned what she needed to know and been able to act as she did if she had been dependent exclusively on formal school and university classrooms. Segregated classes like segregated buses in Montgomery were the long-standing and accepted practice in Alabama schools and colleges at the time. It is unlikely that their content would have encouraged anyone to challenge that practice and face certain arrest. 5) Not all useful peace research goes on in libraries and think tanks. Some can take place while browsing in a bookstore!

There are questions which come immediately to mind as we consider this story of Rosa Parks. What was it that was known by such an "ordinary person" that enabled or motivated her to act and face certain arrest? What was it about the education at Highlander and other learning experiences (including discussions with her civil rights activist husband, Raymond) that strengthened her resolve and gave shape to her action? Do public schools and universities talk about or teach these things? If they don't, why don't they?

Given our earlier discussion of the nature of education and of peace, we are in a position to identify the actions of Rosa Parks in the civil rights movement as linked to non-formal education and positive peace. Part of her inspiration no doubt came from her association with educators and ordinary folk at what is now called the Highlander Research and Education Center; her church and her own black community likely played a role as well. She had been a secretary for the local chapter of the NAACP (National Association for the Advancement of Colored People) as early as 1943. Her action and her life are not peaceful if by peaceful we mean placid and tensionless. Her's is a life of bravery, full of uneasiness and danger – which is what it takes, sometimes, to really make a contribution to positive peace.

The Rosa Parks story indicates something of the benefits of non-formal education: the learning that takes place in structures and situations quite apart from institutionally-sponsored school and college classrooms. Here is another story which illustrates and develops that point even more forcefully.

The account is given by Robert Coles, the pediatrician, child psychiatrist, and lifelong student of children in challenging situations, and it illustrates in quite a striking manner the everyday settings in which peace education takes place. Coles tells the story of Tessie, one of three six-year-olds, who, during the anti-segregation fight of 1961, was accompanied daily by armed federal marshals to her New Orleans school. Each day Tessie walked past a long line of jeering white adults. It was the constant encouragement of Tessie's grandmother, and sometimes even the federal marshals, that formed her educated resolve. Coles later heard Tessie explain:

> If you just keep your eyes on what you're supposed to be doing, then you'll get there – to where you want to go. The marshals say, "Don't look at them; just walk with your head up high, and you're looking straight ahead." My granny says that there's God, He's looking too, and I should remember that it's a help to Him to do this, what I'm doing; and if you serve Him, then that's important. So I keep trying.[14]

After two months of constant jeering and angry threats Tessie had become well known through the newspapers and was the recipient of supportive letters from across the country. One day she received a letter from her home town that was quite different. Coles describes it as "anonymous and brief."

> Dear Little Girl,
>   I stand there with them and sometimes I've shouted, along with everyone else, but I feel sorry for you, and I wish all this trouble will end, soon. You're good to smile at us, like you do sometimes, and I

want you to know I'm praying this will be over, and my kids will soon be back in school with you and the other two.

Sincerely, X

Later Tessie told Robert Coles:

I think of that letter a lot. It shows you, people will be nice even when you expect the worst of them! I guess that lady wants to change how her people are acting, but she can't, so she's upset. Now when I go to school, I'll glance over at them, and I'll be wondering which one of them is her; and I'll be wondering if there are others like her, thinking as she does, only not daring to open their mouths![15]

Tessie's ordeal illustrates the wider arena in which peace education can take place and the varied sources of learning. Tessie's education comes first of all from her grandmother, who in turn witnesses to the learning of her black community and her church. The streets leading up to the school serve as the physical setting for this peace education. Here even armed federal marshals and the words of a former adversary are an essential part of Tessie's education on how to handle this painful and angry situation in a constructive way.

"Learn what you can, where you can" – the educational philosophy of William Carlos Williams is one Robert Coles values intensely.[16] Cole tells another story, this one about his own education while attempting to work alongside members of the Student Non-Violent Coordinating Committee (SNCC) in the early days of that movement. It is a story which illustrates both the strengths of non-formal education and the limitations of formal education.

Coles had spent hours with SNCC leaders Stokely Carmichael, James Foreman, and Bob Zellner, trying to convince them of his well-meaning research interests, but to no avail. As they walked down a corridor and away from the unsuccessful meeting Coles begged one more time for an opportunity to research and help with something – anything! SNCC leader Foreman broke a long silence by suggesting to Coles: "You can help us keep this place clean." Coles accepted and became SNCC's dedicated janitor, not unlike half of the black parents he knew who held identical full-time jobs. In time he came to realize that the SNCC leaders were neither testing him nor putting him in his place, rather

... they were teaching me – or, better, enabling me to learn, putting me in a situation where I had plenty to do, yet could listen to my heart's content. I was constantly learning by experience rather than through abstract discussions.

When Jim Foreman asked Coles one year later what he had learned from his "janitorial research," Coles realized that it had enabled him

... to connect with a group of young people bent on connecting with impoverished, voteless, legally segregated blacks. In doing my everyday tasks, I was able to observe, learn, and come to some understanding of how life went for the SNCC workers and for people in the communities where they were living and "organizing."[17]

Robert Coles has a keen appreciation of the non-formal learning that makes a profound difference in the development of our values and capacity to act constructively. His "methodology" stresses experience or "vantage point" as much as it includes a definition of terms. These vantage points are crucial to peace education in that they allow us to "dive in" to learning opportunities, wherever they arise, rather than merely to "dip in" the protected formalized environments.[18] Diving in without making *too* big a splash avoids drawing attention to ourselves. Furthermore, plunging in does sometimes place us in a position to hear, see, and experience more.

The story Robert Coles discloses is a lesson about methodology, about being in the right place to learn. It is both a sobering reminder of the benefits of common everyday learning experiences as well as an indication of the limitations of much formalized learning. This "ordinariness" of peace education is also clearly depicted by Elise Boulding, who, along with her husband, Kenneth, serves as a founding parent of Peace Studies. She reminds us that we already know a great deal about peaceable living on a daily basis. Peace education becomes an activity focused on a "finding of the peace that already exists."[19] Conflicts are constantly present but so are the everyday ways of resolving quarrels, refereeing squabbles, practising patience, speaking kind and supporting words, apologizing for aggressive actions, turning one's back on challenges to fight it out, and joining with others in a shared cause.

2. A Specific Example: Learning Through the Mass Media

The role of the *mass media* in our non-formal learning experiences related to conflict and peace is immensely important. Elise Boulding has claimed that any society "learns about itself from looking in the mirrors its culture holds up to it." In the case of modernized societies this mirror is largely the mass media. We see and understand ourselves in the reflections of our television programs and popular magazines and newspapers. Boulding goes on to say that a significant distortion occurs in the West, where the media are furthest developed. Here we have "a mirror held up for societies in all parts of the world" and what we see in that mirror is "a Western stereotyping of other cultures, and much of it involves depiction of violence."[20]

A host of problems are associated with this mass media mirror by which we interpret ourselves and our cultures. Our news stations have become competing channels of entertainment, exploiting a market for rivetting images; many of the images so provided have to do with human disorder and suffering. The rival outlets and their sponsors compete for high ratings, focusing on the perceived glamour and excitement of violence. Our reporters seek out what is contentious and often fail to perceive, let alone take hold of, their own potential role as knowledgeable intermediaries. The constant focus on contention reduces every issue to two sides. Journalists portray belligerency and quarrels even when they are difficult to find. All too rarely do they expose the fragmentary and deficient nature of a presentation of merely two positions.

The cultural mirrors provided by our mass media and the preoccupations reflected back upon us help shape what all of us see and understand about ourselves and the world around us. Fortunately, when we pay attention to diverse cable channels and community papers, alternative news magazines and films, and the electronic discussions and web pages of a range of groups, we take hold of a different, wider mirror. Non-formal education of the kind that touches us through various news and entertainment media is a powerful means of forming attitudes, values, ideas, and opinions and inspiring our actions. Its effect can be every bit as lasting as a formal classroom curriculum, a church catechism, or a political party platform. The smaller, less conventional media alternatives may help us imagine ways around problems and violence. The presence of multiple sources of information may help us better understand the complexities of issues.

Closed minds and narrow and uncharitable views are very much a product of dealing with issues as though there were only two sides and limited options in a contest. Take, for example, the old USA-USSR superpower rivalry. Where, prior to 1989, were the sages who could imagine the fall of communism and the Berlin Wall? A concentration on marketable problems – a fixation with major media outlets – makes it difficult for our media and all who are shaped by it to imagine, let alone depict, healthy and constructive alternatives. On the other hand, a multiplicity of information sources rooted in the concerns of unique minorities might move us to a broader knowledge of social issues. Here newfound open-mindedness could allow us to see more intelligent portrayals of the problems and, in turn, to discover more creative avenues to solutions.

Television and film are uniquely influential in regulating our collective cultural identity; much of this is defined for us by the evening TV news. Ironically, the "latest news" may be the most irresponsible form of TV watching since it can lead us to believe we are being educated when we are not. Soaps and sitcoms do not as a rule suffer from such a pretence. What we need to know may not fit the 60 or 90 second bites or "visual and chronological constraints of the genre."[21] These constraints actually deflect us from long-term reflection and respectfully attending to the violence and pain in human experience.

Yet television is capable of setting aside its standard schedule and discourse when it treats the powerful at the time of their weddings, funerals, impeachments, scandalous behaviour, or employment of missile attacks on nations like Iraq. It needs to do the same with long-term violence and social injustice, genocide, and famine. Movies and good documentaries can facilitate such longer-term attention, thoughtfulness, and moral discernment. This might be epitomized in a quiet film like "84 Charing Cross Road," in which a wonderful humour-filled, generous-spirited friendship develops across thousands of miles between people who have a mutual love of books and who contribute to one another's well being while never actually meeting.

3. Why, Then, Are We So Stuck on Schooling?

I introduced the stories above and the example of learning through the mass media because they counter the tendency to associate peace education with formalized learning. This misconception about peace education arises because most of us concerned with education of any kind, including peace education, spend much of our time in classrooms. As a consequence we may confine our understanding of peace education to the formal education or schooling that we regularly experience. Schooling is considered to be very important in most societies, and if peace education is also to be important, then it must take place in schools. Or so we are likely to think.

It is interesting to note that formal schooling — especially so-called "higher education" — tends to disregard and devalue what is indigenous, or non-formal and everyday, even when it takes place *inside the classroom*. I am speaking of the practice of discounting common life experience or cultural context, particularly of students but also of teachers. It emerges partially because of our commitment to objectivity, neutrality or value-free physical and social science. Too much attention in the classroom to the everyday and commonsense understanding of things is considered to be non-critical, naive, and prejudicial or lacking in objectivity. Similarly, in the realm of research the studies engaged in by students and teachers are routinely attempts to dig up deeper causes and more academically respectable explanations. One of my favourite political philosophers once charged that these searches serve to evade responsibility by downplaying or dismissing the more obvious and painful difficulties or differences of which the world is made and with which we all must deal.[22]

The study of peace in formal settings is no less a victim of this underrating of the everyday experience and context of students and teachers than are other fields of study. The choices of "issues" and "minorities" to be focused upon in Peace Studies courses, for example, may emerge from experiences, texts, journals or media resources filtered by the teacher. Such "choices" may ignore popular culture and the smaller familiar or alternative media sources experienced by students.

In considering why we're so stuck on schooling, it is important to take note of an insight of Ivan Illich. He first puts forward this sixty-four-dollar definition of schooling: "the age-specific, teacher-related process requiring full-time attendance at an obligatory curriculum."[23] He then explains our undue attention to schooling and perception of its importance by observing that schools operate with a *hidden* curriculum as well, an unspoken *emphasis* on their own importance. When schools are universal (everybody goes) and compulsory (everybody *must* go) we are enticed by schools to believe that only what is taught or learned in schools is truly valuable, useful or proper. Because of this belief we have the habit of certifying experts in every subject under the sun. "If you didn't learn it in school, it can't be that important and you couldn't possibly be an expert." Public schools and universities also tend to support a notion of scarcity. It is as if knowledge were a commodity in short sup-ply.[24] If you are lucky to get enough of it, you become the certified expert. It is also as if the ideas and questions one has are to be jealously guarded in order to protect the turf of your discipline, your profession, or simply the "good ideas" you want to express in a term paper not duplicated by others.

This constitutes, I think, a convenient but perilous standard for peace education, not to mention any number of other areas, most obviously language-training, music instruction, computer troubleshooting or spir-itual counselling. People can be undeniably competent in these and so many other areas without school certification. The hidden curriculum of schooling limits the value and attention given to non-formal educa-tion, downgrades the gifts of the uncertified, and castigates as "failures" those who are without the requisite years of schooling, or number of courses. Peace education should operate within an opposite climate, one in which there is recognition of the abundance of possibilities, of situa-tions in which every side wins and where good ideas grow and multiply to the extent that they are given up to be shared. It should recognize the value of those non-formal settings away from classrooms, such as the one in which the young internist Robert Coles found himself, or ones in which the influence of the mass media is present. When it comes right down to it, all the discussions about, for example, Peace Studies pro-grams, courses, texts and concepts are best considered in this light. Higher education or schooling by itself, as presently constituted, just can't ensure the knowledge we require or the peaceable action we may want to encourage or empower.

D. Formal Peace Education: Reconceiving the Process

Much of what has been discussed suggests that peace education as presently undertaken in formal contexts – for example, in public schools or university Peace Studies programs – typically faces certain problems and limitations. How might these be addressed? Some of what has already been said is of course relevant to this topic: as we have just seen, schools need to recognize the significance of non-formal peace educa-tion. There may even be non-formal elements which may be incorporat-ed into the teaching of their own formal curriculum. But there are more general matters concerning styles of teaching and learning and ways of conceptualizing the peace education process in formal contexts that need to be considered. I will discuss three approaches or "designs" we may have in mind when we think in this general way about formalized peace education: 1) educating *about* peace; 2) educating *for* peace; and – a somewhat different approach – 3) peace *through education*. I will argue, following James Calleja,[25] that 1) and 2), as actually implemented in our schools, threaten to produce an unhealthy *passivity* in students, while also recommending a way around this danger which may allow us usefully to incorporate elements from these first two options into peace education programs. I will further argue that we naturally arrive at 3) as the overall best option when we generalize to *all* contexts of formal education the pedagogical style – problem-posing education – by which the dangers associated with 1) and 2) may be avoided. It may be noted that, while our aim is to apply what is learned to peace education, in particular, our discussion of these three distinctive approaches should help to bring into focus the weaknesses and (actual and potential) strengths of all formal education.

1. Education About Peace

To learn *about* something is essentially a data-gathering process. Learning about *peace* involves accumulating knowledge, facts, and ideas about peace activity, or about the absence of it.

Students can be quite compliant when simply learning about something and are often encouraged in this attitude by the nature of the process. The teacher or professor is the sole expert, the holder and provider of knowledge. The teacher or expert knows things the student does not know and imparts this knowledge to the student. On this "banking" conception of education, the student is like an empty vessel into which knowledge is poured or a bank account into which facts and ideas are deposited. And so the role of the student can easily become that of a submissive consumer of material. Students simply learning *about* things can be described, says Paulo Freire, as mere "collectors and cataloguers of the things they store."[26]

Learning about *peace*, like any other sort of learning-about, is in danger of becoming part of this obligatory and soul-destroying banking education, in which students learn to accept what they are told and what the texts report. In such circumstances, knowledge is treated as a commodity, as measurable merchandise unrelated to the goals of fulfilling good purposes or cultivating character. Such an understanding of education tends to go along with an uncritical acceptance of the status-quo: having spent all this time learning *about* the way things are with little (if any) investment of ourselves – our lives, interests, aspirations, and fears – it may become increasingly difficult to imagine ourselves as instruments of creative change. Even if we are learning about peace, *about creative change*, the absence of shared responsibility for generating knowledge (which should be appreciated as incomplete or unfinished), may deter us from personal involvement and critical reflection on our own and on our teachers' lives.

Perhaps there are ways around these dangers. Perhaps the typical process of learning-about is only the easiest and could be replaced. Maybe it's the *way* we learn that is creating the trouble here. Consider the way things typically occur in contexts of higher education.

Often there is a substantial lack of trust between students and teachers. Generally speaking, students learn to survive in the classroom or to play "the school or university game" before they learn anything else. Survival techniques may include giving back to the teacher what she or he wants to hear on a particular subject, determining what is likely to be on the exam rather than attending to what is truly compelling or significant, and learning to answer questions posed by an expert pretending not to have the answers. Instead of the foregoing preoccupations a student *might* have been grappling with, and even helping to formulate, questions related to real issues with all their gravity and moral complexity. So the typical way of doing things isn't the only way. What *is* generated is psychological insecurity, kowtowing and a lack of self-respect, timidity, and an acceptance of established ways of doing things, where there *could* be boldness and a healthy revolt against the continuation of the customary.

Teachers, of course, don't exactly trust the students, either. They – we – can be found promoting the very weaknesses that are griped about. Faculty loathe the "is this on the exam?" syndrome, yet it is perpetuated whenever complex social and physical realities are reduced to multiple choice questions and term-paper assignments. Some teachers bemoan the student's incapacity for inventive study and then bitterly complain about work which exceeds the boundaries of their subject matter or course description. Other professors lament the absence of political awareness and social empowerment while rewarding every avenue of competition and individual self-advancement. And, as one of my favourite and delightfully humorous critics has claimed, teachers condemn the maximized access to the total resources of the group and its implicit cooperation by calling it "cheating."[27]

The emphasis on knowing-about as "knowing the material" can

result in a weakening of mental and moral vigour. Students are pushed to answer prescribed questions. What might happen if students were left to develop and refine their own questions? What difference would it make if students were free to take seriously the problems and applications recognized in their own lives as they read material, and, after taking note of these matters, to formulate their own questions and spend their energies augmenting or resolving them? Faculty, meanwhile, might enlarge *their* lives by pursuing the questions which occur to them as they engage all dimensions of their disciplines. As things actually happen, the student is generally hindered from taking seriously his or her own life with all its complexities. She is blocked from gleaning from her reading, study, and interaction with others what is applicable to her own living. The academic obligation is to complete the curriculum – someone else's design. Living with these impediments is not only a distortion of intelligence and the place of knowledge in one's life; it is a form of moral and spiritual suicide. The ultimate result is a disciplined process of ignoring all relevance to one's own situation, avoiding all practical applications to the intricacies of one's own life, and a disregard for any attempts at making improvements either in one's own behaviour or to one's opportunities to contribute to the well-being of others.

But as has already been suggested, things don't have to be this way. The alternative form of learning-about that I've already begun to advocate with a few examples here and there, a pedagogy perhaps especially relevant to learning about peace, is called **problem-posing education**. To appreciate this alternative, we need to recognize that in almost all learning contexts there is a prior condition of not knowing, of uncertainty, and therefore, potentially, of humility. Not all educational contexts are oppressive and hurtful, and not all the people who engage in various forms of learning are oppressed and hurting. But in so many of life's situations we are stressed, uncomfortable, and even the victims of violence. Under all these circumstances, life – our social, political, economic, and cultural life – is problematic. In such a broad social or cultural context the social world can be said to act as a medium or go-between in the learning experiences of all, both so-called teachers and so-called students. Once we see the world this way we will find ourselves engaged in a "problem-posing" education. Here every student becomes a teacher, and every teacher becomes a student, each of us grappling with real-life predicaments. We all share the same world and learn through it and each other. The "problem" – the world with its economic and political structures, many of them exploitative – is common to both teacher and student. Thus the world intercedes in our learning context and provides the opportunity to dialogue as equals about common life-situations.

Developing this model in detail may help us to learn-about, and also to learn about peace, without falling into the dangers of the banking approach. But our model, it may be said, has its own problems. Critics may warn against its lack of neutrality. Indeed, one of the implicit assumptions in banking education is that education can and should be a politically neutral process – just passing on the facts, ma'am! It is as if there were no recognition whatsoever that there often are many particular (and different) *positions and views* on the facts. One evidence of the truth of this often unrecognized "fact" is the argument I am now making with you. I, too, assume a position on what the facts are, with which the proponent of banking education disagrees. Problem-posing education comes right out and denies the possibility of any form of truly neutral education. Even banking education serves particular social and cultural ends, including economic and political ones at times. Consider the nature of most schooling. It is anti-dialogical – there is little interchange between students and teachers as equal participants sharing common purposes and quandaries. As a result, banking education breeds dependency, subserviency or identification with those who already hold knowledge and power – an adhesion or clinging to the cultural values of those with the knowledge-power. In other words, banking education sustains the existing power arrangements by educating the younger generation in the acceptance of dominant values – not, by any criterion, a politically neutral education.

Problem-posing education, on the other hand, erodes dependency and fatalism by allowing us to see and experience the world as problematic, unfinished, and exposed to the change which we can help bring about. Problem-posing education is dialogical and contributes to a "democratization of culture" because it is based on things like mutual trust and a joint enterprise for students and teachers alike.

But you may now be inclined to ask: "Where is the discipline, where is the order? The critique looks too fuzzy, lenient or irrational – problem-posing education lacks rigour." Let us look at this notion of rigour. When we think about a rigorous education, we may associate it with hard work, "stick-to-it-ive-ness," exactitude in results, and a well-disciplined plodding on in spite of all obstacles. Many students find it difficult to associate rigour with a liberatory or problem-posing education.[28] This is likely because in this latter pedagogy the emphasis is on *self*-discipline, learning by pursuing one's own questions, treating one's peers as sources of knowledge and insight, and accepting one's teachers as colleagues. Rigour has traditionally come to be viewed quite differently, as associated with the teacher's demand for large chunks of detailed work – for example, a large number of formulae to be memorized or many books and pages to be read. This latter perception of rigour disconnects it from the quality of our engagement with our comrades or peers in a common pursuit for understanding. The traditional view of rigour may indeed undermine our willingness and capacity to learn from others, particularly in non-academic or informal community contexts. It is revealing to consider the dictionary synonyms for rigour: demanding, harsh, stern, strict, tough, accurate, correct, exact, and precise. In his more general critique of scientific investigation, Abraham Maslow once declared that all such words and conditions are "capable of being pathologized when pushed to the extreme." Maslow argued that the "merely cautious knower, avoiding everything that could produce anxiety (the wild, crazy, loose, uncontrolled, puzzling, guessing, fantastic, playful) is partially blind." The world that such a person is capable of knowing is a much punier one than the realities which can be known and faced by the less cautious person.[29] I recall a very successful political scientist from California who confessed that his work as a psephologist (a student of elections) analyzing state legislators' voting behaviour had all the security of counting money or poker chips, and his new-found work on future studies left all such security behind. If it is *our* world we want to learn about – and this is, if anything, even more obviously applicable to peace education – we may need to follow suit and let go of the false security suggested by traditional interpretations of rigour. Our own demands of ourselves should be as important as the teacher's demands (and, of course, can be as challenging); the accuracy and correctness of our work should have to do not only with our grasp of academic theories and constructs, but with our ability to enter the conversation ourselves, coming to grips with the messy world those (often competing) theories and constructs are designed to understand. Problem-posing education, in other words, requires critical thinking.

It is important to note that applying the problem-posing approach can yield engaging and valuable new experiences of learning-about. Consider some examples relevant to peace education:

- One of America's finest literary critics reminds his own Jewish community that it must come to terms with the Jewish collaborators in Nazi concentration camps and the Jewish leaders who disguised their own names to be the henchmen of Stalin's pogroms and gulags. This critic must risk the censorship of his own community when he describes these hurtful realities.[30]

- A renowned student of human history and archaeology reminds us that symbols – for example, cave drawings traditionally thought to be of bows and arrows, and therefore indicative of endless weaponry, war, and male dominance – can be understood variously. She provides explanations which see the stick-symbols not as arrows representing weapons and dominance but as live branches representing feminine fecundity, rootedness, and wholeness. New, less warlike, explanations emerge when the inquiry is conducted by professional investigators who happen to be women or persons without conventional schooling and traditional religious partiality.[31]

- A famous theologian consciously chooses to study and draw close to the anti-dialogical wing of his own religious tradition in order to further his examination of universal human rights. He wishes to understand the reluctance to accept an enlarged application of human rights in those to whom he is most closely tied. He must risk amending his own views and being isolated from (and unwelcome among) both his more liberal-minded colleagues and his more intolerant new acquaintances.[32]

These are examples of individuals for whom learning about something is a constant challenge in that it exposes them to new and uncomfortable realities. Knowledge is engendered because the cultural structure – the standing place for these searchers – has shifted. They see the world in new ways because they approach it from a different angle, with an atypical set of cultural values or assumptions. They question their own culture – their own community – with values which come from outside that community. The world touches them differently because fresh assumptions or expectations allow them to perceive new realities.

This is, as well, the touchstone for inter-cultural education. Employing diverse cultural principles gives birth to disagreements and apprehensions that are associated with or feed further speculations, understandings, insights, and hopes. So many of our greatest political leaders and creative thinkers have lived on these boundaries of experience or borders of dissimilarities – cultural, political, economic, class –

and different racial and ethnic backgrounds.[33] A proper recognition of differences or diversity motivates a radical openness to what the world reveals about itself – something which will always be part of a healthy peace education.

We have admitted that there are potential weaknesses in an education *about* peace, and it has been necessary for me to dramatize those weaknesses given our susceptibility to them, but I hope it is clear that a thorough knowledge of subjects we care about has not been disparaged. Insight, perspective, and enlargement of our awareness of truth may come through struggles of the sort we have just described. In peace education, we affirm, for example, that learning about different cultures and values may, when approached in the right way, contribute to the avoidance of violence between dissimilar communities. Loraleigh Keashly and Bill Warters have indicated that a good grasp of the reasoning of those with whom we differ can be a foundation for the resolution of conflict. Most of us have those experiences in life where knowing more about something or someone (a competitor or enemy, for example) results in a very changed attitude on our part. Knowing about peace, when approached in the problem-posing manner, can sometimes make all the difference in the world.

2. *Educating For Peace*

This sensitivity to changing our minds, or thinking and believing differently about issues or apparent enemies, has always made an education *for* peace attractive. Knowing as we do that a change in attitude or values leads to quite different behaviour, should we not educate in such a way as to foster deliberately these changes? A problem with learning about something is that we realize that just having more knowledge – let's say about a potential enemy – does not in itself *guarantee* new openness or an understanding attitude on our part. If our understanding does change there is something more at work here – something that has to do with our values, moral standards or the development of our sensitivities and character.

The call to an education *for* peace and not merely *about* peace arises because peace educators recognize the potential for passivity and a lack of motivation to change things when people simply learn *about* something. This may happen no matter how desirable and important that something might be. What they mean by educating *for* peace is that we ought to be educating so that people learn values and attitudes which move them to act effectively in particular ways: against war, for environmental protection, against a particular foreign policy, for disarmament, or for a better hearing for a particular and valuable viewpoint (like a feminist perspective on peace). Educating for peace means equipping people to live peaceably, providing them with *skills* as well as knowledge. It means recognizing that our usual ways of seeing and doing things perpetuate injustice. Many Peace Studies programs are therefore designed to actively promote justice, conflict resolution, service-training, and non-violent action.

But a problem arises as soon as we attempt to define *which* values, attitudes, beliefs, and skills we desire others to learn. Which values and skills should we develop to arrive at what we all value – namely peace? Throughout human history political ideologies and religious dogmas have justified themselves in the name of values and qualities which others were thought obligated to share, since they were held to promote goodness. Now we tend to consider this attitude to be intolerant and controlling. Is educating for peace somehow different? The wish to influence another person's behaviour or shape her or his values may prompt people to assume the role of expert – they know what is good for someone else. This is particularly true in formal education where the lines between students and teacher are clearly drawn, and the power of position or status comes into play. Compliance results when the expert – the teacher – has the knowledge and the student simply listens and takes notes. In such a setting, as we have seen, learners may be told what it is important to know about. But submissiveness is also bred when someone tells us what to value and how to live. Indoctrination in the name of god, country, and goodness may simply be replaced by talk of the right way to make peace and build justice, end war and structural violence, enhance social justice, deepen environmental security, and expand creative forms of dispute resolution. The higher or more sacred the values, the more certain we are of the virtue of our position. Is education for peace, therefore, little more than a newfangled version of indoctrination?

Again it seems that the answer depends on the style of pedagogy used. If it is possible to promote an education for peaceful social change without violating the freedom of those involved in the process and imposing values upon them, then indoctrination can perhaps be avoided. My contention is that problem-posing education helps us achieve this goal. It is, again, only if we succumb to the temptations of banking education and its implicit hierarchy that problems arise.

Before developing this point, though, let's consider once more the way in which no formal education is value-free or politically neutral. When we were comparing banking and problem-posing education we made the point that the former simply transfers existing knowledge and upholds the accepted ways of doing things. Neither is problem-posing education neutral since it openly challenges the status quo. In both cases certain power arrangements are supported. As peace educator Robin Burns has put it, formal schooling either fosters good citizenship, critical thinking, and social literacy or indoctrinates into the status quo.[34] Public education in particular is designed to socialize or even politicize citizens in a given social order. Consequently, it is no more politically neutral than an education for peace.

We can now develop this insight a bit by enlarging our notion of what is meant by "political." Politics is essentially the exercise of power. Educating for any purpose is a practice intended to promote preconceived social designs. The existence of socially accepted "purposes" presupposes a political reality. Of course, government and the acts of governing or challenging government are the touchstones of a definition of politics. But we can generalize from this by considering the *political culture* of people — their ideas, skills, awareness, values, opinions, beliefs, and loyalties in any social context inasmuch as they relate to the execution of, and challenges to, power or social control. The settings for the exercise of these qualities may include business offices, political parties, religious institutions, even the home, the family, and the classroom. Wherever judgments, beliefs, and values are put forward to exercise or achieve wider social purposes or control we have a political culture.

Educating for peace is a process much like education for any other social purpose. It is an exercise of power, of social management. It is therefore political. The process has its political origins in its social design and the intent of its designers. It has its own political culture of larger social or political purposes, principles, and ideals. So the question in this, as in other cases, is not *whether* we will educate for certain purposes and with certain values, but *how*.

There are different approaches to the implementation of socially-designed purposes like higher education (and here we return to the matter of alternative pedagogies). Two of the most common styles are 1) to further the purpose (enlarging or making peace, in our case) by obediently following a blueprint of *projected ideals* and "program or party principles" for the future; and 2) fashioning future social arrangements and institutions in accordance with *past practices*. Both types are built on "certainties" and perceived security. In the first case the certainty lies in the apparent obviousness of the (yet unrealized) ideals or goals contained in the blueprint. In the second case security lies in the assurance we feel with regard to the value of things already known and experienced and the predictability of similar experiences in future. The temptation for most peace educators and many students of peace is to incline towards the former approach and enthusiastically support a blueprint of unrealized or only partially realized peace and justice ideals. On the other hand, we have those who would achieve "peace through strength," and advocate that students should be trained in values which support individualism, free enterprise, and a robust defence or nationalism – strategies that have "worked" in the past.[35]

But there is a third, and radical, political style. It is a posture less damaged by the hunger for certainty and fear of ambiguity, and it grows instinctively out of problem-posing or liberatory education. Here the design is neither predetermined – a blueprint of ideals (and means to their achievement) to be implemented – nor is it a completed past – a template on the basis of which to replicate history and its values. Rather, in this third situation, students (or just as conceivably peasants or urban workers) are "considerers" of the political and economic world around them, they are "readers of the world" or partners in transforming a world which is incomplete and can be refashioned in part by their activity and struggles for peace. As we saw in our previous discussion of the world as mediator or go-between, the social world is unfinished and can be made and remade by all participants with each one learning from that incomplete world and from others. The design is not predetermined; nor is it based on a completed past. The world is still un-ordered, its builders uncertain as to its eventual shape but moved by their interdependence, mutual trust and faith in the possibilities of the future. What Mary Catherine Bateson describes as the approach for the personal lives of women in our day is generalized by the problem-posing approach to all individuals and to larger social and political contexts.

> [W]e are engaged in a day-by-day process of self-invention – not discovery, for what we search for does not exist until we find it – both the past and the future are raw material, shaped and reshaped by each individual.[36]

These are three quite distinct and significant styles of knowing and doing. The third option of problem-posing education amounts to learning in a context which is not dependent upon projecting past values. While it may mean constantly replacing old ideals with new ones, it also means gaining knowledge in a context in which a fixed set of ideals and blueprints are unsuitable or absent. What is called for is to live with uncertainty and moral ambiguity; to know that you do not know, and to face your own limitations and conditioning openly and critically along with others.

The ingredients which make such learning activities possible are qualities like humility, dialogue, and critical thinking, all of which grow out of the absence of a clearly defined order and an unwillingness to contrive one. The recognition of one's own dehumanization in the existing order may just be the key to implementing this pedagogy, just as the willingness to live with moral ambiguity is central to an understanding of lives well-lived. We may need to be able to acknowledge that subtle forms of oppression and disorder are pervasive and that only by a critical awareness of one's own perverted consciousness in the context of this disorder – assisted by others who may not share all aspects of it – is liberation possible.[37] Oppression, dehumanization, and disorder, even when they take the form of boredom, cynicism, and despair, are the unfortunate realities which must be encountered. They must not be denied by the glamorization of the existing order by right sectarianism, nor masked by the glamorization of leftist ideals.

Isn't this still a politically-motivated form of education – this problem-posing style? Can't it, therefore, still potentially contribute to more violence and injustice? In response to this objection we might remind ourselves that this is a pedagogy based on uncertainty and equality. As long as it is dialogical and critical, it is fed by humility and mutual trust. It would appear that such a pedagogy, inasmuch as it is problem-posing, is both engaged in the rough and tumble of politics and peace issues (the political world as mediator) and essentially self-critical and non-sectarian. Keep in mind that an awareness of one's own oppressed or flawed consciousness and conditioning is the starting place for problem-posing education.

This description does not guarantee that any education, no matter what its name – educating for peace, moral education, inter-cultural education, liberatory or problem-posing education – will avoid becoming ideological and instrumental in dividing people. But the *qualities* we have explored seem essential to any education which might contribute to a more peaceful world without proselytization and the need to create enemies.

There is yet a third way of thinking about formal education and peace. As we have seen, particular educational programs about or for peace carry with them the risk of producing passive clients. In the third and final option, education of a certain kind *in and of itself* is considered to be a vehicle for learning peace. What kind? Naturally enough, problem-posing education – but generalized to *all* formal contexts. If problem-posing techniques were adopted for *all* subject areas, students would be learning peace even if peace were not their particular area of study. Put otherwise, when the *process* of learning in other subject areas mirrors the *substance* of peace education, then we don't need to engage in peace education as a separate endeavour to learn and practise peace.

Some of what I have in mind here is already present in some measure in formal contexts of education. The peace that we learn through education includes being willing to dispense with preconceived notions and values for the sake of new and greater knowledge, joining in the communitarian practices of working together for larger truths, treating with respect and openness those who think differently than we do, and applying diligence in verifying findings and testing out new hypotheses – and some of this is already present in formal education at its best. But to round out this third option we should add to these valued practices the critical orientations peculiar to problem-posing education. The emphases on critical awareness of one's own cultural conditioning and an appreciation of the joint endeavour of students and teachers are still often left aside in the competitive world of schooling at all levels.

The claim that people can learn peace *through* education is supported by the idea that formal education is undergirded by fundamental democratic practices and values. What do we mean when we speak of democracy? I would say democracy is exhibited by a process in which all citizens or members have basic rights of participation, which must mean a voice in the determination of the social (e.g., cultural, political, and economic) values which affect them. These rights include the protection of all minorities by structures which militate against an outright tyranny of the majority (in a democratic state, these appear as legal rights, the independence of the judiciary, rights of representation, freedom of speech and assembly). If these are the essential elements of democracy, wouldn't a democratic education in some way help to realize such a social and political reality, both inside and outside the classroom? Peace education, in this view, is what all formal education should be about – a structure and practice which promotes the democratic principles of dignity, equality, and mutual respect and allows individuals to experience and develop their own capacities for cooperation, trust, and commitment.

Peace education may thus be infused in other "school subjects" and this education may instruct us in peaceful ways because of its democratic nature. When this happens it is an educational *experience* that makes for peace, not a platform or a set of ideals or a manual to be followed. But my one concern with regard to this emphasis on democratic education or education for democracy is that in fact it *will* be treated as a set of ideals to be followed, rather than the problem-posing, problem-solving process which constitutes democratic action.

What's wrong with ideals? Ideals can be escape mechanisms – escapes from reality and from uncomfortable truths. We are often unable to live with the insecurity of *what is* (the way things really are) because it introduces our failings, uncertainties, fears, and general incompleteness and places boundless demands upon us. In place of what really is, we – individuals and nations alike – hang on to fixed moral ideals, a *what should be* instead of the ever-changing present. In so doing we attempt to shape the present and future by ideals often rooted in past experience or political and religious doctrines. This effort to clutch ideals and avoid insecurity and its attendant fear may well be the root of all conflict. Where there is fear there will be conflict, either within the person or between the individual and others who stand in the way of security or the absence of fear. In other words, the ideal becomes the enemy of the good. The tendency to project an ideal, the *what should be*, even in the form of nonviolence and democratic principles, may prevent people from facing what really is. As Jiddu Krishnamurti has said, "Ideals have no place in education for they prevent the comprehension of the present."[38]

In short, all ideals and all strategies based on an ideal or set of principles (and here I would include spiritual exercises) may serve to prevent us from confronting what we really are – our social conditioning. The "right kind of education" allows us to face what we are without the screen of idealism. This form of education resists ideologies and systems of any kind. It fosters attention to what we are without the idealistic gloss. It promotes world peace by attending to our conditioning and disavowing all allegiance to authorities, political leaders, and spiritual and educational gurus. Such a disavowal or refusal of dependency prevents such definitions of ourselves and our security as those rooted in nationalism, religiosity, and comparisons with so-called enemies. The clarity which results is a form of action. Better yet, it *is* action. When we move forward in awareness of our conditioning and cherished certainties, this is action par excellence. It may well be the most significant educational and political accomplishment possible. From it grows, not just knowledge, but wisdom.

> Knowledge is not comparable with intelligence, knowledge is not wisdom. Wisdom is not marketable, it is not a merchandise that can be bought with the price of learning or discipline. Wisdom cannot be found in books; it cannot be accumulated, memorized or stored up. Wisdom comes with the abnegation of the self. To have an open mind is more important than learning; and we can have an open mind, not by cramming it full of information, but by being aware of our own thoughts and feelings, by carefully observing ourselves and the influences about us, by listening to others, by watching the rich and the poor, the powerful and the lowly. Wisdom does not come through fear and oppression, but through the observation and understanding of everyday incidents in human relationship.[39]

I cite this commentary on knowledge and wisdom because it summarizes so much of what we have examined in a problem-posing peace education – the openness of mind, the critical awareness of one's cultural position, the joint enterprise with others of all stations, and an appreciation of ordinary, everyday events and relationships.

This is not to say that reading books and garnering information is a waste of time. Not so! If we go back to the stories with which we began we would find that "Parks," Rosa Louise's "uneducated" activist husband, had the wisdom, gleaned from his experience in the NAACP, to encourage Rosa's peace and civil rights education inside and out of formal classrooms. Robert Coles has written, at last count, 53 books. But those books are informed by his capacity to observe and understand the "everyday incidents in human relationship." I wish I could comment further on Tessie. My guess is that, like Rosa Parks, she has grown in knowledge and wisdom from formal classrooms as well as non-formal settings. When Rosa Parks came to our campus she did so, as she insisted, to support a program of "Pathways to Freedom" for disadvantaged but promising youngsters 11 to 17 years of age. If attention had been focused on her alone she would not have come.

Now there may seem to be an assumption in the above that a properly conceived "education for democracy" won't be a passive education and will, to put it simply, help build a peaceful world. If, however, you were to take the trouble to look at what philosophers of education have to say about this element of peace education – cooperation or education for democracy – you might be surprised at all the disagreement. The issues which seem to divide these educators are not just the extent to which democratic principles are desirable and applicable in the classrooms of our nations. More accurately, they quarrel over distinctions between democratic education and other forms of developmental education. They question whether there is any carryover from a democratic classroom and its values to the student's experience in the world outside the classroom. So we may wish to ask: If we learn democratic values and practices inside the classroom, will we be more apt to apply them in our wider social and political lives?

The answers vary. The most positive conclusions may not be satisfying just because those supplying them have been trying to prove too much. Perhaps the most accurate conclusion is that while democratic classrooms do not *guarantee* democratic values and practices outside the classroom, they do at least encourage some familiarity with them and provide some experience of their workability.

Of course much depends on our continually shifting understanding of what constitutes contemporary democratic practice. We may mistakenly regard the development of democracy inside the classroom as a correlate of the broader political order, where an ever narrower representative form replaces something demanding some level of increased participation and a defence of the voice of the least powerful. At such a time it may be important to encourage the ideas and practices of a positive peace which spring from the peace education we have been examining. Such a focus may help students and teachers to examine a real-life context and to consider ideas which can be applied to other dimensions of their lives for a reconsideration of the significance of democratic values and practices generally. This reconsideration allows us not only to take stock of our political posture broadly understood inside our education or schooling experience, but also to prompt questions and considerations beyond it.

And what might we have learned? The educational practices we engage in may not be essential or even relevant (always) in other contexts, but they will have focused on some styles and values worthy of attention. Something does happen in dialogue: one can learn from someone else other than the certified authority; there is a practical application of humility, critical thinking, mutual trust, even love. And those values that were talked about as we experienced this new mode of schooling may be recalled as we engage in political life, and that very engagement may take place in part because we saw things differently. Meanwhile we have come to appreciate that everything we have learned about peace and peace education within the school, college or university, however valuable, is small indeed standing next to the settings beyond the formal classroom. Problem-posing education (by definition and practice democratic) makes peace *through* education both desirable and possible.

E. Celebrating Peace Education: A Conclusion

In the end there is much to celebrate in the area of peace education, taken as a whole. A report card on its growth and effectiveness might include, for example, the massive and quite remarkable educational processes which many of us were engaged in world-wide as we opposed nuclear weapons in the 1980s. (Nigel Young comments on this in his discussion of peace movements.) I think also of the vast movement for mediation programs which today make use of student-chosen peers to help settle fights and anger among fellow students. In my local area the League for Peaceful Schools is mushrooming in growth and success. A creative networking and sponsorship between this League and another new educational enterprise – the Pearson Peacekeeping Training Centre – is now a reality. Alex Morrison, one of the contributors to this book, presides over this new direction in peacekeeping training and its networking enterprise with the public school interests. Parents are amazed at the lifetime skills their daughters and sons have learned through such school programs. In the United States the National Institute for Dispute Resolution estimates that there are over 8,500 school-based conflict resolution programs in the nation's 86,000 schools.

Those of us who follow a listserv (electronic discussion group) like "dispute-res" are overwhelmed at the depth and breadth of concern and activity among lawyers, social workers, and psychologists who use alternate dispute resolution methods. Peace education includes these directions and the practical knowledge of the many non-violent organizations and programs world-wide. Loraleigh Keashly and Bill Warters, along with Jo Vellacott, provide illustrations of these conflict resolution programs and the educational practices of the various people and organizations that have promoted nonviolence. From the US civil rights movement and Rosa Parks in Montgomery, Alabama to Greenham

Common, Berkshire, England to the townspeople of Osijek, Croatia – mediation skills, nonviolent action, and just plain "sharing and mutual help" are all witness to the vitality of peace education and its achievements at the beginning of the twenty-first century.

One might also comment on peace education's new regard for how environmental degradation results in social insecurity and warring over growing scarcities, or how sustainable development results in increased security and peace. Such environment and development concerns enlarge the scope of peace education. This enlarged range expands to include educational and research agencies like the International Institute of Peace through Tourism. I mention this particular agency because it witnesses to the expanded reach of contemporary reflections on peace. Some of those emphasizing ecological considerations, such as ecofeminists, teach us about the link between the traditional stations which women and children fill and the preservation of their immediate surroundings. Their natural environment faces corporate and global attempts to exploit land, forests, water, and holy places for short-term economic purposes. Their peace education includes political, economic, and highly technical knowledge about the long-term spoilage of their surroundings. It also includes organizational skills and nonviolent practice.

Such are the new and enlarged arenas of peace education. If it remains conscious of the shortcomings of standard formal approaches, and open to a problem-posing, problem-solving, democratic pedagogical style, there is a rewarding future for this age-old process of human and social transformation.

Notes

1 My co-editor and philosopher colleague John Schellenberg wisely prefers to say: It is important to remember what "non-formal" means here – to avoid confusing it with "unstructured and undesigned" or "*in*formal." Look carefully at the definitions and you will see that humanly-imposed structure or design in a learning situation is *necessary but not sufficient* for it to count as formal (to be formal it must also be institutionalized), and that a learning situation's *lack* of such structure or design is *sufficient but not necessary* for it to count as *non*-formal (since a non-institutionalized situation of learning may still be designed for learning by someone or other).

2 We may mention again the valuable resource which most peace educators return to as the key source for these distinctions: Johan Galtung, "Violence, Peace, and Peace Research," *Journal of Peace Research* 6. 3 (1969): 167-91.

3 Valerie Dovery, "Exploring Peace Education in South African Settings," *Peabody Journal of Education* 71. 3 (1996): 146-7.

4 Aline M. Stomfay-Stitz, *Peace Education in America, 1828-1990: Sourcebook for Education and Research* (Metuchen, NJ: Scarecrow Press, Inc., 1993) 166.

5 James Calleja, "The Future of Peace Education: Orientation and Evaluation," *Peace Education and Human Development: To Professor Ake Bjerstedt: A Book of Homage*, ed. Horst Lofgren (Lund, Sweden: Dept. of Educational and Psychological Research, 1995) 108.

6 Emilia Sokolova, "Peace Education: From Person to Person," Lofgren 344.

7 James Collinge, "Sharing our Foodbaskets: Some Thoughts on Peace Education and School Subjects in New Zealand," Lofgren 112.

8 Frank Hutchinson, "Towards Cultures of Peace: New Literacies for the Twenty-first Century," Lofgren 233.

9 Toh Swee-Hin and Virginia Floresca-Cawagas, "Weaving a Culture of Peace," Lofgren 400.

10 Gene Sharp reviews these kinds of situations in his invaluable work, *The Politics of Nonviolent Action* 3 vols. (Boston: Porter Sargent, 1973). See especially *Part One: Power and Struggle*, 75-6, and *Part Two: The Methods of Nonviolent Action*, 191.

11 For a brief and useful review of these positions see Thomas A. Shannon ed., *What Are They Saying About War and Peace?* (New York: Paulist Press, 1983).

12 Stomfay-Stitz 4-5 and 56-58.

13 You probably don't want the names of the bookstores but the two new books are valuable resources. David Halberstam, *The Children* (New York: Random House, 1998) and Taylor Branch, *Pillar of Fire: America in the King Years, 1963-65* (New York: Simon and Schuster, 1998). The balance of this discussion is enriched by Rosa Parks's autobiography, which is quite instructive when it comes to peace or civil rights education. See Rosa Parks, *Rosa Parks: My Story* (New York: Dial Books, 1992). Books and articles on the Highlander Folk School (now the Highlander Research and Education Center) are summarized on the ERIC database with public access via: http://venuse.galib.uga.edu (click on "Databases"). One useful book on the center is John M. Glen, *Highlander: No Ordinary School* (Knoxville, TN: University of Tennessee Press, 1996).

14 Robert Coles, *The Call of Service: A Witness to Idealism* (Boston: Houghton Mifflin Company, 1993), 4-5.

15 Coles 51.

16 Coles 18.

17 Coles 12-13.

18 Coles 26.

19 Elise Boulding, "Learning Peace," *The Quest for Peace: Transcending Collective Violence and War Among Societies, Cultures and States*, ed. Raimo Vayrynen (Beverly Hills, CA:

Sage Publications, 1988) 318.

20 Boulding 321.

21 The phrase and much of this discussion of television is based on arguments made in Michael Ignatieff, *The Warrior's Honour: Ethnic War and the Modern Conscience* (Toronto: Penguin Books, 1998) 9-33.

22 Hannah Arendt, "Civil Disobedience," *Crises of the Republic* (New York: Harcourt, Brace Jovanovich, 1972) 73.

23 Ivan Illich, *Deschooling Society* (New York: Harper and Row, 1972) 38.

24 One of the finest treatments of the notion of knowledge as a commodity and of the overall failures of modern schooling at all levels is Ivan Illich's *Deschooling Society*. There are few thinkers who offer such a radical examination of the place of schooling in the modern world and how it perpetuates dependency and a sense of failure, particularly in so-called "third-world countries." Illich today would say the enemy isn't schooling, it's all education because of a certain orientation in it — that is, education "as learning when it takes place under the assumption of scarcity in the means which produce it." See his "Forward" in *Deschooling Our Lives*, ed. Matt Hern (Gabriola Island, BC: New Society Publishers, 1996) ix.

25 Calleja 99-111, esp.104.

26 Paulo Freire, *Pedagogy of the Oppressed* (New York: Seabury Press, 1974) 58. Reprinted in 1991 this is the most important source for Paulo Freire (1921-1997) and his work. The material presented here is a digest of his ideas from the above and many other sources. One illustration of the style of his early work is contained in Cynthia Brown, "Literacy in 30 Hours: Paulo Freire's Process in Northeast Brazil," *Social Policy* (July/August, 1974): 25-32.

27 Neil Postman, "Telling It Like It Ain't: An Examination of the Language of Education," *Alternatives in Education: OISE Fifth Anniversary Lectures*, ed. Bruce Rusk (Toronto: General Publishing, 1971) 27. I highly recommend this most readable and humorous essay in which Postman would add new language to the schools, subtract most of the old language, and rename problems as the answers. It is as relevant today as the day he delighted an audience with it back in the fall of 1970.

28 Paulo Freire and Ira Shor, an American educator who shares Freire's views on higher education, provide an excellent discussion on the question of rigour in their joint book *A Pedagogy for Liberation: Dialogues on Transforming Education* (South Hadley, MA: Bergin and Garvey, 1987). See pages 4-7, "Rigor and Motivation in a Liberating Course" and chapter 3, "Is There Structure and Rigor in Liberating Education?" 75-96.

29 Abraham H. Maslow, *The Psychology of Science: A Reconnaissance* (New York: Harper and Row, 1966) 30-32.

30 Alfred Kazin, *A Lifetime Burning in Every Moment* (New York: HarperCollins, 1996) 55-6, 255-7, and esp. 296.

31 Riane Eisler, *The Chalice and the Blade: Our History, Our Future* (New York: Harper and Row, 1987) 4-5.

32 Harvey Cox, *The United Nations and the World's Religions: Prospects for a Global Ethic* (Cambridge, MA: Boston Research Center of the 21st Century, 1995) 97.

33 One of the most useful twentieth century discussions of this cross-cultural phenomenon of learning which comes about because we live in more than one world or on the borders is Paul Tillich, *On the Boundary: An Autobiographical Sketch* (London: Collins, 1967). The same has been said of creative political leaders like Winston Churchill and Franklin Delano Roosevelt, whose roots are in more than one country or class.

34 Robin Burns, "Peace Education, the Representation of Participants and the Presentation of Conflict through School Textbooks," Lofgren 80.

35 The most focused discussion of these sectarian positions is found in Freire's preface to his *Pedagogy of the Oppressed*. The material here is based on the discussion in the preface, especially pages 21-23.

36 Mary Catharine Bateson, *Composing a Life* (New York: Penguin Books, 1990) 28.

37 Freire 33.

38 Jiddu Krishnamurti, *Education and the Significance of Life* (New York: Harper and Row, 1953) 22.

39 Krishnamurti 64.

EPILOGUE

Conrad G. Brunk:
On Theory and Practice, Realism and Idealism

An important debate runs throughout this book. Sometimes it is under the surface; at other times it emerges into explicit argument. It is the debate about whether the various approaches to peacemaking and conflict resolution put forward by different theorists and practitioners are "idealistic" and "purely theoretical" or "realistic" and "practical." In contemporary, technologically advanced societies, no criticism of an idea is more damning than the charge that it is "idealistic" or "impractical" – the overriding criterion of the worth of an idea is its usefulness in the accomplishment of human goals. If it doesn't "work" then it is of no value. This mode of thinking is often referred to as "instrumental" because it is interested only in the way certain *means* are instrumental in the accomplishment of *ends*.

Of course, one need not be very clever to notice that the instrumental way of thinking is fraught with difficulty. It assumes that we already know the ends or goals we ought to pursue and that the only problem is the technical one of finding the most effective and efficient means of attaining the goals. It has no way of helping us to decide what are the most appropriate goals for us to pursue, and so it has to rely simply upon what people desire as ends. This, then, raises the question of who gets to decide what are the appropriate ends for a group, a society, a nation, or a world to pursue.

The question of whose ends will be realized is, of course, the primary question at issue in most human conflicts. We get into fights about whether a piece of land should belong to my group or to yours, whether we shall have this form of government or that one, whether the laws should protect this group or that group, and so on. Like most matters at issue in conflict situations, these are questions about ends, not just about the means to achieving ends. This is why, when we think about the peaceful resolution or management of conflict, we have to think not only about the most effective and efficient means for one party to realize its ends, but also about how to help conflicting parties rethink their ends. We also have to think about how the means we choose in the pursuit of our ends help to shape our thinking about those ends.

People who like to call themselves "realists" usually mean by this that they are concerned with practical ways of achieving realizable goals. They pursue goals that are "realistic" in the sense that they are reasonably achievable, given the available means and given all the predictable limitations that are likely to get in the way. Realists pride themselves on the fact that they understand, and take seriously, the nature of the world as it *really* is. They don't adopt ends that they can't achieve, and they don't choose means that are ineffective in achieving the realistic ends.

Realists like to call "idealists" those whom they consider not to have a very practical attitude toward the world. Idealists don't take seriously enough the way the world really is. They build romantic theories about how the world *ought* to be, without taking seriously the fact that human nature and social institutions stand in the way of reaching that *"ought."* Idealists pay a great deal of attention to ideal ends, but little attention to the practical means for achieving those ends. The realist says to the idealist: "Don't bother me with your proposals about how to change the world unless you can show me that the state of the world you propose is consistent with what I know about human nature and the world *and* that there is a workable means for getting from where we are now to where you think we ought to be."

The trouble with realism is that it tends to see *every* new idea and every proposal for doing things differently as idealistic. So, in an interesting irony, the same realists who pride themselves on being so effective and efficient in getting things done also tend to be very conservative and resistant to creative change. The reason for this is easy to understand. Realists say they know how to be effective in the world because they understand the world as it *is*, not as they think it *ought* to be (which is the idealists' habit). And so, in order to understand the world, they tend to study very closely how things have been done in the past. The patterns of the past are assumed to predict reliably the patterns of the future. Realists expect the future to be pretty much like the past, and so they tend to act in ways that make it look like the past. Then, of course, they can always say, "Look, we were right!," in a self-fulfilling prophecy.

In the late 1980s the nuclear buildup by the superpower blocs at the height of the Cold War made the world a very dangerous place, in which the East and the West had thousands of nuclear warheads poised in readiness to attack at the slightest hint of a possible attack from the other side. During this period the anti-nuclear protest movement also reached the peak of its public opposition to the proliferation of these weapons of mass destruction. There were widespread public demands for the superpower nations to enter into disarmament negotiations to achieve massive reductions in the numbers of warheads and delivery systems. The world would be a much safer place, these critics argued, if there were fewer and less dangerous nuclear weapons poised at the ready. Those who called for disarmament were dismissed by the political realists as idealistic dreamers, who did not understand the true nature of the political world, in which, like it or not, nuclear weapons were "here to stay" as essential tools of deterrence.

Within a few short years, the world was transformed in ways the political realists of the time did not foresee. With the collapse of communism in the Soviet Union, and its dissolution, the international strategic situation changed dramatically almost overnight. The following decade saw the conclusion of nuclear disarmament agreements and the reduction of nuclear weapons inventories, which surprised even the "idealists." It also saw the proliferation of nuclear weapons and fissionable material to smaller nations and possibly even to non-state terrorist groups in the world, making the earlier claim of the realists that nuclear weapons are effective weapons of deterring aggression even more suspect than before. Nuclear weapons in the hands of secretive terrorist groups are hardly weapons of deterrence, nor can they be deterred by the threat of other nuclear weapons.

So, it is evident that what may appear to be idealistic at one point may turn out to be realistic only a short time later. More importantly, the ability to think creatively about new ways of doing things is what makes real social change possible. Social, political, and even technological innovations, especially the momentous "paradigm shifts" that revolutionize human history, are rarely the work of realists. They are often, instead, the work of people who appear at first to be idealistic dreamers. Their thinking is not constrained by the way things have always been done or the way things have always appeared to be.

This is what many of those who are working in the field of peacemaking and conflict resolution are trying to do. They challenge some of the old entrenched ways of thinking, and in doing so they risk being dismissed as dreamers who are out of touch with reality. Many of their proposals may well turn out to be "unrealistic." Others, however, will likely lead to profound changes in the way conflict is handled at local, community, and even international levels. Already this has proven to be true in many contexts.

One example of this is the proposal made by a group of "idealists" in the late 1970s in Kitchener, Ontario, who proposed to local criminal justice authorities a whole new way of responding to young offenders. Instead of the usual course of a trial, conviction, and traditional punishment, these people suggested using new, mediational approaches to conflict resolution. They proposed bringing offenders face to face with the victims whom they had wronged, to hear what harmful effects their actions had imposed and to work out proposals for redressing those harms acceptable to the victims. At first this "victim-offender reconciliation" idea was scoffed at by lawyers, judges, prosecutors, and criminologists, as completely unworkable and as "idealistic" about offenders as well as victims. Such an approach will not be a sufficient deterrent to crime, they said, and victims will never want to meet with the persons who have wronged them, to say nothing of reconciling with them.

Today, "restorative justice" approaches to crime, with adults as well as youth, have been initiated in communities across Canada, the United States, Australia, and New Zealand, allowing offenders to be re-integrated into their communities as socially productive, law-abiding citizens, instead of being subjected to the dehumanization and debilitation of prison or social ostracization. Governments are even mandating such things as "sentencing circles" for certain kinds of crime, which involve victims, offenders, families, and community members in the resolution of the conflict involved in a criminal offense. What appeared "idealistic" to the realists in the legal system now is sober, "realistic" practice.

So, it looks like the debate between idealism and realism, between theory and practice, is more complicated than some realists like to make it appear. They are quite right in their insistence that it is important to translate ideas and theories into practice. In order to do this, it is also important that they will not do more harm than the good they intend. Idealism that is so out of touch with reality that it is harmful in this way is bad – for exactly the reasons the realists say it is. The trick, as in so many things, is to find the right balance between the two extremes – between an idealism that is out of touch and a realism that is blind to new possibilities. This is what the theory and practice of peace is all about.

Loraleigh Keashly and Bill Warters:
The Conflict Resolution Continuum

As we reflect on the other chapters and the conference session in early October at Mount Saint Vincent University, we are struck by what can be called a *conflict resolution continuum*. Developing this concept may help to broaden our thinking when studying peace and conflict to the point where we acknowledge that a variety of strategies and approaches are in service of dealing with conflicting interests. People may, of course, have mixed (or very clear!) feelings about the morality or workability of some of these approaches. In our own discipline of conflict resolution, for example, there is a definite bias in favour of consensual, multilateral, and nonviolent approaches to managing, resolving, and transforming conflict. Yet a full appreciation and understanding of conflict and those who participate in it requires an attempt to empathize with those whose approaches are *not* consensual or multilateral or nonviolent – it requires the recognition that there are "places" in every conflict's life where other approaches are used, for the reason that they seem the most effective in achieving one's goal.

That raises an important question: What are the relevant goals? This question is related to Conrad Brunk's point in Chapter 1: an important consideration is *whose definition of peace* is being utilized. As observers of a conflict, our goal is often to have it stop as quickly as possible so that all of us can return to a more peaceful – i.e., more *negatively* peaceful, less disrupted – life. Yet to those involved, initial or evolving goals may include the goal to have inequities and harms acknowledged *and* redressed. When dealing with someone very powerful who is either unwilling to meet this need or who does not recognize that there *are* important inequities and harms, something other than a consensual, nonviolent, and multilateral approach may seem necessary to increase the chances of that goal being met. Indeed, unilateral approaches like nonviolent resistance, vocal activism, and various forms of "violent" protest may be seen as important steps in getting parties in the conflict to the place where they become *committed* to consensual, multilateral, and nonviolent approaches such as negotiation, mediation, peacebuilding, and peacemaking. So not only may we have different goals, we may also have different ideas as to how to achieve the goals we share. And the views taken by conflict participants, innocent victims, and observers such as scholars, other countries, or the public on goals and the best approaches to achieving them may very well *change* at various points in the life of the conflict. The point we would like to make is that truly working with conflict requires a sensitive appreciation of all this. As we contemplate the fate of others, we must recognize and "take on" as much as possible their perspectives, treating the goals and approaches selected as ones that "make sense." Thus, while it may feel morally repugnant to include violent protest as a form of conflict resolution, it is important to recognize that this revulsion comes from one perspective, and that from another it may seem a path necessary to follow.

Now having said that, it is important to add that we are not arguing that one should agree with approaches like violent protest, homicide, genocide, or war, whose costs are very high. What we are suggesting is that to not understand what drives these approaches (and, indeed, what drives our more favoured consensual, multilateral, and nonviolent approaches) is to prevent ourselves from truly understanding conflict and hence being able to manage, resolve, and transform it. Without understanding these perspectives, any efforts to encourage and support alternative paths to achieving parties' goals will fail. Such a lack of understanding also sets the stage for us to make huge and costly blunders when we seek to impose our desired approaches. We may inadvertently be party to continuing disenfranchisement of disadvantaged groups or become an active party to the conflict itself.

We think the chapters in this book provide insight into the array of "conflict resolution" approaches and some of the underlying values and functions they may serve in dealing with conflict and keeping, making, and building peace. Most importantly, the authors of all these chapters challenge each and every one of us to examine our own motives in selecting and rejecting paths to peace. What we will discover in this process may initially dismay us, yet at some point also help us by improving analysis *and* empathy — both of which are needed when facing the complexities of conflict.

Alex Morrison:
Theorists and Practitioners — Antagonists or Partners?

There always have been, and always will be, differences of opinion between those who devise theories in Peace Studies and related fields and those who are charged with implementing governmental decisions in the areas of peace, security, and stability. The conceptualists generally begin with a clean slate. They formulate a thesis and then attempt to indicate its practical consequences. They have the freedom to set out assumptions and to make claims such as "If X occurs, then Y will surely follow." They are not constrained by the dictates of the world in which the practitioners operate; thus they can produce new and innovative theories. That is perhaps how it should be: imagination should be given free rein and theorists should be permitted to be innovative, in order to arrive at possible new solutions to perennial problems. Theoretical models must, however, pass through a rigorous sieve before they are implemented — the multifaceted reality of the world in which the theories are transformed into practical instruments of dispute resolution.

These theories are often presented to governmental and international offices by those who devise them, acting in official or unofficial capacities. The problem lies in the fact that their concepts are rarely directly applicable to a specific situation. They represent only the starting point for discussion in which various potential courses of action must be taken into account. Hence the contribution towards the final decision by academics may be great or it may be incidental – often this judgment is impossible to make at the start. (Of course, not all theoretical models are devised by academics. They are often the result of work by members of non-governmental organizations who strive to create situations for non-military intervention and peaceful conflict resolution.)

On the other hand, the practitioners – be they operational personnel, politicians, diplomats or military personnel – are not all free to act in the same "clean slate" manner. Local, national, and international pressures often combine to guide if not force them to make certain decisions. These pressures are the reality of the world in which we find ourselves living, and they shape responses to crises. The practitioners will never be able to fully implement theories into practice due to these constraints.

Let us consider a generic international conflict to which a national government has been asked to respond by contributing a military force to an international, perhaps UN or NATO, armed force. To be borne in mind at the outset is the fact that, by and large, the use of military force does not indicate a failure on the part of politicians, diplomats and parties to the dispute to solve either the underlying or surface problems of the conflict. The role of the military is to create a certain degree of stability that can be used as a firm base from which civilians can negotiate a more permanent settlement. Furthermore, the use of military force is the instrument of last resort in a democratic society; very rarely, if ever, will the military advocate the use of force. In fact, military leaders know the horrors of war; thus they set virtually unattainable preconditions to be met before placing the lives of their troops in danger.

When their government leaders ask for proposals on the options for the use of force in our scenario, the chiefs of defence staff will set out, from the military point of view, the advantages and disadvantages of each option. However, the actual decision is, quite properly, left to politicians. Once the civilian leaders give their instructions, the military may point out the consequences of the option, but it may nonetheless have to be accepted. Following a government confirmation of the task, the military authorities set out to implement the orders. They then apply themselves to assembling the necessary resources in sufficient types and quantities to carry out the job with a high chance for success.

It is in this way that policies are evolved and implemented. One can see, for obvious reasons, the need for the defence community to be more practical than theoretical in order to suffer minimum casualties and to achieve maximum gain from their past experiences. However, for the military to evolve it must also incorporate new ideas. Nevertheless, one must always remember what is at stake and the fact that, in order to accomplish what is expected, the military must hold itself in a high degree of preparation and readiness. If it does not, it will surely incur the wrath of its civilian masters.

In conclusion, it seems that the conflict which, from time to time, erupts between theorists and defence practitioners is due to the fact that one understands the other so little. This may indicate, not mutual intolerance, but missed opportunities. What is needed is greater acceptance by each of the other and acceptance of the true task of the other. For this to exist, we may require the implementation of practical measures aimed at acquainting one group with the realities of the environment within which the other exists and works. This would, at least, constitute a good beginning.

One thing is certain: dwelling on our differences, philosophically and practically, will increase the difficulty of envisioning and creating a new, peaceful, secure, and stable world.

Jo Vellacott:
Dynamic Peace and the Practicality of Pacifism

Reading the other chapters of this book has been a good experience. I find the connections and interrelations fascinating; I shall not detail them, as they are there for all to see. I want to focus on thoughts which for me grow out of the whole.

First, a general reflection. The issue of the academic respectability of Peace Studies because of its possible political nature has been raised in more than one chapter. For the political content, I make no apology. The political slant is not to be regretted, but should be recognized. As Larry Fisk suggests, any true education is transformative. The process by which this occurs involves engaging with the material – not passively accepting what is set out before you but bringing your own context to it, interacting with others around it, deciding what to take, what to reject, on what to reserve judgment, and trying it experimentally in your own living.

I struggle with the concepts of "positive" and "negative" peace. My own inclination, as will have been apparent, is towards acceptance of the value of studying and working for positive peace, as defined by Adam Curle, my mentor in Peace Studies. Like Curle, I find it hard to see as peaceful a situation in which social justice is absent.

I find, however, that "positive" and "negative" peace as usually defined are constricting terms, the more so if we have to choose between them. Perhaps we need a third term. If a true state of peace cannot be attained without social justice and this, as Conrad Brunk suggests, is so broad a goal as to be meaningless, that should not force us to reduce our aim merely to putting a stop to fighting. (In any event, I believe this to be an equally unattainable goal: if we can do nothing to remove the causes of conflict, fighting will soon break out again.) I see a need to look not only at social injustice, or at systemic violence, but also to explore attitudes and to work for continuing change and communication. Perhaps "dynamic peace" is a term we could use for this ongoing process of laying a solid foundation for peaceful relations between people, groups or nations. I can illustrate what I mean with an anecdote.

In the early 1970s a park in Ontario was occupied by people of a regional First Nation. A small group of Quakers camped between the armed police and the occupiers (also believed to be armed) and managed to establish communication with both parties, which led after some days to an end to the stand-off, possibly preventing violence. Is this the end of the story? It is only if we are observing a strict dedication to the idea of negative peace. The aboriginal leaders had taken the action to draw attention to serious problems that were being ignored by the press and the authorities; if nothing further was done, yet another avenue of communication, however flawed, would have been denied them. The intervenors recognized that they had no right to help deprive people of what they had seen as a last hope of making themselves heard, unless they could follow through by helping to open up other ways to make the grievances known. Toronto-based, the Quakers had access to media attention, and as their own understanding grew, they worked for a number of years with the people of the two most affected communities to expose the effects of mercury pollution and of debilitating powerlessness in the face of arbitrary government decisions and to open up better communication with levels of government.[1] Can it be said that any real contribution to peace would have been made had they dropped the issue at the park gates as soon as the stand-off was over?

From this point of view, it will be no surprise that one of a number of difficulties I have with the type of military "peacekeeping" described in Alex Morrison's chapter is that it can simply be a means by which the nations with most influence and power in the international arena serve their own interests, or clamp the lid on a conflict which has its roots in serious injustice, or perpetuate the "us and them" attitudes of two parties to a conflict rather than facilitating communication.

Again introducing a large concept which there is no room here to explore in depth, but which may be deserving of further thought, I put forward the following question for peace students to consider. Is it possible – or desirable – to develop a truly "transnational" organization, whose servants' prime loyalty would be to peace and justice between nations and among people and not to getting the best deal possible for their own nation? "Transnational" may not be the best term, but it will serve for an idea that has seen some realization in NGOs and even in less high-profile areas of the League of Nations and the UN, but so far has had little impact in those intergovernmental structures concerned in major decisions. Again, I can give an historical example of the contrast between traditional international attitudes and what I have called transnational thinking.

In 1919, when the Peace Conference convened at Versailles to work out a peace treaty and the Covenant of the League of Nations, the negotiations were in the hands of the leading statesmen [sic] of only the victorious countries, who struggled jealously for terms that they thought would sell well to the voting public in their respective homes. The defeated governments and peoples were not represented.

Meanwhile, a nascent NGO, the Women's International League for Peace and Freedom, convened, fortuitously just as the terms of peace were published; the League Covenant had come out a few months before. The WILPF gathering was held on neutral territory (in Zurich, Switzerland) and brought women together from both sides of the recent war. Meeting each other face to face, they were directly in touch with the suffering of wartime and the postwar era. Their interests were as near as might be truly transnational. To them it seemed clear that the long-term interests of the people of the victorious nations, as of the defeated, could be served only by a peace that would last. In their one short week together they produced an analysis of the treaty and of the Covenant which unerringly identified just those areas which over the next twenty years would prevent healing, perpetuate hatred, make the international economy unviable, and contribute to the failure of the German experiment with democracy. Who can say what would have happened had the statesmen had a similar width of vision – and the conviction to take it back and sell it to their voters? Instead, we are often presented with a simplistic history that suggests that the peace failed because the League did not have enough power to enforce the provisions of the treaty and because the peace movements of the 1930s emasculated the military power of the western nations.

One of the difficulties that often arises in Peace Studies and peacemaking at all levels is the sense we are given by critics that it is all "pie in the sky," unpractical stuff that must give way to a realistic view. I want to give the last word on that to Ursula Franklin, a leading Canadian thinker and pacifist. I heard Dr Franklin explain that, while she had always been a pacifist, she had until lately accepted as understood "that there are the moral people and there are the practical people," and the moral people have good ideas "like being for peace ... but in practical terms you can't really do those things, but practical people do things, and it comes out right." Now, she said, "It has become very clear to me that this whole vision is wrong. That in fact the mess we are in in this world has been made by the practical people. It hasn't been made by the people who are concerned about ecology, about social justice, about peace. It has been made by people who say 'we are realists, we know the world, we know what's going on.'" But in fact, she pointed out, the practical people have not given us solutions. "The practical people have given us problems. And what has come to me absolutely firmly is that in the end ... what is morally wrong is practically dysfunctional and it isn't worth doing it; that the argument for a moral, caring, pacifist world is not a philosophical argument any more but is intensely practical ... I am convinced that caring and pacifism ... is an essential part of survival. It isn't a luxury of the feeble-minded."[2]

Nigel Young: Peace Studies at the Millennium

The field of Peace Studies has been divided over approach before. In the 1970s, for example, there was a tendency to emphasize social justice and structural violence as issues on the one hand, as against the scourge of physical (direct) violence and the need for an absence of war on the other. Some felt war might be a necessary *means* to social justice and that poverty and repression were more crucial problems. Right now the field seems again to be bifurcating around a different set of anti-war versus justice-related or liberatory tendencies. Oddly, the roles are somewhat reversed in the 1990s. This time those emphasizing social change and conflict transformation are emphasizing *nonviolent* means and the role of social movements — we have here an emphasis on peace culture. The "pacificatory" approach, however, emphasizes structural peace, conflict management and resolution; techniques of interpersonal and corporate mediation and stronger security structures (e.g., the United Nations) and international law and inter-state peace and security schemes (e.g., the Organization for Security and Cooperation in Europe, the OSCE).

In the 1970s the context was the Vietnam War and its aftermath. In the 1990s it is Bosnia, Kosovo, Rwanda, and the Middle East, as well as the violent fragmentation of urban societies. The pacificatory approach sees itself as hands-on and realistic as opposed to the visionary idealists who focus on consciousness and identity through critical, feminist, and alternative approaches to creative change. The latter see the state paradigms, or managed peace, as largely outdated, missing the role of media and consciousness. What both approaches lack is a sufficient concern with weapons of mass destruction. What both share is a concern with the state. The pragmatists see the state as here to stay (at least in the foreseeable future); the idealists see the state and nationalism as at the core of peacelessness and the work on movement in civil society as fundamental if peace is to be built cell by cell.

Indeed, the examples of recent wars and genocide suggest that culture – the symbolic sphere (e.g., religion, media) – can be manipulated by state and non-state actors to deepen destructive conflict. The task of creating peace culture – the construction of images and memory for peace – becomes paramount, and the NGOs and peace movements are, in my view, more likely to sustain this work effectively than are traditional political or bureaucratic structures. International governmental linkages like the UN or the federal Europe that is emerging are only as peaceful as the culture which sustains them, one that is constructed by movements from below. In this process communication with the other is essential. A *lingua franca* is highly desirable, be it English or some variant of it, since the less dialogue, the more violence we will see. Nonviolence has to be preemptive, not waiting for UN or state initiatives (like that of the USA), and it must encourage the empowerment of the weak in such action. "We are the peoples" requires a practical translation at The Hague conference of May 1999 and its follow-up conferences, and again at the peoples meetings of 2000 to reinvigorate the areas of peace building, making and keeping.

Larry J. Fisk:
Last Thoughts and First Principles

One of the contemporary thinkers mentioned in this book, Ivan Illich, counts among his very best friends a twelfth-century monk! I make this observation for two reasons: first, to indicate how wide a base may be needed to support a discriminating perspective on the modern world, and second, because I wish to allow the monk in question – Hugh of St. Victor – to inform our last words. Indeed, Hugh has something to say about the *idea* of "the last word"; that is to say, about the idea of an epilogue. He speaks of an epilogue as related to memory, as a "gathering" of the essence of what has previously been said. It articulates the "principle upon which the entire truth of the matter and the force of its thought rest, ... to this principle everything else is traced back. To look for and consider this principle is to 'gather.'"[3]

The study of peace is, like medical science, a transdisciplinary focus both on what is troublesome and on what may lead to health. The title and contents of our book reflect this two-fold emphasis. We have seen both empirical examination of what is problematic and the deployment of discipline and moral imagination in the consideration of possible constructive alternatives. The task is an enormous one that must be undertaken in a spirit of openness to all relevant perspectives and (therefore) with a willingness to concede one's limitations and set aside cherished certainties if the evidence so requires. This is not to say that we should be reduced to observers, watching the parade of competing alternatives go by. We must commit ourselves to some view or other in order to get anywhere, but in our complex world we must do so in humility – recognizing that learning and being changed go hand in hand.

This may come close to a fitting epilogue for our book in Hugh's sense. All of its chapters in one way or another reflect the need for humility in our conflict-ridden world and in Peace Studies as well. Putting it another way, the approach we take in Peace Studies – more generally, the *manner* in which we do Peace Studies – must mirror its content and hoped-for achievements. (As you have seen, many of the epilogue pieces echo this point, thus providing some confirmation of my claim here.)

Let me develop the point a bit. If we had had another 200 pages, we might well have spent more time examining the global problems that beset us. One of these is environmental destruction and the widespread insecurities and even warfare which are a direct consequence of depleted and misused resources. Another is the frightening prospect of nuclear war. In spite of an end to the Cold War and some important steps towards a dismantling of nuclear weapons there are new threats to international security. Increased military expenditures, even on nuclear missile systems, are part of American post-Cold War budgets. In Russia and other countries of the former Soviet Union the dismantling process is plagued not only by questions of its cost and eventual safe disposition, but also by an international "mafia" ready to inherit discarded nuclear devices and plutonium and to use such material for purposes of blackmail and terror. Yet another problem is posed by the "new wars" of an intra-state nature, which are deliberately pitched to the indiscriminate destruction of anything holding social meaning. Such warring demands a whole new understanding; previous notions of orderly warfare with international rules and objectives are replaced by what appears chaotic and primitive.[4] We might attempt, given more space, to understand these anarchic "patterns" in the hopes of distinguishing pre- and post-conflict management in the face of such horrors.

Now if you think about problems of this sort for a while, you may see that they very quickly raise indignation in most of us. And most of us believe they can be dealt with. We may, indeed, be quite certain that we've figured out how. Our certainties about the twenty-first century may include the notions that we will make the world peaceful by our global caring and responsibility and by our choices of – for example – paying attention to the news, obtaining a higher education or joining a political party. But what if "caring and responsibility" are sophisticated shields from encountering horror? What if newswatching is erudite entertainment? And what if higher education is exalted commodity accumulation, career advancement, and a corruption of moral fortitude; and joining a political party an escape from grassroots social and community struggle? They very easily can be – and we need humility and openness to diverse perspectives to ward against such possibilities.

Illich, for one, would remove global "responsibility and caring" from his life inasmuch as it involves a psychic shield that prevents us from considering disturbing details, as it were, close up, and allows us to carry on relatively normally in "our world." Illich does not want to rule out experience of the horror of the starving and war-ravaged children of Africa. Quite the contrary. He does not want to hide behind the mask of, as it were, arms-length caring or of responsibility.[5] Paul Goodman many years ago noted that we grow more powerless to the extent that we identify with society with a capital "S." Perhaps Illich today is arguing that we grow more politically ineffective to the extent that we identify ourselves as responsible for global problems of the kind I have just mentioned.

But, you say, this book is full of suggestions and illustrations of those who have fought for some far-reaching peace. I suggest you look again at all those examples. I believe what you will find is that people – whether Adam Curle, Rosa Parks, Catharine Marshall or six-year old Tessie – faced situations which they saw as contiguous to their lives and those of their friends and families and in which they were strengthened by colleagues, congregations, and communities. This is not to say that they lacked all concern for events elsewhere, but peaceful living for them began and grew from situations in which they were intimately involved.

It may be said that my point is accommodated by the slogan, quite common where peace is a concern, to "think globally and act locally." But what does it really mean to "*think globally*"? Michael Ignatieff recently reminded us that the advent of world-wide atrocities witnessed in our living rooms via television may stretch the traditional emotions associated with our sense of wishing to *help*. But just how adequate and pertinent are our feelings of guilt, shame, outrage, and remorse, he asks. What if global responsibility and caring – really fixing the troublesome situation – would require us to turn to actions and policies which cannot be supported by our liberal values? What if our righteousness and confidence blinds us to the tenacity of those we oppose? What if our moral revulsion turns back upon us as disillusion or cynicism – "let the brutes destroy themselves." What if our attention to ethnic problems elsewhere conceals our inattention to similar problems in our own communities? Humility is needed here too, to dispose us to notice, let alone answer, these questions.

Our feelings of responsibility, caring, and moral outrage may feed what Ignatieff in the context of Eastern Europe calls an assumption of omnipotence.

> Very often in these liberal interventions the moral reflex – "something must be done" – was sustained by the unexamined assumption that we had the power to do anything. This assumption of omnipotence often stood between indignation and insight, between feeling strongly and knowing what it was possible to do.[6]

Perhaps the admonition to think globally and act locally should take the form of "*think imaginatively and humbly, act similarly, and reverberate globally.*"

It is quite unfashionable, if not downright heretical (perhaps irresponsible!) to say that we do not control the future, but that is precisely what is being said here. We need to examine our certainties, and perhaps learn to live with uncertainty. I mention this so that we are stripped to the bone, and move with humility in our various fields of endeavour, whether that be the community of friends and neighbours out of which grows a politics of genuine interest and accomplishment or an education and discipline which imbues us with sensitivity and enables our appropriate action. I promised the last word to Hugh of St. Victor. The one I have chosen suggests that Hugh not only had insight into the idea of an epilogue, but also some sympathy with what happens to be the content of ours!

A certain wise man, when asked concerning the method and form of study, declared:

> A humble mind, eagerness to inquire, a quiet life,
> Silent scrutiny, poverty, a foreign soil,
> These, for many, unlock the hidden places of learning.[7]

Notes

1 Jo Vellacott, "Origins of QCNC," *Canadian Friend*, 92. 1 (1996).

2 "Technology and Pacifism," lectures given in the Bertrand Russell series at McMaster University, February 1995, quoted by permission of Ursula Franklin.

3 Jerome Taylor, *The Didascalicon of Hugh of St. Victor: A Medieval Guide to the Arts* (New York: Columbia University Press, 1961) 93.

4 Two of the finest discussions in this area are John Keegan, A *History of Warfare* (London: Hutchinson Random House, 1994) 1-10 (although the entire first chapter, "War in Human History," constitutes a critique of the Clausewitzian view of war); and Mary Kaldor, "Introduction," *Restructuring the Global Military Sector: Volume 1, New Wars*, eds. Mary Kaldor and Basker Vashee (London: Pinter, 1997) 3-33.

5 In an interview with Canadian broadcaster David Cayley, Illich explains the way in which caring becomes a "mask of love," impairing one's capacity for confronting what is horrible and disabling one's willingness to act with those close to one, or doing what one is capable of accomplishing which does impact on those far off. See David Cayley, *Ivan Illich in Conversation* (Concord, ON: House of Anansi Press, 1992) 215-18, 282-85.

6 Most of these questions of global responsibility, "the seduction of moral disgust," and "the assumption of omnipotence" are discerningly examined in Michael Ignatieff, *The Warrior's Honour: Ethnic War and the Modern Conscience* (Toronto: Viking, 1998) 90ff. The quotation is found on page 96.

7 Taylor, 94. See also footnote 61 on page 214. The verses are quoted in John of Salisbury's *Policraticus* and are there attributed to Bernard of Chartres.

LIST OF CONTRIBUTORS

Conrad G. Brunk. Professor of Philosophy, Director of Legal Studies and Criminology, and former Director of Peace and Conflict Studies, Conrad Grebel College, University of Waterloo, Waterloo, Ontario, Canada.

Larry J. Fisk. Associate Professor of Political Studies, Mount Saint Vincent University, Halifax, Nova Scotia, Canada. President of the Canadian Peace Research and Education Association.

Loraleigh Keashly. Academic Director, Masters program in Dispute Resolution, College of Urban, Labor and Metropolitan Affairs, Wayne State University, Detroit, Michigan, USA.

Alex Morrison. President of the Lester B. Pearson International Peacekeeping Training Centre, Cornwallis Park, Clementsport, Nova Scotia, Canada. President of the Canadian Institute of Strategic Studies. Former Minister-Counsellor at the Canadian Mission to the United Nations.

John L. Schellenberg. Associate Professor of Philosophy and Coordinator of Peace and Conflict Studies, Mount Saint Vincent University, Halifax, Nova Scotia, Canada.

Jo Vellacott. Author and historian of women and of women's efforts for peace, Kingston, Ontario, Canada.

William C. Warters. Associate Director of the Mediating Theory and Democratic Systems Program, a Hewlett Foundation-sponsored conflict resolution theory-building center at Wayne State University, Detroit, Michigan, USA.

Nigel Young. Cooley Professor of Peace Studies and Director of Peace Studies Program, Colgate University, Hamilton, New York, USA.

INDEX

objectivity, 15, 60, 172

Operation Restore Hope, 81, 87

Organization for African Unity (OAU), 82, 91

Osijek, Centre for Peace, Nonviolence and Human Rights, 122-26, 136, 138, 190

Oslo NGO Forum, 99

Overy, Bob, 149-50, 154

Owen, Robert, 156

pacifism, 15, 72, 120, 147, 152-53, 202-05

Pankhurst, Christabel and Emmeline, 106-07

Parks, Rosa, 114-15, 165-66, 187, 189-90, 208

passive resistance, 111, 129. *See also* nonviolence; nonviolent action; Tolstoy, Leo

patriarchy, 120, 131. *See also* Marshall, Catharine; militarism

Pax United Nations, 77

peace, 11, 13, 15, 16, 98, 148, 151, 155-57, 161-62, 181, 190, 206, 208; conflict and, 25, 31, 67-68, 87-88, 92; definitions of, 20, 24-25, 30, 145, 148, 207; education and, 177, 181, 185, 189. *See also* negative peace; positive peace

Peace Brigades International, 135

peacebuilding, 19, 85, 88-89

peace culture, 150, 152-57, 205-06

peace education, 125, 143, 161-64, 169, 179-80, 185-86, 189-90; achievements and limitations, 162, 167-68, 171, 173, 180, 187, 189-90; definitions of, 160-62, 164-65, 173, 188; formal education and, 101, 165, 171, 173, 186. *See also* problem-posing education

peace enforcement, 87-88, 92

peacekeeping, 15, 19, 83-85, 88-89, 92, 98, 101, 156, 189, 203; definitions of, 25, 74, 76, 81, 90-91, 93; history of, 74-75, 79, 82-83, 98

peacekeeping umbrella, 90

peacemaking, 23-26, 29-32, 85, 128, 195, 197

peace movements, 143-57, 162, 164; campaign issues, 121, 136, 147, 149-51, 154

peace research, 23-24, 144, 162, 166

peace studies, 14-20, 23, 25-26, 32, 67, 143-44, 155, 159, 205-06; approaches of, 24-25, 27, 29, 181, 205-07; challenges to, 13, 23, 156, 172, 202, 205-06; higher education and, 32, 142, 156, 172-73, 181

Pearson, Lester Bowles, 68, 74

Pearson Peacekeeping Training Centre (PPTC), 85, 90, 101, 189

peer-mediation, 189

People's General Assembly, 70

people's power movements, 151

periodization, phases of peace movements, 150-51

P-5 (UN Security Council permanent members), 70, 71, 93

picketing, 104, 106, 117-18

Pinochet, Augusto, 97

police, 89-90, 106, 117-18

political culture, 182

political ideology, 15, 152, 181

political power, 26-27, 107, 133. *See also* power

politics, 15, 182, 209

positive peace, 20-25, 29, 31, 103, 145, 155-56, 159, 202-03; peace education and, 161-64, 188; views of, 131, 133, 166-67, 202-03

post-Cold War, 77-79, 82-83, 85, 88-89, 91, 95, 157, 207

Postman, Neil, 192